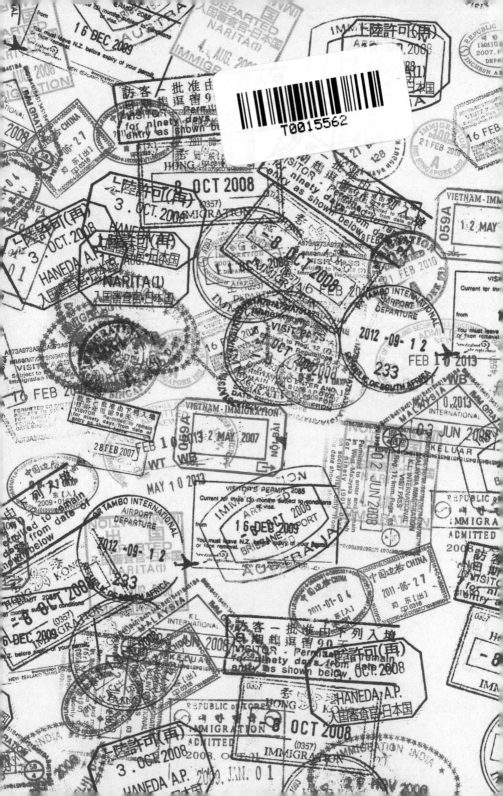

The publisher and the University of California Press Foundation gratefully acknowledge the generous support of the Constance and William Withey Endowment Fund in History and Music.

License to Travel

License to Travel

A CULTURAL HISTORY OF THE PASSPORT

Patrick Bixby

UNIVERSITY OF CALIFORNIA PRESS

University of California Press
Oakland, California

© 2022 by Patrick Bixby

First Paperback Printing 2023

Library of Congress Cataloging-in-Publication Data

Names: Bixby, Patrick, author.
Title: License to travel : a cultural history of the passport / Patrick
    Bixby.
Description: Oakland, California : University of California Press, [2022] |
    Includes bibliographical references and index.
Identifiers: LCCN 2022000984 (print) | LCCN 2022000985 (ebook) |
    ISBN 9780520375857 (cloth) | ISBN 9780520976276 (ebook)
Subjects: LCSH: Passports—History.
Classification: LCC K3273 .B59 2022 (print) | LCC K3273 (ebook) |
    DDC 342.08/2--dc23/eng/20220531
LC record available at https://lccn.loc.gov/2022000984
LC ebook record available at https://lccn.loc.gov/2022000985

ISBN 978-0-520-37585-7 (cloth : alk. paper)
ISBN 978-0-520-39789-7 (pbk. : alk. paper)
ISBN 978-0-520-97627-6 (ebook)

Manufactured in the United States of America

31   30   29   28   27   26   25   24   23
10   9   8   7   6   5   4   3   2   1

For Nicole

CONTENTS

ILLUSTRATIONS

ACKNOWLEDGMENTS

This book was dreamt up in a different world, where no one had ever heard of the Covid-19 virus and the pandemic-to-come always seemed distant, far more distant than it actually was. But by the time I sat down to write the pages that follow—in a hastily arranged home office furnished with a card table and a folding chair—we were living in a new reality, where nation-states around the world had begun to close borders, restrict internal movement, and require quarantines for visitors and returning citizens alike. Almost everywhere, it seemed, emergency measures had dramatically slowed the accelerating pace of mobility and migration that has defined our age of global interconnectedness. Our collective freedom of movement had been restricted in fundamental and pervasive ways.

Many would-be travelers found themselves confined at home for months on end, balancing thoughts of distant destinations with fears of infection and forced quarantining; others were stranded far away, kept from their loved ones by travel bans or canceled flights. Of course, restrictions on freedom of movement had more dire consequences for migrants, refugees, and other vulnerable populations who must cross borders to find the conditions necessary for their very survival. All of us who roam the planet are compelled to possess a passport, though the universal requirement affects some of us very differently than others. In the midst of the pandemic, our travel documents seemed to take on new meanings, almost by the day, as passport power indexes were turned on their heads, as vaccine passport proposals began to emerge, as passport applicants experienced lengthy delays in receiving their papers.

It was a strange time—at a moment when global mobility had all but ceased—to be thinking about the long history of travel documentation. It was more than a little odd to be writing of the wanderers whose stories make up this book, to be reliving their experiences of crossing borders and spanning cultures, while being obliged to sit still. But it was also, in a curious way, the perfect occasion to dwell on these narratives of travel and mobility, migration and dislocation. I hope my readers will share this sense with me as they travel through this book, whether in some quiet, motionless space or, perhaps better, gliding high above the earth in the cramped coach section of an airliner, rushing backward through an unfamiliar landscape in a high-speed train, or bouncing along in the back of a bus somewhere out there.

Despite the physical isolation prescribed by the virus, I was hardly alone in writing this book. First, I must thank Niels Hooper, executive editor at University of California Press, for his immediate enthusiasm in response to my proposal and his unstinting encouragement (and open lines of communication) as I turned this project into a book. Also integral to the process were his wonderful editorial assistant, Naja Pulliam Collins, and my fantastic copyeditor, Anne Canright, whose clear and consistent guidance helped bring this idiosyncratic project to press.

Many others kept me company along the way. I would like to express my gratitude to Steven Beschloss for welcoming me into a highly edifying workshop on writing for audiences beyond academia, part of his Narrative Storytelling Initiative at Arizona State University (ASU). There I had the great fortune to meet Christopher Schaberg, whose savvy advice as both a writer and an editor has been crucial to the publication of this book. During the period that followed, I also had the wonderful luck to befriend Leo Bersani and Sam Geraci, who moved to Phoenix just in time to brighten up the place as the gloom of the pandemic descended. As I wrote, I received invaluable feedback and support from friends across the country and across the ocean, including Douglas Atkinson, Bree Beal, Anne Ní Choirbín, José Francisco Fernández, Seán Kennedy, James McNaughton, Lois Overbeck, Mark Quigley, Jean-Michel Rabaté, Eric Wertheimer, and Feargal Whelan; and closer to home, Christopher Hanlon, Sharon Kirsch, Richard Lerman, Annika Mann, Matt Simonton, Michael Stancliff, and Bonnie Wentzel. This project made me more grateful than ever to be part of an interdisciplinary academic unit at ASU, where I can call on colleagues who know far more than I do about ancient history or eighteenth-century literature or any number of other things. I am especially thankful for the kind contributions of Arthur Sabatini, whose talent for conjuring obscure details and surprising anecdotes never failed as he indulged me with his thoughts during the composition process.

I would also like to give special thanks to Nadia Louar, Claudia Villegas-Silva, and Saleem Jassim, all of whom graciously shared their own passports stories with me. Our conversations, ranging across the United States, Europe, Latin America, and the Middle East, taught me more about the emotional resonance of the passport than anything I encountered in the historical archive. Nevertheless, this book also benefited greatly from the thoughtful assistance of a number of archivists, including Rachel Detzler and Carrie Hintz at the Stuart A. Rose Library, Emory University, and Jennifer Thorp at New College, Oxford University. As the book neared production, it also profited from the generosity (and wonderful photographs) provided by some of the artists and activists discussed in these pages, including Antoine Cassar, Callum Clayton-Dixon, Susan Robeson, and Helena Waldmann.

As ever, my biggest debts of gratitude are owed to members of my family, both near and far, including my mother-in-law, Jeri Richardson; my aunt, Nancy Foerster; and the many Bixbys who listened to my passport-themed ramblings, offered unfaltering encouragement, put up with my general absentmindedness—and even promised to read this book someday: my father, Patrick; my brother, Brian; my children (and officemates, for a time), Claire and Owen; and most of all, my fellow traveler of more than two decades, Nicole.

INTRODUCTION

"The Most Precious Book I Possess"

A LITTLE BOOK CONTAINING thirty-odd pages of sturdy paper, it is
bound with a grainy cardboard cover and embossed with the name of a
country, a national symbol, and the word *PASSPORT* or its counterpart in
another language. It might be red, green, blue, or black, depending
on the issuing country, but it is always the same easily grasped size—
according to an international standard first established nearly a century
ago—and it always includes a data page containing a serial number, a
photograph of the holder, and a range of personal details. When the
edges and corners are noticeably worn, when the pages are creased and
smudged, adorned with colorful entry stamps and sought-after visas, the
document becomes a talisman for the global wanderer and the précis of
a life story, whether for the privileged tourist or the desperate migrant.
It possesses the strange power to control exactly where we may go and
where we must not. A passport can offer the promise of secure passage to
a new life far away; it can enable flight from the dangers, the restrictions,
or just the mundanity of familiar surroundings; it can garner one a fast
pass to the head of the line or unwanted scrutiny in the backrooms of
officialdom. It can give us license to cross borders of every description—
geographical, but also cultural, linguistic, economic, legal—in search of
something unattainable at home, and then bring us safely back again.

In *Step across This Line* (2002), Salman Rushdie claims without irony
(his native tongue as a global migrant and master storyteller) that "the
most precious book I possess is my passport."[1] Although he acknowledges that such an assertion about a seemingly commonplace object

might seem like hyperbole, it is no overstatement for him. Yes, the passport has its practical function as an indispensable travel document (do *not* lose it); yes, it may contain a photo of which we are not particularly fond (ignore it if you can); yes, it may lull us into a complacent sense that it will do its job and pass inspection by the border control officer (or now, the automated passport-control kiosk). But if we do give it some attention, the passport begins to accept much more psychic investment, to bear more emotional weight, becoming in the process a "precious" object carrying more than mere practical or material value. For Rushdie, this is largely due to the recognition that not all passports do their work so easily or unobtrusively. The novelist relates vivid memories of his first passport, an Indian one he carried in the 1960s, which stated in its pages that the bearer could visit only a painfully brief list of countries. When he received a British passport in his teens, he felt as if the world suddenly opened up to him, and soon enough the little book took him far away from home to a Cambridge education and the literary circles of London. It was also the book that told the story of his bifurcated Anglo-Indian identity most directly and concisely; it was the one book that accompanied the wandering writer everywhere he went around the globe; it was a book that, in demanding freedom of movement for its holder, declared a whole cluster of promises about what would be possible in his life.

A passport is thus the most personal of artifacts, and yet, as Rushdie's story demonstrates, the little book takes on its private value only against the broader history of nations and empires. His possession of an Indian passport was engendered by the fact that, just a few months after his birth in June 1947, India gained its independence from the United Kingdom and discontinued the use of British Indian passports. At almost the same moment, the partitioning of the subcontinent and the founding of the new state of Pakistan placed an international border between Rushdie and much of his extended family. Soon passports would be necessary for reunions on either side of the frontier. But for decades the wider geopolitical order would not see fit to grant broad access to holders of passports from the newly sovereign dominion of

India, and even today other nation-states provide far less visa-free entry to citizens of India than to those of most Western countries.

To be sure, the passport is an object closely associated with the rise of the nation-state and the evolution of international relations, and has thus been continually implicated in the regulation of citizenship status, global migration, asylum seeking, national security, and related concerns. It is an object that assigns an individual an official identity and advances state efforts to monitor and control the movement of certain peoples and populations. This is the unyielding paradox of the passport: even as it promises independence and mobility, adventure and opportunity, escape and safe haven, it is also an essential tool of government surveillance and state power, ostensibly assuring homeland security and regulated traffic across national boundaries. It is, in other words, an object that occupies a place at the very nexus of the personal and the political.

This unique positioning means that passports, these little books, have a capacity to tell stories like few—perhaps no—other documents in the historical archive: they offer a tangible record of our displacements, which is alternately personal memoir and travel narrative, but always caught up in the wider currents of cultural and political history. Rushdie's early passports tell a story of the relationship between his formative identity and the collectives in which that formation inevitably took place. Years later, his British passport would also tell the story of his period in hiding from the *fatwa* brought against him by Iran's Supreme Leader, who called for Rushdie's execution after the publication of *Satanic Verses* (1989); and then, the story of his global celebrity, academic appointments, high-profile friends, and cultural exchanges around the world, after fears of the death sentence waned. Passports thus recite the seeming imperative that we must be "attached" to one place and only "allowed" to enter into others. They tell stories about some of the most consequential ideas of our time, such as "modernity," "nation," and "globalization," though the narratives they offer are far more intimate than these lofty abstractions suggest. They remind us that, at some point in our history, human beings became dependent on the nation-state as a

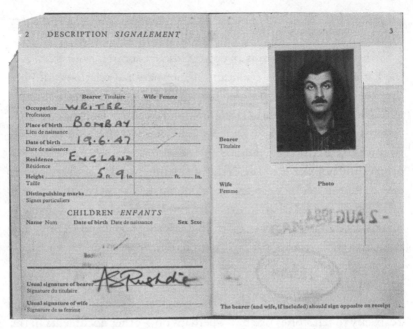

	Bearer Titulaire	Wife Femme
Occupation Profession	WRITER	
Place of birth Lieu de naissance	BOMBAY	
Date of birth Date de naissance	19.6.47	
Residence Résidence	ENGLAND	
Height Taille	5 ft. 9 in.	ft. in.
Distinguishing marks Signes particuliers		

CHILDREN *ENFANTS*

Name Nom   Date of birth Date de naissance   Sex Sexe

Usual signature of bearer
Signature du titulaire

Usual signature of wife
Signature de sa femme

Bearer
Titulaire

Wife
Femme

Photo

The bearer (and wife, if included) should sign opposite on receipt

FIGURE 1. Photo page of Salman Rushdie's passport, 1974. Image courtesy of Stuart A. Rose Library, Emory University. By permission of Her Majesty's Passport Office.

source of identity and protection and that this dependence has only become more difficult to shake in this era of rapid worldwide travel and instantaneous electronic connectivity. As we will see, looking at these precious objects closely—reading these little books carefully—can help us to better understand the emotions and imaginings associated with mobility and migration in our ever more "globalized" epoch.

The rise of the modern territorial state in the eighteenth century gave new impetus to the delineation and control of international borders, along with new means to track and manage the mobility of its citizens. If the nation-state has not yet met its long-heralded demise, it is nonetheless part of an increasingly mobile and interconnected world, where the passport plays a crucial role in facilitating the flow of people and capital across frontiers. The September 11 terrorist attacks led governments around the world to harden their borders, with enhanced passenger screening by trained security personnel, increased identification requirements, and other new surveillance techniques. The years since have also witnessed a rise in nativist and populist movements, exhibiting xenophobic attitudes toward new arrivals and calling for reactionary measures such as travel bans and border walls. But none of this has stemmed the flow. Perhaps no other statistic illustrates our age of global mobility better than the United Nations World Tourism Organization estimate that there were 1.5 billion international tourist arrivals in 2019, more than a twofold increase from the 681 million arrivals in 2000 and a sixtyfold increase from the 25 million arrivals in 1950, just as global travel began to recover from the devastation of the Second World War. Although reliable statistics on undocumented individuals are difficult to compile, most indices also mark a dramatic upturn in "irregular" immigration over the last two decades, to about 260 million border crossings in 2019. Never in the history of our species have so many been so capable or so compelled to cross these manmade lines; never in the history of the nation-state have those lines been more permeable. Not even a global pandemic could slow the pace of global mobility for long.

The less-little book that you now hold in your hands is about those who traverse frontiers, who travel over borders, who step across lines, and the documents they depend on to make these crossings possible. As Rushdie reflects on this theme, he notes the archetypal significance of traversing frontiers, citing an example from Persian myth: the avian god Simurgh summons the birds of earth for a congress in his home atop Mount Qâf, though only a handful of his feathered friends muster enough courage to travel so far. Their journey across the divide between here and there is not a matter of some base need but of religious devotion and divine obligation. The story allegorizes something Rushdie locates deep in our natures: an impulse he sees in Christopher Columbus navigating the Atlantic in search of a new world and (a less problematic instance) Neil Armstrong striding out onto the surface of the moon. This is an impulse we will witness repeatedly in the chapters that follow, whether in Marco Polo traveling the distant reaches of the Silk Road; in Sir Philip Sidney initiating the tradition of the Grand

Tour; in Mary Dods pursuing a life beyond the constraints of social expectations and gender norms; or in James Joyce, Gertrude Stein, Willa Cather, Langston Hughes, Marc Chagall, Paul Robeson, Hannah Arendt, Ai Weiwei, Elon Musk, Yasiin Bey, Sarah Ahmed, and many others traversing the frontiers of the nation-state over the last century in search of novel ways of being in the world. Their journeys involve not just literal movements across geographical borders but metaphorical movements across other boundaries, between home and away, familiar and foreign, belonging and exclusion, sameness and difference, self and other. Their journeys necessitate moving beyond the limits within which they can claim the rights of nativity or citizenship—and thus they entail all manner of dislocations and dangers.

Significance accrues to the passport largely because it is the key prop in the modern ritual of border crossing. "At the frontier," Rushdie writes, "liberty is stripped away—we hope temporarily—and we enter the universe of control. Even the freest of free societies are unfree at the edge, where things and people go out and other people and things come in, where only the right things and people must go in and out."[2] Here we must identify ourselves: our documents proclaim our names and nationalities, our birthdates and birthplaces; the border control officer supplements these details with questions about our activities and intentions, our resources and destinations. The officer examines the document we hand over, looks closely at the picture, at the face of the holder, asks a few more questions. The nation-state he represents offers a form of hospitality that Jacques Derrida calls "conditional," generating interrogations, tensions, dramas related to who we are and where we come from. We are wise, in these circumstances, if we play along with the routine and present ourselves as plainly as possible: no reason to add to the drama with political opinions, smart quips, seditious irony, or anything else that might attract attention. But we are also liable, in these circumstances, to sense our own estrangement from our homes and ourselves: Am I so easily reduced to a set of dates, place names, and biodata? Do I have any ownership over my identity? Am I somehow someone to be feared? Do *I* have anything to fear? It is telling that the passport inspection ritual makes an appearance in just about every major work of travel literature from the last century—from Robert Byron's *The Road to Oxiana* (1937) to Paul Theroux's *The Great Railway Bazaar* (1975), Bruce Chatwin's *In Patagonia* (1977), Pico Iyer's *The Global Soul* (2001), and Elizabeth Gilbert's *Eat, Pray, Love* (2006)—as an unavoidable, and often anxious, episode in any journey across borders. Here, in this interstitial space between one domain and the next, the passport makes its promises to shield us from harm and accompany us to the other side.

· · ·

In *Joseph Anton* (2012), a memoir of his years living in hiding under the fatwa, Rushdie tells a story of the passport ritual gone wrong. Shortly after arriving at Benítez International Airport for a literary fair in Santiago, Chile, on a hot, airless day in 1993, the novelist and his companion (and future wife), Elizabeth West, were surrounded by local police, relieved of their travel documents, and ushered off to a nearby law enforcement building for questioning. This was at a time when Chilean security forces were still under the control of the brutal Augusto Pinochet. As Rushdie recounts the episode, his detention resulted from a struggle between competing factions within the security forces over whether he should be admitted to the country with a death sentence hanging over his head—whether he should receive protection from a nation-state of which he was not a citizen. Held for hours in a small room, with armed guards posted outside, the writer and his partner made repeated requests for the return of their passports, which had no effect on their Spanish-speaking captors. The dire circumstances briefly turned comic when their guards wandered off and Rushdie decided to "take a little stroll" through the streets of Santiago, though he was soon intercepted by an English-language interpreter who respectfully, but stubbornly, demanded his return to the holding room.[3] The situation was only defused when a staffer from the British embassy arrived to retrieve the world-famous author and his companion and deliver them to their hosts in the city.

This episode involving Rushdie's "precious book" can be viewed as a recent, and rather extreme, example of what American literary scholar Paul Fussell has called "the passport nuisance" (borrowing British novelist and travel writer Norman Douglas's phrase).[4] For Fussell, "that ritual occasion for anxiety so familiar to a modern person, the moment one presents the passport at a frontier," is emblematic of a new kind of experience arising shortly after the First World War, when passport requirements were standardized and universalized for the first time. In his classic study *Abroad: British Literary Traveling between the Wars,* Fussell points to a telling instance of "the passport nuisance" in a brief memoir written by D. H. Lawrence, which describes his year-long relationship with the "half-gentleman and debtor" Maurice Magnus. In 1916, before meeting the English novelist, the colorful American had run off to join the French Foreign Legion, only to run away from his regiment and eventually run afoul of Italian authorities for his financial misdeeds after the war. In the spring of 1920, Lawrence accompanied Magnus on a steamship voyage from Italy to Malta, where he witnessed the American's consternation while queuing up for passport inspection. The roguish Magnus, who had managed to swindle his way into fine hotel rooms and first-class train cars across Europe, was reduced to a nervous wreck during the bureaucratic routine. But as soon as he passed "examination"— "Yes, he passed all right. Once more he was free"—his trepidation was quelled and his demeanor again became "quite superb and brisk."

Fussell describes the passport "ritual" at the Maltese port as a "debased" version of the mythic journey across the threshold that divides home from the wider world beyond: "For the hero, it is a moment of triumph. For the modern traveler, it is a moment of humiliation, a reminder that he is merely the state's creature, one of his realm's replaceable parts."[5] In this regard, the scholar suggests, the return home is even worse for "the modern traveler," enduring the sustained scrutiny of a customs and immigration official, who briefly confiscates the passport as he thumbs through a registry of political dissidents, escaped criminals, and other offenders against the state to cross-check the name on the document.

When Hollywood first turned its attention to the border control ritual, it did so with this debasement very much in view, playing the new passport regime for laughs and thereby countering, if not exactly allaying, our anxieties with mirth. *Monkey Business* (1931), the third feature film starring the Marx Brothers, finds the four siblings stowed away on an ocean liner steaming across the Atlantic toward America. The long sea voyage gives them plenty of time to get up to their trademark high jinks: insulting the captain, tormenting the passengers, and generally running amok throughout the ship. These antics rise to a crescendo when the ship finally arrives in New York and the passengers line up for passport inspection and visa stamping: without travel documents of their own, the brothers resort to misdirection and bribery to disrupt the workings of state bureaucracy. But when their initial attempts fail, they turn to a frantic ruse. Each of the siblings, in turn, attempts to pass himself off as one of the paying passengers—the iconic French entertainer Maurice Chevalier—whose passport they have somehow managed to pinch en route to America.

Predictably, as the brothers force their way one by one to the front of the line, the passport officials are neither convinced by their resemblances to the passport photograph nor impressed by their attempts to sing Chevalier's hit, "You Brought a New Kind of Love to Me." The situation reaches a kind of manic absurdity when Harpo (with his wild eyes and mop of curly blond hair, so unlike Chevalier's placid features and slicked dark mane) mounts the passport inspection table and struts about, jauntily wagging his cane, before jumping down and wildly tossing official papers in every direction, as an officer tries to restrain him. Demanding his passport, another passport officer is handed a pasteboard, a washboard, and then finally the Chevalier passport, which the stowaway somehow produces from the depths of his baggy coat. Since the mute Harpo cannot sing Chevalier's tune, he instead lip-synchs to the sounds of a phonograph that has been strapped to his back, though as the machine winds down and the record slows the charade collapses altogether. A brief wrestling match with the officers ensues, ending only when Harpo puts one of them in a headlock, knocks off his service cap, and proceeds to imprint his bald head with a visa stamp.

Waiting in a long line at customs and immigration—at JFK airport or Paris's Charles de Gaulle or Dubai International or wherever—half-dazed from jetlag, we might have fantasized about disrupting the proceedings in a similar way. The comedy of the scene lies precisely in the incongruity between the highly ordered structure of the passport control process and the uninhibited actions of the Marx Brothers, which transform this modern ritual into an anti-rite by parodying, mocking, and utterly deriding it. Nonetheless, all of the "monkey business" performed by the brothers does stage a rather serious critique of the passport regime that had taken hold around the world by the time the film was made. In its carnivalesque reimagining of the border control ritual, the scene announces a protest against the administrative processes of the nation-state that demands not only to know our identities but also to regulate our mobility and migration. If only momentarily, the reeling objections of the Marx Brothers rock the Ship of State, their comic routines undoing its bureaucratic routines, as we laugh in recognition at the contingency and conditionality of its power.

Yet we might also sense in the episodes above that the passport ritual can be more than a mere nuisance. What Fussell does not tell us about the aftermath of the scene witnessed by Lawrence in Malta changes the mood of the whole affair dramatically: Magnus, who faced criminal prosecution for fraud in Italy, as well as general persecution for his homosexuality, would later commit suicide by ingesting hydrocyanic acid rather than submit to extradition. He was a desperate fugitive at the mercy of two sovereign powers. But, like any passport holder, he faced particular pressure as he passed from the domain of one nation-state to another, requiring him to proclaim his personal and national identity, to open himself to inspection and interrogation. We are all vulnerable at the frontier, though some of us are much more so. The anxiety Magnus feels epitomizes the emotions of many travelers facing the ritual of border crossing, as whatever sense of individual sovereignty we hold on to confronts this plainspoken assertion of state sovereignty. We are answerable to bureaucratic procedures that may often seem mundane or tedious but can escalate to the level of tense drama (or tragedy or comedy or tragicomedy) as the passport holder is deemed safe or dangerous, legitimate or illegitimate, free to pass or subject to detention and deportation. The emotions associated with this drama—anxiety, angst, desperation, or relief and perhaps even gratitude—adhere to the passport.

Although he does not remark on the life-or-death significance of the episode in Malta, Fussell nevertheless concludes that "the wartime atmosphere which nourished the passport as an institution hangs about it forever," suggesting not just that "human creatures are conceived as personnel units" by our governments but that we are subject to historical vicissitudes far beyond our control.[6] This sense of vulnerability and contingency, brought on by the horrific clash of nation-states in the First World War, is conspicuous in one of the great works of fiction inspired by the conflict, Ernest Hemingway's *A Farewell to Arms* (1929). The plot of the novel pivots on whether its young American protagonist, Frederic, can flee the destruction and bloodshed of the Italian campaign with his pregnant British lover, Catherine. As the couple make plans for their escape to neutral Switzerland each is asked, "You have a passport, haven't you?"[7] During the war, the passport had become a key means for the nation-states involved to identify their own citizens, while keeping spies, saboteurs, and other potential threats out. For the lovers, the document comes to represent the opportunity (but also a potential obstacle) to leave behind the terrifying world of the conflict, which, as Frederic tells us in an iconic line, is all too ready to kill "the very good and the very gentle and the very brave impartially."[8]

To put this all another way, the very possibility of saying "a farewell to arms" depends on their passports. When Frederic and Catherine make their attempt to escape the war—by rowing across Lago Maggiore to the Swiss shore on the other side—they are confronted by armed soldiers and brought to a customs house. There, the lovers are told to produce their passports and asked a litany of questions that might still sound familiar to our ears: "'What nationality are you?' . . . 'Why do you come here?' . . . 'What have you been doing in Italy?' . . . 'Why do you leave there?'"⁹ The neutral country is hardly welcoming. As we know, the hospitality of the nation-state is always conditional, even in times of peace, receiving guests only when they have been asked to guarantee their identities and testify to their intentions. In Hemingway's novel, the officials eventually allow the couple to enter the country, but require them to relinquish their passports, obtain provisional visas, and report to the police wherever they go in Switzerland. Although Frederic and Catherine have made their escape across the frontier and away from the war, there is still something ominous in these demands: their passport-less status, deprived of the protections offered by the document, portends their inescapable fate in the thrall of powerful nation-states and their internecine conflicts.

A Farewell to Arms offers us a clear view of just how prominent the passport had become at the intersection of personal desire and state power. A few years later, Graham Greene's novel *The Confidential Agent* (1939) would commence from the insight that the passport had also become central to specifying the self—to dictating the identity of the individual in official terms—even in the furtive realm of espionage on the eve of the Second World War. Attempting to disembark after a third-class passage across the English Channel, Greene's protagonist (identified only as "D") is detained by police officials at Dover because his face does not seem to match the photograph in his passport. Years of strife in Spain, including imprisonment, near death in an air raid, and the murder of his wife, have rendered D's visage almost unrecognizable even to his own eyes: "He looked down at it; It had never occurred to him to look at his own passport for—well, years. He saw a stranger's face—that of a man much younger and, apparently, much happier than himself."¹⁰ Taken aside for questioning and provoked by the official to inspect his face in the only reflective surface available—the glass protecting "a picture of King Edward VII naming an express train 'Alexandra'"—he has to confess that the official's doubt is not unreasonable.¹¹ The photograph in the passport becomes more legitimate than the all-but-anonymous individual it is supposed to represent. Moreover, as English literary scholar Leo Mellor points out, D is also compelled to compare himself to the twin emblems of the British Empire in the picture behind the glass—its royalty and its technology—and he is found wanting. Suddenly, confronted with these various images, he discovers that his identity is no longer under his control, but is now dependent entirely on his document: "the object in his hand makes *him* into a thing."[12]

The demands to present oneself for inspection, to be compared to an estranging photograph and a standardized description, to be interrogated regarding origins and aims: all this contributes to a sense of being at the mercy of nameless officials and overbearing governments. Rushdie also writes of how, during his time hiding from the fatwa, he read *The Confidential Agent* and marveled at the economy of the effect it achieved by beginning with this simple device: "A man does not look like his passport photograph, and that's enough for Greene to conjure up an uncertain, even sinister world."[13] In its riotous, inverted way, the passport scene in *Monkey Business* also draws our attention to the power of the passport in certifying the identity of its holder. To gain safe passage across international borders, travelers have to prove not so much the authenticity of their papers as their own coincidence with those documents—a function that not even the manic efforts of the Marx Brothers, supplemented by disguises and masquerades, can subvert. Indeed, their raucous behavior can also be seen as a frenzied response to the sense of anxiety and alienation generated by the passport control ritual, which still has the capacity to "conjure up an uncertain, even sinister world" for us, if only for that brief moment when we hand over our documents, smile cautiously at the passport control officer, and hope for the best.

. . .

Perhaps we should not be surprised that border crossings and passport controls would become something of a staple—and often a source of high drama—in Hollywood films. This is nowhere more evident than in movies about US citizens attempting to escape the perceived horrors of rogue regimes overseas. And nowhere is this more viscerally rendered than in the 1978 film *Midnight Express,* which tells the "true" story of an

American college student, Billy Hayes (Brad Davis), and his attempt to smuggle several kilos of hashish through the Istanbul airport in 1970. The foolhardy young man arrives at passport control in a barely concealed panic, sweating profusely, the only soundtrack his rapidly accelerating heartbeat; the stern customs officer takes a slow pull on his cigarette, inspects the passport, and assesses Hayes with a sidelong glance. The young man makes it through the checkpoint only to be detained a few minutes later as he attempts to board his plane. The remainder of the film serves to underline the stakes of the passport ritual, as Hayes is subjected to a (largely fictional) living hell of physical torment and deprivation in a Turkish prison.

We have moved from nuisance to nightmare. A similar scenario plays out in the 2012 Ben Affleck film *Argo,* based on the story of the so-called Canadian Caper—a covert mission to rescue six US embassy staffers from Tehran in 1979, shortly after the culmination of the Iranian revolution. This time, however, the anxious passport scene plays out at the end of the film, when the staffers attempt to pass themselves off as Canadian filmmakers (using fake Canadian passports) who have been in Iran to scout locations for a *Star Wars*-like sci-fi film. Cue tense music and close-up after close-up of worried glances from the Americans as they approach the airport checkpoint. Although they are waylaid by passport control officers and ushered into a backroom for questioning, the staffers manage to board their flight by using of a copy of *Variety* magazine and some storyboards from the imaginary film to corroborate their identities. In classic Hollywood fashion, *Argo* reaches its dramatic climax when the officers discover their error and attempt to chase down the taxiing jet before it can carry the Americans away to safety. Even as their narrow escape offers a sense of closure and relief, it reminds us again just how fraught with peril the passport ritual can be.

In these films, the frontier turns out to be a site less of mobility and migration than of stress and surveillance (as well as xenophobic distress regarding Americans abroad), where bodies are subjected to enhanced policing techniques, with only their precious travel documents to protect them. If we cannot rely on Hollywood for cultural sensitivity or historical accuracy, *Midnight Express* and *Argo* do tap into the hopes and fears that cling so closely to these documents. Although passport problems may not always land the traveler in a dark prison cell awaiting some ancient, and always inventive, form of torture, they do threaten to strand the traveler in a kind of modern purgatory with no escape in sight. In this sense, the airport-as-frontier becomes a kind of intermediary zone where the traveler is handed off from the legal protections of his own nation-state to those of a foreign government (and then back again at some later date), but only if the transactions are successful. Steven Spielberg's 2004 film *The Terminal* shows us what can happen if they fail: a new kind of nightmare for the passport holder. The film is based in part on the real-life story of Mehran Karimi Nasseri, an Iranian refugee who spent more than eighteen years living in Terminal One of Charles de Gaulle airport after his passport was stolen in 1988. But *The Terminal* casts Tom Hanks in the lead role as Viktor Navorski, a man from the made-up Eastern European country of Krakozhia (Кракожия), who is stranded at JFK airport after his passport is invalidated by the collapse of his government back home. He is thus the generic "foreigner" requesting hospitality at the frontier.

If casting Hanks, "America's Dad," in the role of Viktor Navorski and providing him a fictional homeland blunts the political commentary of the film, *The Terminal* nonetheless seeks to make a general, though sanitized and sentimental, statement about the fate of the unwanted guest in the current world order. The film opens with images of canine patrols making their way through a baggage claim area as uniformed agents rearrange the passport inspection lanes and take their places behind the security desks. These scenes of national security in the post-9/11 airport are soon disrupted by roiling crowds of recently deplaned travelers, spilling through the baggage claim area and into the passport control queues. When Navorski presents himself to the officer at the passport control station, the limits of hospitality quickly become apparent. After a terse "Welcome," he receives the standard interrogation—"Purpose of your visit? Business or pleasure?"—but as Navorski mumbles something (in a bastardized Bulgarian devised for his character), it becomes clear that the foreigner, the guest, does not comprehend the language in which he is interrogated. To make matters worse, when his passport is scanned into the computer network by the officer, it brings back an "IBIS hit"— that is, the document has been flagged in the Interagency Border Inspection System, which provides the United States law enforcement community with information about criminal history, terrorist ties, and other security concerns. A team of Customs and Border Protection (CBP) officers quickly appears and escorts Navorski to one of their pro-verbial backrooms, where the uncomprehending Krakozhian is sub-jected to further interrogation: "What exactly are you doing in the United States, Mr. Navorski? Do you know anyone in New York?"[14]

Viktor Navorski is no savvy former-CIA assassin like Jason Bourne. The hero of *The Bourne Supremacy* (2004) intentionally triggers an IBIS hit with a flagged passport in order to infiltrate the backrooms of Naples International Airport: once there, he mutely resists questioning, then assaults an American consular agent and copies the SIM card from his cell phone, all so that he can listen in on CIA communications. This inversion of the usual border control scenario (a kind of action-movie update of *Monkey Business*) plays out the fantasy of the lone individual resisting the control of state power by turning the passport regime against itself. But it is just that, a fantasy, and a particularly American one at that, even though this brand of rogue individualism would seem to represent a distinct liability in "the war on terror."

The passport registry that Fussell identifies as a part of the "passport nuisance" has evolved into a network of national security databases that may well, at some point in the near future, achieve the aim of creating a single interconnected digital archive of all passports, capable of tracking them with complete visibility as they move around the globe. The passport is no longer a self-contained object, with all vital information clearly inscribed in its pages; instead, it is increasingly a networked object, linked to databases via microchips and antennas— with all the concerns about personal privacy, information security, and identity theft that such connectivity entails. Meanwhile, techniques of cataloguing the body of the traveler have also become more and more sophisticated, developing from subjective descriptions and irregular photographs to electronic fingerprinting, retinal scans, facial recognition, and other biometric data gathering. A great deal of anxiety has stemmed from the dystopian implications of these new protocols at the border, which have significantly augmented the tools of state power used to monitor the individual traveler. Italian philosopher Giorgio Agamben sees these protocols as a sign that, after September 11, we have entered into "a new biopolitical era" of state control and management of our bodies, now increasingly prey to extrajudicial force: the new security paradigm initiated by a state of emergency has become a regular governing technique. In 2004, the same year that both *The Terminal* and *The Bourne Supremacy* were released, Agamben protested what he calls "biopolitical tattooing"—the requirement that those entering the United States on a visa must have their fingerprints and photographs on file—by refusing a post at New York University, rather than submit to the new measures.[15]

All Viktor Navorski wants to do is to see a bit of the city: to go, as he says in a few memorized phrases, on a "Big Apple tour," which includes "Brooklyn Bridge, Empire State, Broadway show *Cats*." But the steadfast CBP officer, Thurman (Barry Shabaka Henley), has already asked Navorski to relinquish both his return ticket and his passport. The scene is initially played for laughs, but it becomes gradually more poignant as it unfolds (a woman's scream in the background reminds us that the backrooms of the airport are a place of jeopardy), reaching a climax when the officer extends his arm to collect the passport from Navorski, who mistakes the gesture for one of hospitality and attempts to shake the outstretched hand. When Thurman corrects him and points to the document—"No, no. Mr. Navorski. That. Passport"—the traveler reluctantly presents it to the officer, who has to forcefully jerk the precious book from the grip of his counterpart.[16] We immediately cut to a close-up of Thurman slipping the burgundy-colored Krakozhian document into a plastic envelope for safekeeping by the authorities of the

FIGURE 2. Viktor Navorski (Tom Hanks) reluctantly hands over his passport in *The Terminal* (2004). Amblin Entertainment.

nation-state. Navorski is now marked as "simply unacceptable"—a "citizen of nowhere," he is later informed—who does not "qualify for asylum, refugee status, temporary protective status, humanitarian parole, or non-immigration work travel or diplomatic visas," though he still fails to understand what he is told. With no valid passport, no recognized status, and no functioning nation-state to call on for help, he will remain stranded at the frontier – this no-man's-land with no way out.

. . .

Much of Rushdie's writing is concerned with the delights and distresses of mobility, with the transformative effects of travel and migration, with the experience of encountering both open hospitality and defensive hostility at the border. No doubt the most fanciful example of frontier traversing in his fiction is to be found in the opening pages of *The Satanic Verses:* we encounter his protagonists, Gibreel Farishta and Saladin Chamcha, plummeting from a great height toward the English Channel after their hijacked jetliner has exploded en route to London Heathrow. Here is a modern myth of border crossing. As they tumble through the atmosphere, like "bundles dropped by some carelessly open-beaked stork," each character undergoes a miraculous rebirth: Gibreel, the famous and flamboyant Bollywood star on his way to visit a lover in London, transforms into his namesake archangel; Saladin, the Indian-born, British-based voice actor returning from a gig in Bombay, metamorphoses into a horned and hooved devil.[17] Equally miraculous, as Saladin clutches onto Gibreel, the latter begins to sing and flap his arms as if they were angel wings, thereby slowing their descent and bringing them to a soft landing in the Channel. Eventually, the two wash ashore on a snowy English beach, the only passengers from the ill-fated flight to survive.

Of course, this is not the whole story. The novel takes place amid the xenophobia of the Thatcher era, not long after the passage of the British Nationality Act of 1981, which dictated that only UK citizens had a right to live there—throwing the fate of residents from the former British colonies up in the air, as it were. It should be no shock, then, that a team of policemen and immigration agents soon apprehend Saladin and demand his passport, even as they laugh derisively at his unlikely account of survival. Through a miraculous frontier crossing, Saladin has avoided the passport ritual at Heathrow, and yet, even in these fantastical circumstances, the passport nuisance-turned-nightmare remains part of the narrative.

How did we get here? How did the world arrive at this universal requirement and what have been the consequences for how we traverse geographical and cultural boundaries? What impact have passports had on the emotions and imaginings of those who use them and are, often reluctantly, defined by them? How have these documents inflected the way we feel about home and away, travel and migration, belonging and dislocation, citizenship and exclusion, national conflict and international cooperation? What can the passport tell us about the uneasy intersection of the personal and political over the course of its long history? These precious books, held close to our vulnerable bodies as we cross borders, carry with them intimate stories about us that, nonetheless, testify to our place in much larger narratives. They speak to the aspirations, uncertainties, and spiraling movements of individuals who have long since come to rest; they give material form to the rights and privileges, restrictions and pressures, that steered these movements. But even as the archive of our passports and their various precursors makes visible where we have come from, it also provides a glimpse of where we are going, as the pace of international travel and global migration continues to accelerate, carrying us toward more and more pressing questions about our place in the world. To investigate the cultural history of the passport, then, is to consider something crucial about the promises of mobility, structures of feeling, and instruments of state power that, perhaps more strongly than ever, affect us today. So let us embark on our journey and cross over the frontier.

PART ONE

———

A Prehistory of the Passport
as We Know It

ONE

Ancient Bodies, Ancient Citizens

ON THE AFTERNOON OF SEPTEMBER 26, 1976, a French military transport plane carrying an Egyptian ruler touched down at Le Bourget airport, just outside of Paris, after a five-hour flight from Cairo. In recognition of his royal station, the traveler was met by Alice Saunier-Seïté, the French secretary of state for universities, and received full military honors from an air force detachment and the Republican Guard, wearing their dress uniforms, complete with red-plumed cavalry helmets and white leathers. The Egyptian sovereign had come to France for what was expected to be a stay of several months in a sterile enclosure on the grounds of the Musée de l'Homme, where he would undergo a series of scientific tests and advanced treatments designed to slow the deterioration of his corpse. For this was Ramesses II, a pharaoh of the Nineteenth Dynasty, whose soul had passed into the afterlife more than three millennia before his French sojourn. Ascending to the throne as a teenager and reigning for more than six decades, Ramesses II is remembered as one of the most powerful rulers in Egyptian history, not least because he led a series of military campaigns in Syria, Nubia, Libya, and neighboring domains that helped to extend his influence throughout the region. But despite the illustrious history associated with Ramesses II, many accounts of his posthumous journey to France focus on a detail that seems utterly incongruous with both his royal station and his mummified state: the long-dead pharaoh reportedly arrived on French soil that early fall day in 1976 with a recently issued Egyptian passport.

No doubt the arrival of the Egyptian ruler was a sensitive matter of international relations. French president Valéry Giscard d'Estaing had proposed the transfer of the mummified pharaoh during a state visit to Egypt in December 1975, as he sought agreements with Egyptian president Anwar Sadat on topics such as international arms sales and the entrance of French industries into the Egyptian economy. Following on the recent Sinai Interim Agreement between Egypt and Israel, which had committed the countries to resolving their conflicts by peaceful means, the French visit was also intended to lay the groundwork for a successful dialogue between oil-rich Arab states and their Western European counterparts at a conference to be held in Paris at the end of December. Initially, d'Estaing had suggested that the mummy of Ramesses II should be transferred to Paris for an exhibition on his reign at the Grand Palais museum; but, "out of concern for Egyptian sensitivities," he later abandoned the scheme in favor of this archeological effort to preserve the "glorious past of Egypt." He was aware that French Egyptologists were already collaborating with Egyptian specialists in Cairo, where they had identified a startling deterioration of the mummy, which had been disinterred nearly a century earlier. Perhaps betraying a bit of condescension, the French president suggested that it would be "very useful" for the mummy to be "treated in a sterile environment" in the laboratories of the Musée de l'Homme, where the specialists were "particularly trained in the application of these treatments."[1]

After a rival Egyptologist in the United States alleged that the deterioration diagnosis was simply a pretext necessitating the venerated relic to travel abroad, the *New York Times* suggested that the mummy may have been suffering from nothing more than "a case of 'diplomatitis.'"[2] Nonetheless, upon his arrival in France, the long-deceased Egyptian sovereign endured numerous scientific analyzes and then underwent intensive treatments to eradicate insects, fungi, and bacteria, which *Le Monde* reported, rather glibly, would surely give him "a new lease of life."[3]

In these circumstances, it is all the more curious that the mummified remains of Ramesses II would require a passport for international travel. Today, stories about "the mummy with a passport" can be found in every corner of the World Wide Web, whether one searches with English, French, or Arabic terms. As might be expected, such accounts are published on sites dedicated to the paranormal and "strange-but-true" history, though they are repeated on seemingly more reliable, or at least more reputable, sites such history.com and nationalgeographic.com. They have also circulated widely on Facebook, Twitter, and Instagram. That being said, the presumed reasons for the passport requirement vary substantially across these sources: we are told that international law would not allow for the transport of human remains without proper identification; that French law necessitated anyone entering the country, whether alive or dead, to carry a passport; that Egyptian law required even deceased individuals to have proper documentation in order to leave the country; that Egyptian officials believed the documentation would afford the pharaoh legal protections abroad, ensuring his safe return home in due time. Even the body of the deceased sovereign, that is, needed the protections offered by a valid passport. Given the long history of European plundering in the region, dating back to the Napoleonic invasion and the "discovery" of ancient, pharaonic Egypt at the end of the eighteenth century, this final rationale is neither unprovoked nor unwarranted—to be sure, colonial infrastructure had facilitated the removal of countless archeological treasures by the French-run antiquities service and by museums across Europe and North America through the course of the nineteenth century.

Yet for all its notoriety, the passport of Ramesses II does not reside in any archive. Reporting on the transfer of the mummy in 1976 makes no mention of the passport, and no such document is to be found in the records of the Egyptian Museum, Cairo, or the Musée de l'Homme, Paris. The collective will of the internet has been content with several widely circulated "mock-up" versions of the document, which integrate a stock photo of Ramesses's ghoulish mummified face, derived from a museum catalogue, with a stock image of the biodata page from a recent Egyptian passport, filled out with the appropriate details: "Date of Birth:—/—/1303 BC . . . ; Nationality: Egyptian; Sex: M; Date of Issue: 09/03/1974; Date of Expiry: 09/03/1981; Profession: King (deceased)."[4]

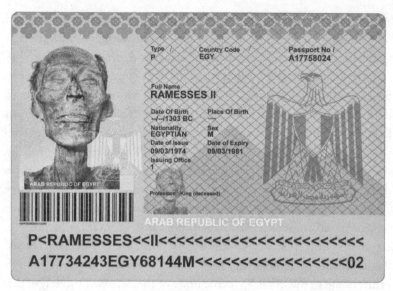

FIGURE 3. An "artist's creation" of Ramesses II's passport, 2020. Image courtesy of HeritageDaily.

But the creators of these mock-ups missed an opportunity to generate more "authentic" fakes, for the examinations carried out in Paris succeeded in establishing a number of physiological details for the pharaoh: he stood some five feet seven inches tall and had fair skin and (to the astonishment of many) red hair, a trait that would have associated him with the deity Set in ancient Egyptian religion. If not an outright hoax, then at the very least the story of the "mummy with a passport" has become an example of collective false memory or what other corners of the internet have dubbed Mass Memory Discrepancy Effect, or MMDE. The phantom passport of Ramesses II may not reside in any official archive, but it nonetheless maintains a shadowy presence, one that troubles the historical archive as an accumulation of memory with its capacity to generate alternative narratives.

The case of the mummy with a passport thus provides us a clue to the mystery of how collective emotions attach themselves to these little books and evoke a shared fascination with the travel documents of the dead. The faux passport of an ancient pharaoh can be summoned to demonstrate the absurdity of national bureaucracies or international law or, more subtly, the anxieties generated by the persistent disparities in international relations and brutal histories of colonial exploitation. In its own way, the mock passport also evokes memories of those amulets that were placed on mummies or wrapped in their bandages to protect the deceased on their transit to Duat, the realm of the dead. In still another way, the modern passport and its many precursors are crucial components of the historical archive, promising to bring us into proximity with the dead and hence stoke the desire of the historian to bring them "back to life." Yet these elusive documents also attest to the fragility of memory, which we seek to preserve against the threat of forgetfulness and oblivion, against the threat of death itself. They are collected and interpreted; they are subject to loss and preservation, to practices of sorting, storing, and deploying information; and yes, they are prone to fakery and forgery. They help to tell stories about the individuals who carried them, but also about the international relations that they signified and facilitated, or even, as in this strange fantasy of a passport-carrying mummy, about the body of a long-deceased sovereign and its implication in a drawn-out afterlife of political intrigues.

. . .

Most histories of the passport, whether scholarly treatises grounded in international law or journalistic pieces composed for a quick online skim, locate the earliest references to travel documents—proto-passports, as it were—in that foundational text of the Western tradition, the Bible. Betraying the desire for a site of origin, these accounts point to the Old Testament—Nehemiah 2:7–9 (dating from about 445 BCE), to be precise—where the eponymous royal cupbearer requests a "letter of safe conduct" from King Artaxerxes I of Persia, so that he may travel to Judea and help to rebuild the walls of Jerusalem.

Pursuing the same nostalgic impulse, we can identify another potential site of origin in the world of Ramesses II, even going back several generations prior to the reign of the great pharaoh. For the archive of Egyptian culture bears what are arguably the oldest documents of international relations to come down to the present day, dating all the way to the mid-fourteenth century BCE. The so-called Amarna tablets or Amarna letters were first discovered in 1887 by a local Egyptian woman at the site of the ancient palace of King Akhenaten. Western archeologists soon arrived in droves, including the pioneering English Egyptologist Flinders Petrie, who unearthed many more tablets over the subsequent decade. Ranging from five to eight inches (12.5 to 20 cm) in height and three to four inches (7.5 to 10 cm) in width, the 382 tablets were imprinted with cuneiform characters by a reed stylus that has managed to convey their messages for more than three millennia. The tablets include a large number of diplomatic communications written in Akkadian, the regional lingua franca of the period, and sent to King Akhenaten by rulers of other states around the eastern basin of the Mediterranean Sea. The communications address commercial dealings and the exchange of gifts, strategic matters and the formation of alliances, as well as dynastic affairs and the procedures of diplomacy, especially the arrangement of marriages among the nobility of various kingdoms. While the letters have been of great importance to biblical studies, providing insight into the culture of the Canaanite people prior to their appearance in the Old Testament, they have only recently been of interest to research on the emergence of early "states," as administratively ordered communities, and of early international (or, more properly, interstate) relations. Together, as a trove, the clay tablets have conjured a potent strain of what Jacques Derrida calls "archive fever," that burning desire to preserve memories, to collect and catalogue all the remnants of human experience, along with the repetitive impulse to return to a site of alleged or assumed origin. And yet most histories of international relations still fail to mention—much less offer any detailed discussion of—the ancient Near East.

This is perhaps even more surprising when we consider that the Amarna letters include a document (catalogued as EA30) that can be identified as the earliest surviving safe conduct pass, a precursor to the

FIGURE 4. One of the cuneiform-imprinted clay tablets discovered at Amarna. Image courtesy of the Metropolitan Museum of Art.

modern passport that provided the bearer secure transit through the lands of the issuing sovereign—and sometimes beyond. The letter takes the form of a command from King Tushratta of Mitanni:

> A message to all the kings of Canaan, the subjects of my brother (the King of Egypt). Thus (says) the King (of Mitanni): I am sending herewith my messenger Akiya to the King of Egypt, my brother, on an urgent mission (traveling as fast) as a demon. Nobody must detain him. Bring

him safely into Egypt! (There) they should take him to an Egyptian border official. And nobody should for any reason lay hand on him.[5]

Royal envoys such as Akiya were a vital means for orchestrating the complex political alliances and economic affairs that developed across the eastern Mediterranean during the Late Bronze Age. Maintenance of these relationships depended on the ability of messengers to move freely throughout the region, not just to mediate diplomatic communication, but to carry goods, conduct transactions, escort royal brides, and serve as informants, even spies. This was, of course, an often arduous and sometimes dangerous profession. Overland travel for the couriers, usually alone but occasionally in caravans employing mules to carry gifts and other goods, was extremely slow in the time of the Armana letters, especially in the brutal heat of the summer months. Oversea travel was not much faster and was subject to the whims of the wind and the hazards of storms and pirates. *The Satire of the Trades,* a book of teachings written during the Egyptian Middle Kingdom, several hundred years earlier, describes the burdens of the vocation in drolly fatalistic fashion: "The courier goes out to a foreign country, after he has made over his property to his children, being afraid of lions and Asiatics."[6]

The clay tablet carried by our imperiled Akiya could not do much to ward off ravenous beasts of prey or even the roving bandits that threatened areas of the region not under sovereign control. Nonetheless, the message it carried can be seen as an early example of sovereign authority seeking to tame violence and assert order in its relation with other sovereigns or sovereign states. Such a document could spare the royal envoy from assaults, robberies, and demands for payment of taxes by both brigands and officials in kingdoms along the way. Certainly, it would have been kept handy in the event of a challenge by the guards, soldiers, or emissaries of a local ruler. It could also prevent the courier from being waylaid or otherwise abused by representatives of the king upon his arrival.

Of course, we can only conjecture about the emotions and sense of personal significance that Akiya may have attached to this small clay tablet, symbolizing the protective power of his sovereign, King Tushratta. But if we look to this distant past for traces of our present, it is possible to envisage the significance of the tablet for him: more than any weapon or piece of armor, even more than a caravan of other messengers, merchants, and mules, the letter guaranteed his bodily safety. For, almost magically, by virtue of a series of markings on its surface, the tablet embodied and mobilized the authority of the king to protect his courier on a toilsome journey into foreign lands. Did Akiya clutch it close to him in the sturdy satchel where he carried the items most crucial to his well-being? Did he reach into the satchel and run his fingers nervously over the cuneiform characters, seeking reassurance, when he sensed the presence of danger? Did he feel a moment of panic when, setting out one already-sweltering morning, he rifled through the satchel to be sure it still contained the precious object? What sentiments adhered to this little piece of clay? Again, we can only imagine, perhaps projecting some of our modern passport anxieties onto the ancient messenger, but there can be little doubt that, in addition to its diplomatic purpose, the clay tablet functioned as an amulet of sorts: an object believed to protect a person from trouble or harm, as if by some powerful enchantment. We know that amulets—of metal, stone, glass, and clay—played an important role in ancient Near Eastern religious beliefs regarding the safety of both the ambulant living and the mummified dead, but few of these charms could have possessed the additional rhetorical and political force of EA30.

According to an agreed practice, the message that the ancient passport holds is formulated to order the representatives of another sovereign power to let this messenger pass freely through their lands: "A message to all the kings of Canaan, the subjects of my brother (the King of Egypt). Thus (says) the King (of Mitanni): I am sending herewith my messenger Akiya. . . . " In this sense, the cuneiform inscription on this early travel document functions as what British philosopher of language J. L. Austin calls a "performative"—that is, a message that *does* something rather than merely *saying* something. When the king utters, "Nobody must detain him. Bring him safely into Egypt!" he performs an act, namely, issuing a command or order. In a contemporary US passport, analogous language persists more than three millennia later, though it has morphed into a slightly milder entreaty: "The Secretary of State of the United States of America hereby requests all whom it may concern to permit the citizen/national of the United States named herein to pass without delay or hindrance and in case of need to give all lawful aid and protection." According to Austin, such a message cannot be judged according to whether it is true or false, but rather according to whether it is "happy" (successful) or "unhappy" (unsuccessful), depending on if others play along with this verbal assertion of sovereign authority or not. In this sense, as other theorists have suggested, the repetition of happy performatives might even be seen as productive of such power.[7]

What is more, the message on the cuneiform tablet (that early technology of mediation) extends the authority of the king beyond the reach of his voice, of his bodily presence, of his sovereign domain, and perhaps even beyond the end of his life, so long as it survives in material form. Upon arrival, then, Akiya would either have been welcomed with hospitality, a bountiful feast and comfortable lodging, perhaps a gift for himself and a few more to return to King Tushratta, or have been subject to robbery, imprisonment, and even murder, if the command on his passport was unsuccessful—unhappy—at his destination.

Matters of sovereign authority like these were often negotiated between various rulers in the Amarna letters. But the system of rules ordering relations between kings in the ancient Near East was believed to come under the jurisdiction of the gods, who served as the ultimate arbiters on such concerns. Due to this divine jurisdiction, scholars debate whether the rules that bore on documents like EA30 should be considered in terms of theology or rather as the earliest forms of international law, since there was no effective distinction between the two domains in the ancient Near East.[8] Everyone involved, as legal scholar Raymond Westbrook has emphasized, worshipped gods and believed them to be involved in their affairs. This meant that constituent power of religion did not just establish the power of the king in each domain and order the political map of the entire region; it also effected the general transition from the state of nature to the state of law across these societies. During the rule of Akhenaten, however, Egypt witnessed the emergence of early forms of international relations, as well as a number of radical, though generally fleeting, social and cultural transformations: the renovation of artistic and architectural styles, the transfer of the capital to its new site in Amarna, and, for the first time anywhere, the establishment of a monotheistic religion, dedicated to the sun god, Aton. The legacy of these transformations has been a topic of much speculation. In his final book, *Moses and Monotheism* (1939), Sigmund Freud would venture, based in part on evidence derived from the Amarna letters, that Aton was in fact the original god of the biblical prophet and thus the basis for both Jewish and Christian theology.

We should not forget that the letter of safe conduct referenced in the Book of Nehemiah almost a millennium after the rule of Akhenaten performs a similar function to that among the Amarna tablets. The document mentioned in the Old Testament—called a *halmi* ("sealed document" in Elamite) or *miyatukka* (in Old Persian)—was a travel permit (and ancient meal voucher of sorts) required to traverse the royal roads of Persian Achaemenid Empire as early as the sixth century BCE. The requirements were a significant administrative function of what French Iranologist Pierre Briant has called "a monolithic State as vast as the future Roman Empire," stretching from Upper Egypt to central Asia, from the Danube to the Indus.[9] Halmis are mentioned on many occasions in the so-called Persepolis Administrative Archives (clay tablets discovered in the ceremonial capital of the Achaemenid Empire), though a particular Aramaic papyrus from ancient Egypt (a letter provided by Aršâma, an Achaemenid satrap during the fifth century BCE, for his steward Nehtihôr) has allowed historians to reconstruct their use with great precision. In general, the documents indicate the number of travelers in the caravan, the path they were to follow, and the rations they should be supplied along the way. During the fifth and sixth centuries BCE, the royal roads were divided into stages across each province, with storehouses and postal relays positioned along the way; when reaching the end of each stage, the caravan leader was compelled to present a halmi, which entitled the travelers to the exact quantity of provisions specified on the document. For instance, Aršâma declares in his letter: "Behold! One named Nehtihôr, [my] officer (*pequid*), is going to Egypt. Do give him (as) provisions from my estate in your provinces . . . every day two measures of white meal . . ., three measures of inferior meal, two measures of wine or beer, and one sheep, and hay according to (the number of) his horses."[10] Of course, in addition to dictating their menu, the halmi also allowed Nehtihôr and his companions to carry on to the next stage of their journey.

The Book of Nehemiah tells us about something more than these practical matters. Living in exile as a high-ranking official in the court of King Artaxerxes, the sixth monarch of the Achaemenid Empire, Nehemiah learns—to his considerable alarm—that the walls of Jerusalem have been knocked down and the Jewish inhabits of the city have been thrust into great jeopardy. After several days of fasting and prayer, the dismayed Israelite comes before Artaxerxes, who inquires about the cause of his worry and what might be done to alleviate it. Nehemiah immediately lodges a request for the travel documents, which accompanies an appeal for the materials he will need to rebuild Jerusalem when he returns:

> 7 I said to the king, "If it pleases the king, let letters be given to me for the governors of the region beyond the River, that they must permit me to pass through till I come to Judah, 8 And a letter unto Asaph the keeper of the king's forest, that he may give me timber to make beams for the gates of the palace which appertained to the house, and for the wall of the city, and for the house that I shall enter into."

What is perhaps most extraordinary about the request is that it is preceded by a lengthy prayer to God that, receiving heartfelt repentance from Nehemiah for the sins of the Israelites, He might grant the exile favor in the presence of Artaxerxes. The utterly remarkable fact is that the Israelite does not appeal to his God directly for safe passage through "the region beyond the River" (i.e., west of the Euphrates), but rather for help in securing a letter of safe passage expressing the temporal authority of the Achaemenid sovereign. Such, apparently, was the rhetorical and political force of a halmi from Artaxerxes in the province of Avar-nahra ("Beyond the River") where the embattled district of Judah lay.

The Book of Nehemiah also testifies to the emotional energies circulating around the letter of safe conduct. The biblical text has an extremely complex and sometimes conjectural history: its chapters circulated as independent works, combined with other materials to form Ezra-Nehemiah around 400 BCE, received additional editing during the Hellenistic era, occasionally broke off into a distinct book in Latin translations after the ninth century, eventually becoming a standard book of the Paris Bibles in the thirteenth century and then of Hebrew Bibles nearly three hundred years later. But it is generally agreed that the early and late chapters, which present the action in an animated first-person voice, are based on the memoirs of a historical figure named Nehemiah; and it is undeniable that, as the narrator relays his own story, he provides these sections of the text with a rapt immediacy. As he tells it, "I was very sore afraid" when approaching Artaxerxes with his request, and the Israelite both exclaimed, "Let the king live for ever," and "prayed to the God of heaven" one last time before lodging his request with the Achaemenid sovereign. When his passport request is granted, the overwrought Nehemiah identifies it, with evident relief, as a sign that "the good hand of my God [is] upon me."

．　．　．

As important as this early reference of travel documentation has been for scholars and journalists, and as compelling as the emotional revelations of the desperate exile have been for readers of the Bible, the Book of Nehemiah is perhaps more important to the history of the passport for what it tells us about ancient conceptions of citizenship. At the beginning of the book, the majority of Israelites are subjects of the Achaemenid Empire, scattered across lands far from their home, even as they continue to nurture a common identity and a shared affiliation to Judah. It is this affiliation, of course, that drives Nehemiah to return home to the city of his ancestors in the hope of rebuilding its walls and restoring the community to its former integrity. As this work proceeds in later chapters, he faces formidable antagonists and witnesses new divisions arise among the people of Jerusalem. But soon after he assumes the role of provincial governor, the defiant Nehemiah institutes a series of social and liturgical reforms designed to unite the community and protect it from its enemies, both internal and external. He plans a census of the inhabitants of Jerusalem and establishes a register of genealogy, which includes the names of those families that have returned to the city from their captivity in Babylon. Driven by his sense of righteousness, Nehemiah also assists in the efforts of his fellow reformer, Ezra, to mend the community by promulgating the teachings of the Torah, which form a binding agreement among the Israelites: the book of law becomes the law of the land. In these chapters, the two men thus work to establish a form of citizenship based on both the celebration of common bonds and the recognition of communal laws, but this conception, as many have noted, is also dependent on excluding others beyond the walls of the city.

Commentators up to our own time have seized upon this unfortunate chauvinism to promulgate their own ideas of citizenship. When, just hours before the inauguration of Donald J. Trump on January 20, 2017, agitational Southern Baptist pastor Robert Jeffress delivered a sermon at St. John's Episcopal Church in Washington, DC (a National Historic Landmark that was later the site of a rather infamous photo op for the Bible-brandishing president), he called on the Book of Nehemiah to affirm that "God is not against building walls!" Speaking directly to Trump, who sat there in the front pew, Jeffress enthusiastically summoned the biblical figure: "When I think of you, President-elect Trump, I am reminded of another great leader God chose thousands of years ago in Israel."[11] The pastor, known for his boyish smile, went on to announce cheerfully that the first step to rebuilding the community in Jerusalem was for Nehemiah to reconstruct "the great wall" around the city, which he succeeded in doing, according to Jeffress, because he refused to bow to his critics or to allow the disapproval of his own citizens to deter him.

Admittedly, the idea of citizenship has often emphasized this logic of exclusion, insofar as the concept draws its significance from the opposition between in-groups and out-groups, citizens and aliens who do not enjoy the same rights and privileges. If histories of citizenship typically begin across the Mediterranean in ancient Greece, it is largely because that is where an idea of the *polis* (or "city state") emerged to help define the bond between favored men and their native city—to the exclusion of women, slaves, foreigners, and other subordinates, judged unfit for political participation. In recent years, with an eye toward our modern political situation, Giorgio Agamben has also called attention to the ancient Greek distinction between the "good life" of political participation (*bios*) and the "bare life" of mere bodily or biological existence (*zoē*), which was considered to be excluded from the polis in any strict sense. Indeed, for Agamben, the exclusion of bare life is crucial to establishing the polis as a properly political space, and yet despite this exclusion, the city state continued to exercise power over *zoē* precisely through the abiding potential to transform it into *bios*. Those brought within the embrace of polis citizenship enjoyed certain rights, such as owning land and holding political office, though they also shouldered civic responsibilities, including participation in the assembly and defense of the city state in times of war.

For these reasons, citizenship in ancient Greece was closely regulated. It was only within a narrow range of circumstances that the polis would bestow the status of citizen on an outsider, who might benefit the community with his valuable talents or financial assets. Even more than its neighboring city states, Athens was restrictive in granting citizenship, and in the middle of the fifth century BCE (nearly simultaneous with the events described in the Book of Nehemiah) the polis passed a measure limiting citizen status to freeborn persons whose fathers *and* mothers were both Athenians. All other inhabitants of the city state were considered "illegitimate."

A few generations later, when Plato set out his vision of an ideal polis in *The Republic* (c. 375 BCE), he maintained the notion that citizenship should be inherited. Nonetheless, he also imagined an inclusive class structure—with room for merchants, traders, sailors, soldiers, and a ruling elite of philosopher-kings—that would promote justice precisely by allowing each group to pursue its own endeavors, without disrupting the efforts of others. But, infamously and rather capriciously, his argument concludes by excluding most poets and artists (of all people) from his ideal polis, because their work, trading as it does in illusory images, threatened to excite passions that might overwhelm the self-control of average citizens and rulers alike. It might also be noted here that the philosopher, with his totalitarian tendencies, would prohibit any citizen of his ideal republic from traveling outside the polis for private reasons and anyone under forty years of age from leaving the city state at all, not even to conduct public business as heralds or ambassadors. So much for the educative benefits of going abroad.

In actuality, most Greek citizens could travel freely around the Mediterranean without so much as a letter of safe conduct or other such document to ease their way. Yet there were exceptions. The Athenian Agora excavations of 1971 unearthed a number of terra-cotta tokens that have been identified by American classicist John H. Kroll as "*symbola*," "credentials," or "passports" for official couriers and private individuals sent out from Athens to military headquarters across the region during the fourth century BCE. Fashioned of fine Attic clay and pressed with an engraved stamp, the twenty-five tokens found at the Agora (the open space at the center of ancient Athens used for markets, religious processions, military drills, and other public assemblies) typically include the demotic of a military commander stationed at the peripheries of Athenian territory. The demotic, a kind of ancient proof-of-residence, indicates the commander's Athenian citizenship, while in a number of cases the commander's military title—for example, "Nikoteles, general for Samos"— suggests that he had authority well beyond the city state proper.[12] Because the clay tokens were apparently produced and distributed in considerable quantities, Kroll concludes that they must have served an integral function in the administration of Athenian military affairs during the period.

One of the most intriguing facets of research into the Agora tokens is that it links their function as passports with the term σύμβολον (*symbolon*). Similar usages of the word can be found in Aristophanes's comedy *The Birds* (414 BCE), when a middle-aged former Athenian confronts the Goddess of the Rainbow for trespassing in the newly founded city of the birds, "Cloud Cuckoo Land": "Did an official provide a symbolon for you in person?"; and in Aeneas Tacticus's *How to Survive under Siege* (fourth century BCE), which outlines the most effective methods for defending the inhabitants of a surrounded city: "Allow no citizen, or immigrant, to leave by sea without a [symbolon]." To be sure, in fourth-century Athens, objects called symbola were used for a variety of administrative purposes by a number of polis institutions. The Greek word *symbolon*, combining σύν or *syn* ("together") and βάλλω or *bállō* ("I throw, put"), originally derived from a common commercial practice: a contract was confirmed by breaking some durable item in two, so that each party could retain a piece of the whole. If it was necessitated at a later date, either party could confirm their identity by putting their half of the object together with the other: thus, *symbolon* initially meant something like a "token employed in comparisons to determine authenticity," and from there evolved into the more general sense of "token," "credential," or "watchword," eventually including "ticket," "permit," or "license" as well. Of course, the word also gives us *symbol*, in the familiar sense of something that signifies or denotes something else.

It was in this same context, fourth-century BCE Athens, that Aristotle developed his influential theory of writing, which views a symbolon *not* as a "representation" or "imitation" of something, but precisely as "a token or tally, directly corresponding to another such item, with which it correlates." As British linguist Roy Harris emphasizes, "It thus constitutes one half of a complementary pair, the 'symbolic' connection between the two being established by agreement and shown by some physical connection between them."[13] Crucial to the idea of the symbolon, whether we have a "symbol" or a "passport" in mind, is that even though it takes the form of a material object, a tangible item, its function depends entirely on the shared agreement of the parties involved. Its use relies on the appropriate circumstances. For a symbolon to serve its purpose, that is, there must be a community of interpretation, be it in the polis or at the distant reaches of its territories, that shares the same understanding of its meaning. Only in this way can a symbolon perform its job successfully (happily); only in this way, as we shall see again and again in the chapters that follow, has the passport taken on a range of outsized symbolic meanings.

With a bit of wishful thinking, some ancient Greeks were already trying to extend the territorial reach and symbolic value of their "passports" just about as far as can be imagined: members of Dionysic and Orphic religious cults used them to facilitate their passage from the domain of the living to that of the blessed dead, Elysium. Befitting their ambitious purpose, these were no utilitarian clay tokens but rather thin tablets or "leaves" of gold, inscribed with the name of the deceased and instructions on how to navigate the hazards of the afterlife. Often, the inscriptions also seem calculated to reassure the dead that their cult membership would guarantee them a pleasant journey. About forty of the tablets (sometimes referred to generically as *Totenpässe* from the German for "passports of the dead"), dating from the third and fourth centuries BCE, have been found around the Greek-speaking Mediterranean, placed in graves near the dead or in casings around their necks as protective amulets. Thus, much like the amulets of their Egyptian predecessors, these gold tablets promised to protect the migrating souls of Greek initiates after their bodies had perished. Their prevalence suggests the solace to be found in such a promise, even if the tablets could offer no assurance of a return passage.

• • •

Ancient Rome was generally more liberal in granting citizenship than ancient Greece insofar as Roman law accommodated individuals who were not born Roman citizens, thus broadening the embrace of the polis to include women, freed slaves, and even inhabitants of Roman client states far beyond the city. The fact that just about anyone might be made into a Roman citizen meant that different communities of people could come to identify with Rome, even if they were not natives of the city or even descended from natives. But like their Greek counterparts, ancient Romans still viewed citizenship as a collection of both privileges and responsibilities that included the rights to vote, to stand for public office, to enter into marriage, to hold property, and to have a legal trial, as well as the duties of military service and paying taxes. This is not to say that all citizens enjoyed the same protections, however. Although Roman law extended a range of potential rights to its citizens, it was only the *cives Romani* who were considered full Roman citizens and who experienced the complete shelter of Roman law—and only the so-called *optimo iure* ("best rights") among this group enjoyed the right to vote and to stand for public office. Under certain exceptional circumstances, citizenship could also be revoked, either temporarily or permanently. For example, Roman law could condemn criminals to the status of *homo sacer* (meaning both "sacred man" and "accursed man"), as a kind of sanctified outlaw: someone who could not be sacrificed according to the decrees of divine law, but who could be killed without it being labeled murder by the laws of the city. The *homo sacer*, whom Agamben identifies with zoē or "bare life," was prohibited from inhabiting the city alongside its legitimate citizens; instead he was exiled to the furthest margins of Roman society, where he existed in a strange (and, for the philosopher, highly significant) zone of indistinction between law and violence, norm and exception, inclusion and exclusion.

The most notorious instance of exile under archaic Roman law involved the great statesman, rhetorician, and advocate (as well as perhaps the greatest Latin stylist the world has ever known) Marcus Tullius Cicero. A hybrid of the treacherous poet and the dependable philosopher-king, Cicero was also an influential political thinker, deeply indebted to Plato in treatises such as *De republica* and *De officiis*. Both texts contemplate the question of citizenship in relation to constitutional theory and the "duties of justice," and have become foundational to the divergent traditions of republicanism and cosmopolitanism (another word derived from the ancient Greek, combining *kosmos,* "world" or "universe," with *politês,* "one of a city" or "citizen"). As a political actor, Cicero played a key role in thwarting a plot to overthrow the Roman Republic in 63 BCE, when he rooted out five of the aristocrats responsible for the so-called Catilinarian conspiracy and saw that they were swiftly executed for their crimes. For his deeds, Cicero was initially hailed as *Pater Patriae* ("Father of the Country"), despite the fact that he had begun his career as a so-called *novus homo* ("new man"), the first member of his family to serve in the Roman senate. Within a few short years, however, his political rival Clodius introduced a bill in the senate to outlaw the execution of Roman citizens without a proper trial, retroactively condemning Cicero's actions and promptly driving him into exile. Adding insult to injury, the very day that the statesman left the Italian peninsula, Clodius put forward another bill—a kind of ancient article of civil forfeiture, combined with a restraining order—that mandated the confiscation of all Cicero's properties and prohibited his presence within four hundred miles of Rome.

Within a year and a half, the political winds had changed again, allowing for Cicero's homecoming and the restoration of his possessions. But he returned to a maelstrom, stirred by a turbulent rivalry between Rome's most powerful generals that eventually forced the statesman from the city once more in 49 BCE, when he fled to join Pompey's forces in Greece ahead of Caesar's advancing armies.

This departure has recently inspired a kind of alternative-history thought experiment by a pair of classicists, T. Corey Brennan (also known for his work as a guitarist with the Lemonheads and other bands) and Hsing I-tien, who transfer our narrative from the Mediterranean world to the far reaches of ancient China: "What if," they ask, "rather than returning to Rome [Cicero] had chosen another path, namely the road eastward to the Han Empire, where he might persuade powerful groups to move against Caesar?" Brennan and Hsing argue that the notion is not entirely implausible; had the exile been so disposed, "he would have had no difficulty finding a guide in Cilicia," where he had once served as governor, or even closer to Rome in Asia Minor. In actuality, by the time Cicero left Rome in 49 BCE, traffic had been moving back and forth along the Silk Road for nearly a century, generating an early form of globalization based not just on the textile trade, but on the exchange of ideas about commerce and governance. It is intriguing to consider how Cicero, that early proponent of cosmopolitanism—who acknowledged obligations not just to his fellow Roman citizens, but to the wider republic of humanity—might have conducted himself on such a journey. What exchanges, agreements, or allegiances might he have sought along the way?

It is also intriguing to consider the role his travel documents would have played. Brennan and Hsing envision the Roman statesman crossing the frontier of the Han Empire and traveling through the countless villages, towns, steppes, and deserts along the Silk Road for months, even years, on his way to the capital in Chang'an (present-day Xi'an).

> He would then have had to pass the frontier control point, probably at the Jade Gates (Yumen 玉門) Pass, near Dunhuang 敦煌, a military stronghold with impressive earthen walls punctuated by beacon towers extending far into the distance. There he would have obtained the travel documents needed for him to continue his journey to Chang'an. . . . The pass (*zhuan* 傳) was a wooden tablet recording his name, place or origin, and title, and his skin color, height, and other physical characteristics. His travel documents would have included a list of his possessions, the names of members of his traveling party, and the weapons, vehicles, and horses he brought with him. Depending on Cicero's powers of persuasion through interpreters, it might also have granted free passage through subsequent checkpoints or free board and lodging.[14]

For the classicists, this scenario is part of a larger imagined narrative that implicates Cicero in a Chinese plot against Caesar, but we can linger here over the implications of his fictional travel documents. In late Republican Rome, a messenger or other traveler of low rank would have likely carried the seal or mark of his patron to ensure his safe passage, although Cicero would almost certainly have moved about without the aid of such an object. This privilege would no doubt have diminished after this once-powerful senator was expelled from the polis. As he traveled east into the administrative regions of the Han Empire, he would have encountered a complex bureaucracy managed with documents such as the zhuan, which played a crucial role in the intricate system of traffic control on the Silk Road.

The zhuan adds an important dimension to the cultural history of the passport, one that reemerges prominently later in this book, because it brings the archive and the body, the document and the traveler, closer together than ever before. It is possible to reconstruct the use and significance of these ancient passports thanks to the extensive use of documents and thorough record keeping during the Han Dynasty (202 BCE–220 CE). Over the last century, a series of discoveries in the ruins of ancient watchtowers scattered along the Juyan and Jianshui border defense lines has provided archeologists and historians with more than 30,000 bamboo strips and other wooden documents. These include detailed registers—ancient databases, as it were—of those granted permission to pass through checkpoints, as well as wooden passports that had evidently been presented at checkpoints but subsequently confiscated from or otherwise relinquished by travelers. These were travel documents, then, that presage the other, bleaker side of the passport paradox, for they were intended not so much to protect or propel the vulnerable body of the holder as to track and control its movement across frontiers.

Perhaps most striking, both the zhuan and the registers contained information relevant to the identification of individual travelers, including, as Brennan and Hsing note, their name, title, height, complexion, age, and other biodata. Records also indicate that borrowed or forged passes would result in punishment of their bearers. The physical description of zhuan holders thus appears to have played a crucial role in guaranteeing that the documents and the broader system of traffic control could be relied on to monitor the movement of people through the Han Empire. In this regard, the passes presage the modern travel documents that emerged some two millennia later. Already, they raise questions about how identity might be "read off the body" with attention to particular physical traits, how travel documents might administer mobile populations, and even how certain sly individuals might seek to circumvent that control, despite considerable risk to their well-being.[15] If zhuan could not yet be understood as identification documents per se, capable of verifying stable features of personal and legal identity, they nonetheless provide a glimpse of what was to come: they served to locate travelers within a larger bureaucratic system of registration and control designed to restrict freedom of movement.

TWO

Great Sovereigns, Grand Tourists

THAT WE KNOW ANYTHING ABOUT the travels of Marco Polo is due almost entirely to his fortuitous imprisonment (if there could be such a thing) not long after his return from China to Italy in 1295, when he was captured during a skirmish between Venetian forces and their Genoese adversaries. Over the course of several months, as a means to pass the time behind bars, he recounted extravagant tales of his Eastern travels to his cellmate, who happened to be the Italian romance writer Rustichello da Pisa. The writer (whom many have called a hack) subsequently integrated the tales with other stories, including scenes from his own Arthurian romances and other recent reports back from China, to produce the tome we now know as *The Travels of Marco Polo*. Versions of the text quickly circulated through Europe in a number of manuscript translations and soon came to play a crucial role in the Western understanding of the Far East. Although Polo is often given credit for being the first European to venture down the Silk Road, other adventurers from the continent had traveled into the Mongol Empire, and a few, including Willem van Ruysbroeck and Giovanni da Pian del Carpine, had even written down accounts of their journeys. But none had traveled as extensively as Polo, who was away from Venice for some twenty-four years as he moved across China, India, Japan, and other far-flung domains; and none had produced such a compelling, entertaining, and widely circulated report of their travels. That any of this happened, that Polo made his journeys and lived to tell the tale, owes much to some rather remarkable travel documents.

Over the course of its long history, the vastness of the Silk Road evoked a variety of efforts to control, secure, and facilitate the movement of peoples and goods (not to mention ideas and other contagions), efforts that foreshadow our contemporary techniques for managing the flows of globalization. During the thirteenth century, after many years of disruption, attempts by the ever-determined, and often brutal, Genghis Khan to reestablish the trade routes and bring them under unified political administration helped to establish the Mongol Empire, which stretched from the Black Sea in the west to the Pacific Ocean in the east. Here, along a seemingly boundless network of roads trod by merchant caravans, the use of travel documents once again took hold. Presiding over the so-called *Pax Mongolica*, the Great Khans that followed Genghis often provided their envoys and other officials traveling the routes with tablets of hard-wearing wood, bronze, silver, or gold, called *paizi*s (Chinese) or *gerege*s (Mongolian), which afforded the travelers secure passage through Mongol lands as well as the right to demand various goods and services from populations along the way. Given such benefits, local Mongol authorities were known to abuse the scheme by issuing unofficial paizis that allowed for the mistreatment and exploitation of roadside inhabitants. But the official golden tablets issued by the Khans were special: they asserted the sovereign's authorization of the holder's movement across his territories and into other jurisdictions spanning the length of the Silk Road. No doubt the best-known recipient of such a tablet was our venturesome Venetian merchant, Marco Polo, although he was not even the first Venetian to be granted its far-reaching privileges: in 1266, his father and uncle, Nicolò and Maffeo, had been presented with paizis by the grandson of Genghis Khan, the much-celebrated Kublai Khan, to assist in their long journey home from Dadu (present-day Beijing).

Among the very first Europeans to travel the full distance of the Silk Road, the Polo brothers had been greeted with both extreme curiosity and extreme generosity by the Great Khan, who was already familiar with "the Latins" but desired additional knowledge about Western political and religious matters, especially the Catholic Church.

FIGURE 5. "The Great K[h]an delivering a Golden Tablet to the [Polo] Brothers. From a miniature of the 14th century," in *The Book of Ser Marco Polo* (1903), translated and edited by Colonel Sir Henry Yule. Image courtesy of Archive.org.

Surmising that he might benefit from the wisdom and authority of the Church in Rome as he sought to quell unrest in his immense empire, Kublai dispatched the Polo brothers, along with one of his own emissaries, to transmit a request to the Pope: that he should send one hundred priests, "able to show by clear reasoning that the Christian religion is better than" his own, along with "oil from the lamp that burns above the sepulcher of God in Jerusalem."[1] To safeguard the brothers on their marathon journey home, the Mongolian sovereign provided the Italian merchants with a golden tablet about ten inches long and three inches wide (25 × 7.5 cm), inscribed with a fearsome command that translates roughly as: "By the strength of the eternal Heaven, holy be the Khan's name. Let him that pays him not reverence be killed." As *The Travels* makes clear, a stranger in a strange land could very well end up at the wrong end of a spear, resulting in imprisonment, enslavement, or summary execution. Not only did the golden tablet provided by Kublai Khan protect the Polo brothers on their journey back to Venice around 1270, thus making possible their second and far more famous expedition to the

Far East, with the teenaged Marco in tow; but two more paizis would permit the three Polos to leave the court of the Great Khan in Xanadu, accompany the wedding party of the princess Kokachin to Persia, and then finally return to Venice for good in 1295.

During their journey home, the Venetians were presented with still more tablets by the Persian ruler (and Kublai Khan's great-nephew) Kaikhatu in the Middle Eastern region of the Mongol Empire, where the Polos tarried for many months:

> he gave them, as emissaries of the Great Khan, four tablets of gold, each a cubit in length and five fingers in width and weighing three or four marks. Two bore the sign of gerfalcon, one of the lion, and one was plain. In these tablets it was written that in reverence to the Everlasting God the name of the Great Khan should be honoured and praised throughout the length of years, and everyone who disobeyed his commands would be put to death and his goods confiscated.[2]

The issuance of these paizis is a testament to the great confidence, and even affection, that Kublai Khan and his family invested in the Polos, who were permitted to travel with a kind of diplomatic status as their trusted emissaries. But these tablets, as impressive as they were, also demonstrated the limits of their issuing authority in the farther reaches of the Mongol Empire, where the strength of the dynasty was in increasing jeopardy two generations after the rule of Genghis Khan. Their power as safe conduct passes was directly proportional to the power of the sovereign who issued them, even as the passes extended the reach of that power precisely by asserting or reasserting his authority in distant lands. But the command they asserted was not guaranteed to succeed. Marco tells us these tablets also entitled the Polos to escorts of horses and horsemen at several points along their journey, "a necessary precaution, because Kaikhatu was not a lawful ruler and the inhabitants might have molested them, as they would not have done had they been subject to a lord to whom they owed allegiance."[3]

The veracity of these accounts has been contested since they were first published in the late thirteenth century, and this skepticism has only grown over the ensuing centuries due in part to the fact that the text exists in about 150 unreliable versions in some dozen languages, the original manuscript having been lost long ago. There can be little doubt that Polo and Rustichello both sought to enliven certain elements of the story, just as there can be little doubt that omissions were made and errors were inserted through copying and translation missteps from version to version over the years.

Here again the tablets play a significant role. When Marco lay on his deathbed in 1324, nearly thirty years after his return from the East, friends and family gathered around and, even as they paid their last respects, sought to elicit a confession regarding what they took to be his tall tales and extravagant lies. As was common practice, a priest was also summoned to the bedside, though rather than receiving a final confession, he served the role of a notary to transcribe a last will and testament, written out on a piece of sheepskin measuring about twenty-six inches by ten inches (65 × 25 cm). In 2018, a team of Italian historians completed a three-year study of Polo's will, and the Biblioteca Marciana (Venice's National Library of St. Mark) published a scholarly book on the bequest, including a reproduction of the nearly seven-hundred-year-old parchment. The bequest distributes the considerable wealth of the merchant-traveler among the guilds and religious institutions of Venice, as well as among his daughters, something atypical in a time of patrilineality. Giving testimony to Polo's journeys in the East, the document also lists items such as the silver girdle of a Tartar knight, the golden parade headdress of a Mongolian lady, and the golden paizis presented to him by Kublai Khan to ensure his safe passage home. (He never did bring back those more perishable items, pasta and ice cream, that he is so often miscredited with introducing to the West.) Scholars have also discovered the will of Marco's uncle, Maffeo, which contains clear reference to arrangements concerning "the three tablets of gold which were from the magnificent Chan of the Tartars" (*tres tabulae de auro que fuerant magnifici Khan Tartarorum*), Kaikhatu.[4] Although researchers have not located the paizis themselves, historians and archeologists have found other tablets matching their description in China and have documented their use (and abuse) by Mongol aristocrats and officials throughout the duration of the Mongol Empire.

One of the most remarkable facts about the golden tablets possessed by Marco and Maffeo is simply that the travelers held on to them for so long. Certainly, these precious tablets had a substantial financial value, but they must have meant more to the Polos—and here we might sense another feature of the passport that still matters to us today. Like the silver girdle or the golden headdress in their collections, the tablets were souvenirs of a sort, material records of their travels, sturdier and more concrete than any tale spun from the experiences they had gathered far from home. Whether it was to prove their credibility to their doubters—that is, to demonstrate that they were indeed the marvelous adventurers they claimed to be; or to recall for themselves in quieter, more sedentary times their many adventures, all they had seen and done on the Silk Road; or perhaps to bring to mind the combined privileges of movement and security provided by these metallic tablets, backed by an imperial, even divine, authority that stretched across most of the known world, both nephew and uncle maintained possession of their golden passports until the ends of their lives.

Beyond their personal value to the Polos, the tablets also possess their own world-historical significance. Without them the brothers might never have survived the journey home to gather up young Marco, along with a message from the Pope and a quantity of holy lamp oil, for a return trip to the court of Kublai Khan. And twenty-four years later, the mature Marco might never have completed the journey home to tell his tale to Rustichello and help inspire the Age of Exploration that followed. Indeed, on his voyages to the New World Christopher Columbus would carry an edition of *The Travels of Marco Polo,* heavily annotated in his own hand: he reportedly viewed the tome as a kind of talisman and would-be guidebook to the East, however misguided his voyages came to be.

• • •

The issuance of safe conduct passes like paizis (though not in the form of precious golden tablets) would become a common practice in Europe during the late Middle Ages as the feudal state system slowly evolved into a collection of sovereign states, with parliaments emerging to negotiate with monarchs on a range of legal and diplomatic questions. Canadian political scientist Mark B. Salter has gone so far as to suggest that "the control of movement" during this period indicates "the beginning of the sovereign state as an international actor—and the formulation of the state as a safe domestic space and the outside as a dangerous international space."[5] The term "sauf-conduit" arose in Middle French at the end of the twelfth century to describe permission to travel to and from a particular place without being detained or arrested. By the end of the thirteenth century, just prior to publication of *The Travels of Marco Polo,* the term had migrated into Middle English as "sauf condut" via *The Metrical Chronicle of Robert of Gloucester,* a vernacular history of England, which also introduced "conduct" or "condyt" into the language in a now obsolete sense: i.e., "provision for guidance or conveyance; a company of attendants appointed to conduct a person safely on a journey; an escort, a convoy."[6]

The term did not come to designate an official document until the late fourteenth century in France and the early fifteenth century in England, by which time it had become customary for English monarchs to provide safe conduct passes for those entering or leaving their sovereign domain. The tyrannical Richard II and his usurping cousin, Henry IV, signed documents granting travel permissions to various lords, their wayfaring parties, and their "necessary horses, etc.," often "with the proviso that no one fleeing the English laws should be in their company." But it was not until 1414, shortly after Henry V took the throne, that an Act of Parliament codified this practice and granted the monarch power to issue these documents to anyone he desired, whether English subjects or foreign nationals. The act also reaffirmed that the holder of a safe conduct pass was protected by the personal authority of the king, and in so doing asserted a sovereign monopoly on violence: any transgression of sovereign authority by killing, robbing, or otherwise "spoiling" the holder of the pass became an act of high treason against the crown, punishable by death.[7]

Henry V is remembered for quelling internal tensions, often rather ruthlessly, so that he could rule England as the monarch of a unified state, and for pursuing foreign campaigns, with no shortage of valor or ambition, so that he could extend his power into France and unite the thrones of the two countries. His legendary status in the story of England owes much to Shakespeare's depiction of the monarch in his history plays, especially the eponymous *Henry V* (c. 1599)—and perhaps most especially to the famous St. Crispin's Day speech in act 4, proclaimed by the youthful monarch on the eve of the Battle of Agincourt in 1415. Although it was penned nearly two centuries later, the rousing oration has been credited with providing vital insight into the leadership of Henry V and all potent medieval monarchs, who ruled not just through divine right, but through the strength of their personalities and the intensity of their convictions. After learning that his cousin, Westmoreland, has wished for another ten thousand troops—those "men in England who do no work today"—to face the vast numbers of the French forces, Henry responds that the glory of his gathered soldiers—"we few, we happy few, we band of brothers"—will be greater for not having to divide it among more men. Then, doubling down on his bold declaration, the king offers any man who does not wish to stay and fight the proper documentation to see him back home:

> No 'faith, my Couze, wish not a man from England:
> Gods peace, I would not loose so great an Honor,
> As one man more me thinkes would share from me,
> For the best hope I haue. O, doe not wish one more:
> Rather proclaime it (*Westmerland*) through my Hoast,
> That he which hath no stomacke to this fight,
> Let him depart, his Pasport shall be made,
> And Crownes for Conuoy put into his Purse:
> We would not dye in that mans companie,
> That feares his fellowship, to dye with vs.

Let us pause for a moment over the mention of a "Pasport" in these lines. In writing *Henry V,* Shakespeare drew heavily on *Holinshed's Chronicles of England, Scotland, and Ireland* (1577) and other Tudor histories (as well as other recent plays about the monarch), but the word is not to be found in any of these historical sources and is in fact an anachronism in the play (especially when we consider that Henry V promoted the use of the English language for official purposes). The word *passeport,* a compound of *passer* (to pass) and *port* (seaport or harbor), did not emerge in French until a few years after the events of the play, in 1420 under the reign of Louis XI, to denote a certificate for the free circulation of merchandise, and it did not come to indicate a document guaranteeing the free movement of a person until 1464. The term made its way into English as "pasportis" at the end of the fifteenth century in the *Registrum Secreti Sigilli Regum Scotorum* (*Register of the Privy Seal of Scotland*), but did not take the form that Shakespeare uses—the one still familiar to us—until much later, in John Baret's *An aluearie or triple dictionarie, in Englishe, Latin, and French* (1574). In both texts it is rendered synonymous with the safe conduct pass: "sauffconductis or pasportis" and "a Pasport or saulfe conduct to passe."[8]

It is clear from the lines in *Henry V* that, even on foreign soil, the passport is an instrument of sovereign power, which could be used quite opportunely to expel a coward from the ranks of heroic Englishmen. But like so much in the play, these lines are double-edged. On the one hand, they indicate a sovereign who is indeed, as the prologue puts it, "a mirror of all Christian kings," leading his men (and the English people) with a charismatic rhetorical energy that binds them together in an invincible comradery (see Kenneth Branagh's 1989 film adaptation of *Henry V* for a glimpse of this capacity). Because Henry's spontaneous offer of a passport to anyone who might desert his ranks demonstrates both his benevolence and his confidence in the campaign, it also serves to bolster the courage and commitment of the soldiers who stand before him. On the other hand, his pronouncements offer an ominous, though rather ironic, foretelling of the monstrously efficient warrior king who orders the preemptory killing of French prisoners of war in transgression of military law. In alluding to the passport, Henry demonstrates a sense of sovereign authority that extends boldly, even brazenly, into foreign territories as he asserts his dynastic claim on them: on the battlefield in France (even more than on the throne in England), that is, the monarch wields an absolute power, which risks its own corruption.

Written in the final years of Queen Elizabeth I's reign, Shakespeare's play has been read not just as a case study of the qualities of an effective ruler, whether king or queen, but also as a knowing missive to the sitting monarch. Like Henry V, Elizabeth presided over a realm that was threatened by deep internal divisions, which called for shrewd and courageous action by the monarch, not least in crafting a public image as a dazzling emblem of national honor. By the end of the sixteenth century, however, the power of the sovereign to require subservience had become more limited and Elizabeth had to rely on the cooperation of an often intractable Parliament in order to acquire the financial means to govern. It was also during the reign of the so-called Virgin Queen that the influential jurist Edmund Plowden retrospectively articulated the essential duality of the English sovereign: "a Body natural," his (or, now, her) physical or biological self, which ages, suffers, and eventually dies, and "a Body politic," an immortal, and even mystical, power uniting the sovereign and his subjects in mutual responsibility, while governing the nation in all things.[9]

As the head of state, Elizabeth still possessed the power to issue safe conduct documents, administered through the Privy Council of England, in order to protect the domestic space from foreign threats and aid in diplomatic affairs, espionage activities, and, if necessary, military campaigns. As later volumes of the *Register of the Privy Council of Scotland* attest, she often received requests from her rival cousin, Mary Queen of Scots, for passes allowing members of the Scottish nobility and their entourages to traverse England en route to conducting diplomatic affairs on the Continent. Meanwhile, subjects of the English queen were obliged to seek a "license to travel" from Elizabeth and her council whenever they desired to leave English territory, whether on official business or for a less venerable reason. Indeed, members of the royal court who lost favor with the sovereign—for some private misbehavior or some public disobedience—often asked for a license to travel abroad as a relatively graceful means to avoid the wrath of the monarch, through a form of voluntary (or at least self-imposed) exile.

But not all such licenses were granted to save the realm from external threats or to save face after some affront to the Crown. During the Elizabethan age, long before modern tourism emerged, documents were issued in certain exceptional cases to allow travel to the Continent for educational or, more broadly, cultural purposes. A license to travel embossed with the royal seal of Queen Elizabeth and dated May 25, 1572, was rediscovered only by chance in 1966, when the ornithologist, scholar of English literature, and Oxford Fellow John Buxton and his colleague, the physician, Officer to the Medical School, and cofounder of the Oxford University Society of Bibliophiles Ben Juel-Jensen, were examining a volume in the library of New College, Oxford, at the end of the Michaelmas Term. They came across the faded travel document, one of the few to survive to the present, lodged among a collection of papers "evidently intended to illustrate the signatures of English kings, queens, nobles, and other prominent persons."[10] The document consists of a piece of velum about ten inches by twelve inches (25 × 30 cm), headed with the bold autograph of Elizabeth herself, but inscribed in the elegant hand of a royal secretary with a variety of sixteenth-century legalese (which nonetheless recalls the letters of safe conduct from previous epochs):

> Elizabeth by the grace of God. Queene of England france and Irland, defendo^r of the fayth &c. To all Justices of | peace: Maiors, Sheryffes, Bailiffes, Constables. Customers Comptrollers and s^{r}chers, & to all other o^r officers ministers and | subiects to whom it shall appartayn, and to every of them, greeting. We lett you witt that we have licenced and by these p̃nts | doo licence our trusty & welbelovid Phillip Sidney esquire to go out of this o^r Realm of England into the partes of beyond the | Seas, and there for his attayning to the knowledge of forrayn Languages to remayn the space of twoo~ yeeres next and | immediatly following after his departing out of o^r Relm. Wherfore we will and commaund you & every of you quietly to | suffer him to passe by you w^{t}out any yor lett or trouble, w^t Three servantes, ffowre horses or gueldinges, & one hũdred poundes | in money or under and all oth^r his and their bagges baguages and necessaryes . . . .[11]

FIGURE 6. A license to travel provided to Philip Sidney, signed by Queen Elizabeth I, 1572. By permission of the Warden and Scholars of New College, Oxford.

Sidney would go on to become an exemplary Renaissance man—a soldier, a statesman, a scholar, and a poet—but he was not yet eighteen years old when he received the royal license, having recently left Christ Church, Oxford, after three years of study (though without taking a degree, as was common among young men of his station). Now, in the spring of 1572, a new peace treaty between England and France afforded him the opportunity to cross the Channel and travel the Continent for the first time.

The license discovered by Buxton and Juel-Jensen is thus of no small significance to literary history, because this piece of velum enabled

Sidney, who would soon be the most dashing man-of-letters in England, to continue his education amid the most revered cultural institutions of Europe. In other words, the document was a ticket for the young man to pursue the ideal of Renaissance humanism: to develop the all-but-limitless capacities of man to the full by incorporating various forms of knowledge wherever he found them, whether across disciplinary boundaries or national borders. The present condition of his license suggests that it was put to good use, since it has been folded several times, worn at the edges of those folds, and apparently subjected to wind and rain on its journey, to judge by the smudges in the ink and discolorations of the velum. In fact, although the document granted Sidney leave "to remayn the space of twoo~ yeeres" outside of England, he did not return to his native land until a full three years later, after traveling across several countries and often staying several months in the cities he visited along the way. If journeys like this were still unusual for an Englishman in the late sixteenth century, they would become increasingly fashionable during the seventeenth and eighteenth centuries for aristocratic youths, who undertook the so-called Grand Tour as a professional rite of passage, often in preparation for a career in diplomatic service or public officialdom. For others, however, the principal value of such travel lay in the aesthetic education, or at least connoisseurship, offered by exposure to celebrated museums, architectural marvels, and august libraries.

In this sense, the journey Sidney embarked upon in 1572 was an important precursor (and even a paradigm) for the Grand Tour tradition. Naturally, his first stop was Paris, where he had the good fortune to become acquainted with a number of prominent Protestant artists and intellectuals, but also witnessed first-hand the infamous St. Bartholomew's Day massacre of French Huguenots. Carrying on through Strasbourg and Frankfurt, he then visited Vienna for several months before an extended trip through Hungary and Italy eventually landed him in Venice, where the young man immersed himself in the social and cultural life of the city. Between excursions to Genoa and Florence, Sidney also spent lengthy periods educating himself at the celebrated university at Padua, where he adhered to the curriculum dictated on his license to travel—"attayning to the knowledge of forrayn Languages"—while also pursuing extracurricular scholarship in many other fields. During this period, as Buxton establishes in his *Sir Philip Sidney and the English Renaissance,* the young man translated the works of "Cicero first into French, then from French into English, and finally [back] into Latin 'by a sort of perpetual motion.'"[12] Sidney simultaneously studied the Venetian government and constitution, treatises on the politics and diplomacy of Europe, and the letters of famous Italian statesmen, as well as books on astronomy, geometry, and Italian poetry. Some years later, this crash course in interdisciplinary studies, combined with his earlier education in the Greek and Roman classics, would result in *Astrophel and Stella* (1591), the first sonnet sequence written in English, and *An Apology for Poetry* (1595), the first landmark of literary criticism in the language, which synthesizes many of the themes of Renaissance humanism.

We know from these writings that Sidney did not discount the role his license to travel had played in his rather extraordinary education. Composed in about 1580, but not published until after his untimely death a few years later at the age of thirty-one, his *Apology* contains one of the first figurative uses of the word *passport* in the English language— as "a quality, talent, or attribute, etc., giving a person or thing the right, privilege, or opportunity to enter into some state, position, social sphere, etc." Arguing stridently that many disciplines depend on poetic language to attract their audiences and convey their messages successfully, Sidney claims that "Neyther Phylosopher nor Historiographer, coulde haue entred into the gates of populer iudgements, if they had not taken a great pasport of Poetry."[13]

. . .

By the mid-eighteenth century, the Grand Tour had become a highly conventionalized affair, with its well-established routes and a well-established literature. Meanwhile, the exigencies of governing modern states had led authorities throughout Europe to more strictly regulate the movement of individuals within and across their borders, often using travel documents as a means of enforcement. Progressively, after the Treaty of Westphalia in 1648, these modern states had also claimed sovereign authority to designate who had and who did not have a legitimate place within their boundaries. Still, there were no passport standards, so travel documents could take the form of a government-issued safe conduct pass or a semiformal letter from some high-ranking individual, though they were almost invariably a single large sheet of paper, with a watermark and a seal to assert their authenticity. Unlike today, these travel documents were often issued to travelers upon their arrival in a foreign country, though they sometimes came at a steep price. British subjects traveling across France and Italy on their Grand Tours often complained of the documentary demands that slowed their progress, regarding them as little more than bureaucratic hassles or even means of extortion. This set of circumstances comes together with amusing effect in Laurence Sterne's great satire of the Grand Tour, *A Sentimental Journey through France and Italy* (1768), which sends its rather hapless but nonetheless buoyant protagonist, Parson Yorick, on an abortive excursion south from England. A riposte to Tobias Smollett's altogether unsentimental *Travels through France and Italy* (1766), Sterne's novel downplays the objectives of the conventional Grand Tour narrative, with its emphasis on social distinction, professional advancement, and classical instruction, in favor of attention to the moral sentiments of its protagonist, even as Yorick's countless romantic dalliances repeatedly obstruct his, and our, moral edification.

Yorick's distracted nature is on display early in the novel when we find that, having forgotten the small detail that France and England were at war, he has neglected to secure a passport before leaving London. Arriving in Paris with the aid of a few casual deceptions, he soon learns from the proprietor of his hotel that the police have inquired after him and his passport. Only then does the absentminded parson realize that he has traveled this far without proper documentation. Passport controls had long been an important feature of governance under the absolutist state of ancien régime France, and by the middle of the eighteenth century, after the implementation of new measures, all travelers entering and leaving the country were required to hold the correct papers. The state of emergency brought on by the Seven Years War between Great Britain and France only added impetus to these measures. Despite all this, and the admonitions of his innkeeper in Paris, Yorick keeps up his nonchalance, buoyed by his confidence that "the King of France is a good-natur'd soul:—he'll hurt no body." Having already paid a month's rent, the parson refuses to quit his lodging "a day before that time for all the kings of France in the world." Meanwhile, his innkeeper fears that the foreign traveler, with his blasé attitude toward sovereign authority, "will certainly be sent to the Bastille to-morrow morning," because "nobody could oppose the king of France."[14] Yorick may maintain a blind faith in the benevolence of the sovereign, but the absolutist state and its passport controls threaten to curtail his Continental sojourn, and with it his peripatetic narrative of moral edification, before they have really gotten underway.

Fortunately, as Danish literary scholar Jesper Gulddal has pointed out, "the authoritarian aspirations" of the absolutist state to control movement in mid-eighteenth France were not matched by its competence or capacity to enforce its laws.[15] To be sure, *A Sentimental Journey* suggests, quite comically, that it was easy enough for the resourceful (or at least fortunate) foreign visitor to secure travel documents from a well-positioned benefactor who did not happen to share in the authoritarian aspirations of his government. Finally convinced to acquire a passport, Yorick proceeds rather grudgingly from Paris to Versailles, so that he might enlist help from the French foreign minister, a Monsieur le Duc de Choiseul. But when he finds the minister otherwise occupied, the parson opts instead to pay a visit to a Count de B—, who is widely known for his high opinion of "English books and English men." Eventually, after several narrative digressions, Yorick is admitted to the drawing room of the count, where he finds a complete set of Shakespeare laid out on a table. The parson proceeds to tell the story of his plight to the nobleman, who responds with a kind acknowledgment, before adding, "very politely, how much he stood obliged to Shakespeare for making me known to him."[16] On the strength of this astounding misrecognition, which somehow casts the parson as his namesake from *Hamlet* (c. 1599), Count de B— is only too happy to supply a passport, "directed to all lieutenant-governors, governors, and commandants of cities, generals of armies, justiciaries, and all officers of justice, to let Mr. Yorick the king's jester, and his baggage, travel quietly along."[17] If the scene (and the entire passport fiasco, for that matter) does little to advance the narrative of the parson's travels, it does go a long way to lampoon the delays, the hassles, even the absurdities associated with the emergent system of passport control. Perhaps most significantly, certainly most amusingly, it represents a complete failure of travel documentation to serve as identification, to link person and paperwork in any secure or objective way, despite the aspirations of the absolutist state to do so.

The facility with which such a document could actually be attained is evinced in an anecdote featuring the always resourceful Benjamin Franklin during his days in France as the first United States Minister to the Court of Versailles. As media historian Craig Robertson tells the story in his study of the American passport, Franklin needed some official way to safeguard another representative from the fledgling nation-state, Francis Dana, on a diplomatic errand from France to Holland. So, during the late summer of 1780, the iconic American polymath (who had begun his career as a printshop owner in Philadelphia) simply created a "passport" on his own press in Paris. Written in French, the one-page document contains a rather tentative appeal from the US representatives: that Dana not be hindered on his journey but instead be granted aid and assistance "as we would do in like circumstances for all those recommended to us."[18] With the addition of Franklin's signature and his official seal, pressed into red wax near the bottom margin, the humble sheet of paper became one of the first US passports ever issued, nearly a decade before the Department of State in Washington, D.C., began producing anything of the kind.

Together, the stories of Yorick and Franklin, one fictional and one factual, indicate a wider set of preoccupations across Europe and North America in the latter half of the eighteenth century, as new calls for individual liberty and freedom of movement confronted the tightened security measures imposed by modern states. Advocates for revolution in France cited internal passport controls as a particularly egregious abuse of power by the ancien régime and called for their abolishment because they impinged on the fundamental human right to travel freely. As American sociologist John Torpey points out, the first right protected by the Constitution of 1791, drafted shortly after the demise of absolute monarchy in France, was the liberty "to move about, to remain [and] to leave."[19] The Constitution was headed by that canonical statement of Enlightenment values, the Declaration of the Rights of Man and the Citizen (*La Déclaration des droits de l'homme et du citoyen*), which sought a basis for these rights in a secular version of natural law, holding them to be universally valid across all times and all places. Article IV of the Declaration proclaimed that "the exercise of the natural rights of each man has only those borders which assure other members of the society the fruition of these same rights. These borders can be determined only by the law." But as latter-day commentators have noted, there were inherent tensions in the Declaration, announced clearly enough in its very title, which recognizes the equality of human beings and the rights of French citizens separately. This foundational document thus inscribes ideals that were not only aspirational for the embryonic nation-state of France, but perhaps at odds with the very idea of a sovereign nation-state as such. In any case, with a rather rich historical irony, passport controls were not only reinstituted as the French Revolution descended into the Reign of Terror in 1792, but bolstered under the "new regime," a process that provided authorities with an ever more invasive technology of surveillance and subjugation.

Torpey begins his groundbreaking book, *The Invention of the Passport,* with attention to the French Revolution precisely because it brought about the "birth of the nation-state," which in turn helped to inaugurate similar developments around the globe. It would take time, after the chaotic rush of events at the end of the eighteenth century, for the new regime to fully assert its authority over movement within France and across its borders. But once the process had been reinitiated, it rapidly became evident that right to travel freely would be curtailed persistently. Torpey argues, moreover, that the emergence of the modern passport in the nineteenth century would become a crucial aspect of the "state-ness" of sovereign states, since the capacity of the document to legitimate subjects and control their movements is a reflection of sovereign authority. Article III of the Declaration of the Rights of Man, as if preempting article IV, had asserted that "the principle of any sovereignty resides essentially in the Nation. No body, no individual may exercise any authority which does not proceed directly from the nation. The state is the political institution in which sovereignty is embodied." No longer imbued in the person of the king or queen by some divine authorization, the sovereignty of the nation-state now found its basis in the nativity (that is, birth or "bare life") that enacts the passage from "subjects" of a monarchy to "citizens" of a nation-state. "Rights" in this formulation, as Agamben points out, "are attributable to *man* only in the degree to which he is the immediately vanishing presupposition (indeed, he must never appear simply as man) of the *citizen.*"[20]

It was not long until French authorities created of the first state-supervised registry of persons to track births, deaths, and marriages across the entire population of the nation-state. And soon they placed all foreigners traveling in France (who had not arrived on an official mission from a friendly power or acquired French citizenship of their own) under special surveillance and subjected them to deportation if their presence was judged "susceptible to disturb the public order and peace." In other words, the tensions intrinsic to the Declaration of the Rights of Man and the Citizen were quickly resolved "in favor of the nation-state" (and its native or naturalized inhabitants).[21] Yet, as Torpey acknowledges, the efficacy of the passport to reliably determine distinctions between citizen and noncitizen, native and foreigner, had to wait on the establishment of an international system of sovereign states, after the many military clashes that afflicted the Continent through the Napoleonic era.

THREE

Modern Bodies, Modern Citizens

WHEN GEORGE GORDON, LORD BYRON, took up lodgings in Venice in the fall of 1816, he quickly fell in love (as was his habit), this time with Marianna Segati, the young wife of his Italian landlord. Rather indiscreetly (as was also his habit), the author of love lyrics such as "She Walks in Beauty" and "When We Two Parted" described his new mistress in a letter to his close friend and confidante, Thomas Moore:

> She has the large, black, oriental eyes, with the peculiar expression in them which is seen rarely among *Europeans*—even the Italians—and which many of the Turkish women give themselves by tinging the eyelid,—an art not known out of that country, I believe. This expression she has *naturally,*—and something more than this. In short, I cannot describe the effect of this kind of eye,—at least upon me. Her features are regular, and rather aquiline—mouth small—skin clear and soft, with a kind of hectic colour—forehead remarkably good: her hair is of the dark gloss, curl, and colour of Lady J[ersey]'s; her figure is light and pretty, . . .

After breaking off the letter, he continued writing under a later date: "You will perceive that my description, which was proceeding with the minuteness of a passport, has been interrupted for several days."[1] We can only speculate on what may have distracted the poet, who, in any case, was interrupted again by some more enticing activities for nearly two weeks before he finally completed the letter. But we can see more clearly the role the passport was coming to play in his poetic imagination, and in the cultural imagination of Europe more broadly during the early decades of the nineteenth century. The male poet, seeking to capture his

FIGURE 7. Detail of *Byron and Marianna*, c. 1840. Engraving by George Zobel after a painting by William Drummond. Published by D. W. Kellogg and Co.

new mistress in words (and, no doubt, to impress his friend), draws on not just the masculinist traditions of love poetry, but also the standard-ized descriptions employed by the emerging surveillance apparatus of the modern nation-state.

As the passport evolved into a means to establish the identity of trave-lers passing across territorial boundaries, it began to adopt physical descriptors meant to translate the distinctive appearance of individuals into a reliable array of details. Gradually, passport holders were situated within what Michel Foucault calls "the field of documentation," which transcribed their bodies into "a network of writing" that recorded specific information about them and allowed the mechanisms of state control to operate on them. Even as Byron betrays an Orientalist fascination with the other, the exotic, the almost ineffable, he also seeks to "read" off the legible surface of the body in order to both portray and possess his mistress. Like a passport, his missive attempts to render her physical appearance—her eyes, mouth, complexion, forehead, hair—as closely and clearly as possible into language, to express a proximity that is at once intimate and invasive.

By the time he wrote his letter to Moore, Byron was a seasoned traveler who had undertaken his own extended and rather idiosyncratic Grand Tour nearly a decade earlier, spending several years roaming through Portugal, Spain, Malta, Albania, Greece, and Turkey. In 1816 he had fled England and the scandals associated with his love life, traveling in a replica of Napoleon's coach (no less) and eventually taking up residence in Venice, where he initiated a succession of new love affairs and began work on his picaresque satire in verse, *Don Juan* (1819–24). His wanderings had introduced him to the passport demands of early nineteenth-century Europe, and the long poem, which crisscrosses the terrain of his travels, registers the paradoxical nature of the document: he refers to "a passport, or some other bar / To freedom," while also suggesting that wealth "is a passport every where."[2] In his missive to Moore, the Romantic poet acknowledges the passport as a powerful new form of representation, even if he tries to evade its increasingly conventionalized and authoritative ways of reading off the body. Byron must resist, though apparently not too forcefully, the objective and objectifying thrust of these passport descriptions. But in his ironic regard for officialdom, he also acknowledges that these descriptions are not quite as objective as they are claimed to be by the authorities that rely on them. Is there anything particularly distinctive about "regular features" or a "remarkably good" forehead? By the same token, who is to say what exactly amounts to "clear and soft" skin, much less skin "of hectic colour," which may be only fleeting? As an identification document, the passport would inevitably confront the inherently subjective—one might even say poetic—nature of any effort to render the body in words, to somehow transmute physical characteristics into fitting language.

At the same time, as attempts to define personal identity or to exercise freedom of movement wrestled with government efforts at control, the passport came to occupy a more prominent place in the literature of the period. Jesper Gulddal, with his sustained scholarly attention to these struggles, has identified a key instance in Stendhal's *The Charterhouse of Parma* (1839). The novel follows the story of Fabrizio del Dongo, an idealistic young Italian aristocrat whose desire for adventure and romance repeatedly run up against the restrictions put in place by the expansive passport system of the Habsburg Empire.[3] Following the Congress of Vienna in 1815, which sought to restructure Europe in the aftermath of the Napoleonic Wars, the Habsburg Empire had extended its power to several possessions in northern Italy, including Parma and the Kingdom of Lombardy-Venetia, where Byron could be found in 1816. Across these domains, the passport system served a disciplinary function akin to that which Foucault identifies in the institutional setting of the panopticon, allowing a limited number of border guards in the region to regulate the movements of the population through strategies of individuation and supervision. Members of this population, in other words, became objects of information.

Set in this fraught environment, *Charterhouse* has long been considered as not only a highly nuanced psychological portrait, but also a canonical depiction of an individual deeply "imbedded" in history—that is, within the social and political forces that define his historical moment. It bears mentioning here that Stendhal, for all his fame as a novelist, was the author of several travel books, including *Rome, Naples, and Florence* (1817)—the first book that Marie-Henri Beyle wrote under his far more famous nom de plume —based on his experiences as an eager tourist, an imperial administrator, and then a temporary exile from the Bourbon restoration. When he sat down to write *Charterhouse* more than two decades later, he revived lucid memories of his time in northern Italy under Austrian rule, with its greatly intensified travel controls and documentary demands: indeed, the word *passeport* appears no fewer than seventy-one times in the novel.

The story of Fabrizio's troubled coming of age begins with his journey from his palatial family estate on Lake Como north all the way to Waterloo, where he hopes to join the battle in support of his childhood hero, Napoleon. The flight from home, the first step in his much longer and even more perilous passage toward personal autonomy, is made possible only with a passport lent to him by one of his plebeian friends, a barometer dealer named Vasi. To gain safe passage across international borders at the time, travelers had to prove less the authenticity of their official papers than their own coincidence with those papers; the travel document (with its detailed physical description of the holder), and *not* the embodied self, became the authoritative manifestation of identity. The borrowed document allows Fabrizio to escape the control of both his conservative father and the local authorities, but the handsome young man hardly makes it to Belgium before he is arrested, due in part to the absurd incongruity between his appearance and that of the middle-aged commercial traveler described in the passport. A series of escapes, evasions, detentions, and further misappropriations ensues. Unfortunately for our boyish hero, when he finally returns to his native Lombardy, his use of the fraudulent passport puts him under the surveillance of the Austrian police force—occasioning another departure from home, which eventually lands him in Parma. There, the stringent movement control of the Habsburg passport system plays a decisive role in Fabrizio's fate: his earlier offenses against the system place him on "the Austrian black list," compelling him to destroy his own documents and move about in constant danger of discovery.[4]

Under these conditions, as we have seen, passports increasingly became tools of identification, fixing the identity of their holders and testifying not just to their nationality, but to their physical characteristics, profession, and other credentials. The capacity—or at least, the official assumption of the capacity—of such documents to affirm the credentials of the holder is demonstrated in another letter by Byron, written from Bologna on August 29, 1819, nearly simultaneous with the action in that region described in *Charterhouse*. Some days earlier, on the recommendation of a friend, the English poet had purchased a horse from a "Lieutenant**," only to discover that the poor animal was suffering from a nasty fungal infection. When Byron attempted to return the horse and reclaim his money, he fell into a spirited argument with its previous owner and, after several provocations, called the man a thief. Greatly insulted, the lieutenant retorted that "he was an *officer* and man of honour," and then "pulled out a Parmesan passport signed by General Count Neipperg," the formidable Austrian military leader and statesman. Provoked even further by this credential-flashing, the exasperated poet had answered that "as he was an officer, I would treat him as such; and that as to his being a Gentleman, he might prove it by returning the money: as for his Parmesan passport, I should have valued it more if it had been a Parmesan Cheese."[5] Perhaps it is no coincidence that a romance with another married Italian woman, Teresa Guiccioli, would soon draw Bryon into the ranks of the Carbonari, a secret revolutionary society then bidding to put an end to Austrian influence in northern Italy.

Apart from its comic value, the Parmesan passport episode is noteworthy because it illustrates both the presumed authority of such documents to testify to the credentials of their holder and the defiance toward such authority from the likes of Lord Byron. In *Rome, Naples, and Florence,* Stendhal had also voiced his frustration with passports and their associated rituals, including the requirement to swear an oath when attaining a visa, as well as with the unwavering insolance of the minor officials who demanded to see his papers. In *Charterhouse,* as Fabrizio attempts to fashion a sovereign selfhood—not least, through a series of ill-fated love affairs—he repeatedly eludes the control of the increasingly powerful passport system with the use of stolen, fraudulent, and otherwise illegitimate documents.

To be a Romantic hero of this sort was to attempt escape from political oppression and other forces of subjugation—or at least the minor indignities of bureaucracy. After Stendhal's protagonist becomes amorously involved with an actress named Marietta, her jealous manager and former lover, Giletti, attempts to run him through with a sword. In the ensuing tussle, Fabrizio kills Giletti and then tries to escape Parma with a passport purloined from his dead rival. But the young man soon becomes mortally afraid that the document will betray him, for it presents certain "material difficulties" ("*difficultés matérielles*"): "Fabrizio's height was, at the most, five feet five inches, and not five feet ten inches as was stated on the passport. He was not quite twenty-four, and looked younger. Giletti had been thirty-nine."[6] This is not to mention the fact that the youthful Fabrizio is smooth skinned, while the older man had been "strongly pitted by small-pox," as indicated on the document.[7] Passports, as we know, were meant to be reliable forms of identification, which meant, among other things, they contained information that could not be erased or otherwise altered without drawing the attention of border officials. Reading and rereading the document as he prepares to leave Parma, Fabrizio thus begins to feel intense apprehension about the discrepancies in the document, for he has no other choice but to use the passport at the Austrian border office as it is.

When the young man is called on to present the document and "undergo an examination," he must rely on a stroke of luck that rises to the level of a deus ex machina in order to make his escape—in a scene that presages the passport anxieties portrayed in so many novels and films of more recent vintage. His mind awhirl with worries, Fabrizio enters a dirty little station at Casalmaggiore and hands his passport over to an "ill-tempered" police official, who peruses the document for a full five minutes.[8] As his inner torment grows, Fabrizio starts to believe that he will be arrested at any moment. But unbeknownst to him, the official just happens to be a friend of Giletti who surmises that the taller, older man must have sold the document to the shorter, younger man standing before him. Not wishing to implicate Giletti in an illegal transaction, the official weighs his options (even as Fabrizio weighs his own options for fight or flight) and then employs another ruse: feigning fatigue, he steps into the backroom of the station and asks his colleague to stamp the passport with a visa when he has the opportunity. Before Fabrizio can steal away in panic, the other officer emerges and murmurs, as if to himself, "Well, let us see this passport; I'll put my scrawl on it." With a quick stamp on the passport and a flourish of his pen, he sends an astonished Fabrizio on his way, while muttering to the young man "in a careless tone: 'A good journey, sir.'"[9] On arriving safely in Bologna, the exhausted Fabrizio wanders into the church of San Petronio to recover his strength. He is quickly overwhelmed by a feeling of gratitude for having avoided discovery at the border station, as he comes to see his escape as nothing less than a sign of divine protection. Then, in a moment suffused with irony, Fabrizio throws himself on his knees and, much like Nehemiah long before him, gives thanks to God in a "state of extreme emotion."[10]

. . .

With its reliance on fallible documents and uneven enforcement, the passport system in nineteenth-century Europe presented certain opportunities for those who wished to remake their identities—not just to elude the authority of the nation-state and its border controls but to step across other boundaries, to create alternative forms of selfhood. If it was not always easy to hide alterations after the documents were issued, it was often possible for determined travelers to embellish or manipulate the identifying information entered into their passports, which would seldom be questioned during their travels.

This was demonstrated rather marvelously during the period by Mary Shelley, whose travels had once taken her, in the summer of 1816, to a famous rendezvous in Switzerland with her lover (and husband-to-be) Percy Bysshe Shelley, her step-sister, Claire Clairmont, and the notorious Lord Byron. It was there, in a rented house on the shores of Lake Geneva, that she first conceived her novel *Frankenstein* (1818). A little over a decade later, after the deaths of both her husband and Byron, Shelley was residing in Arundel on the southern coast of England, when she wrote to a friend in London, the actor John Howard Payne, with a rather unexpected "commission": would he procure a passport for two of her friends who were planning to cross from Brighton to Dieppe in a few days' time? Since, as Shelley acknowledged, the passport office would not issue documents except to the persons themselves, the assignment would require Payne to employ his acting talents to impersonate one of the travelers and to enlist a performer friend to play the other. (It is worth noting here that Shelley is credited with the first use of the compound term *passport-office* in the English language some years later: it appears in her proto-feminist novel *Lodore* [1835], when a disappointed lover, attempting to track down his departed mistress, goes searching for clues to her whereabouts in the records kept there. It seems that she too has run off to France.)

In the fall of 1827, after Payne had agreed to her commission, Shelley sent another letter with detailed physical descriptions of the travelers, not just for the passport applications, but for makeup, hair, and costuming: "Mrs Douglas is short, i.e. an atom shorter than I—dark, pretty with large dark eyes & hair curled in the neck ... Mr Douglas is my height—slim—dark with curly black hair—the passport must be drawn out for Mr & Mrs Sholto Douglas."[11] Shelley supplied the signatures of "Isabel Douglas" and "Sholto Douglas" to aid Payne and his accomplice in forging the passport applications, which were also to include mention of their traveling companions, "Mrs Carter & her two children—boys one ten the other nine—Mrs Percy Shelley and boy."[12] What Shelley fails to mention in her correspondence with Payne is that the Isabel Douglas of the passport application was in fact her friend Isabel Robinson and that Mr. Sholto Douglas was in fact Mary Diana Dods, the illegitimate daughter of a Scottish earl, who wrote under the pen name David Lyndsay. The pseudonym—affixed to widely admired dramas and reviews, as well as stories considered "very much in the vein of Byron's Oriental tales"—had permitted Dods/Lyndsay to pursue a literary career freed from the social prescriptions and professional limitations imposed on women writers in England.[13] Now, the requested passport would allow Dods/Douglas and Robinson/Douglas to embark on a new life together in France, living openly as husband and wife.

The scheme was not exposed until more than a century and a half later, by American literary scholar Betty T. Bennett, whose *Mary Diana*

Dods: A Gentleman and a Scholar tracks the painstaking, twisting and turning archival work required to discover the various male guises adopted by Dods over the course of her life. The archive itself worked to deceive Bennett, for the letters Shelley sent to Payne provided an alternative explanation, primarily monetary, for the travelers not securing the passports themselves. The forged signatures, those testaments to the identity of the document holder, only compounded the matter by demonstrating the potential fallibility of the historical record. Bennett soon discerned that, from the early stages of her writing career, Dods had been able "to assume identities independent of her sexed body" by "sending her author's queries and manuscripts through the post."[14] The passport in question provided an even more powerful means of transformation, because it provided "proof" abroad of the male identity that Dods/Douglas had adopted at considerable peril to herself/himself in England. With the force of state authority and "official" language, it would contribute to the performance of an alternative gender identity. The document, moreover, would allow Douglas, donning masculine dress to complement his close-cropped hair, to pursue a position with the male-dominated diplomatic corps in France or Germany or Italy, where foreign nationals were often employed in high-ranking positions (though sadly, Dods/Douglas died before taking up such a position). But the absence of any record of the fraudulent passport in the Archives de France led Bennett to acknowledge that by 1827 such a document was no longer required for British subjects on French soil. Rather, the misleading letters, the recruitment of actors, the charade in the passport office—in short, the whole passport scheme—"was not to permit international travel; it was for intercultural, intergender travel."[15]

In this respect, then, the passport had come to provide not just an official testament to the identity of the bearer, rendering distinctive physical characteristics legible to state authority, but also a user-friendly means for pseudonymity—or a handy affirmation of an alter ego that might allow Dods/Douglas to slip past the invasive gaze of that authority. Marie-Henri Beyle famously adopted more than two hundred pseudonyms during his career as a writer and diplomat; the story of Fabrizio and his multiple false passports clearly extends this preoccupation with new identities. Calling on Jean Starobinski's influential 1951 essay "Stendhal Pseudonyme," Gulddal suggests that these false passports highlight the quintessentially Romantic idea of a cleavage between "an inauthentic outside and a true inner being," "conceiving 'pseudonymity' as a means of conforming superficially with accepted social norms while at the same time retaining a degree of inner freedom."[16] For Dods/Douglas, conversely, the false passport provided an opportunity to live out her/his "true inner being" with a bit of cover from the bureaucracy of the nation-state, although, as Bennett asserts, her/his "life insists on the mysteries and complexities of existence that are so often oversimplified in the name of order and control."[17] In an important sense, however, this life only became possible once Dods/Douglas crossed the border defined by this "/," leaving her/his home in England behind and entering into a kind of willful exile from its compulsory norms for gendered embodiment.

As the Dods/Douglas case demonstrates, the nineteenth-century passport applicant was almost always a man: when a husband and/or father traveled with his wife, children, servants, or other women under his protection, their details were to be noted on *his* application. A single passport would then be issued to cover the whole group. With the waning of regulations during the nineteenth century, women who desired to travel independently—but who wanted to avoid the expense, inconvenience, or increased scrutiny of a passport—began to do so through much of Europe. Indeed, following the bourgeois revolutions of 1848, passport requirements were relaxed in all the major countries of Europe, although traveling with such a document still offered an official promise of government protection and aide. It was therefore considered advisable to carry travel documents, especially for women traveling alone or with others of their sex, even as they asserted that their place was no longer just in the home—or at home in their native country, for that matter—but out in the wider world. Through the course of the century, the advance of social and economic liberalism spurred on the free circulation of people around the Continent, with less interference from documentation requirements and border officials (which more cosmopolitan travelers often saw as an impediment to the development of European civilization). There were exceptions during times of war, pandemic, and civil unrest, but the general trend was toward eased enforcement, even as the exponential growth of railroad infrastructure, as well as the mounting speed and comfort of ocean travel, resulted in rapidly increasing numbers of border crossings.

. . .

Across the Atlantic, the United States had not yet developed a comprehensive system of border control, in part because levels of immigration were still relatively low and in part because the perceived need to build a labor force and populate the western frontier was ever increasing. These circumstances were compounded by tensions between the federal government and individual states during the antebellum period. Although the Department of State began issuing passports to American citizens traveling overseas in 1789, it had shared this function with state and local authorities until Congress passed an act in 1856, amid the mounting sectional antagonisms that would eventually lead to the Civil War. During this entire period, the federal government did not require travelers or immigrants to present their passports on entering the country, nor did it compel citizens to acquire travel documents before leaving its territory. Nonetheless, the National Archives contain a rich trove of passport applications, which tells us much about the means and motives of Americans who participated in foreign travel through the course of the nineteenth century. Passports were usually issued with the understanding that they were optional for cross-border travel and merely provided their bearer an extra layer of protection against impediments or inconveniences, along with identification for collecting mail when abroad, presenting on social occasions, and accessing private libraries, museums, archives, and other cultural institutions.

Even this modest degree of bureaucratic constraint could be considered irksome (and reason for procrastinating or otherwise postponing the application process) by a well-traveled and moderately successful writer of high-seas adventure tales, who was about to set off for London with the proofs of his latest novel under his arm:

New York Oct: 1st 1849

Hon: John M Clayton
Secretary of State.

Being about to travel to Europe, I solicit the favor of a passport from your Department. Accompanying are the items of personal description—which I trust will prove sufficient.
As the vessel sails on the 8th Inst: may I beg, that the passport will be forwarded in time—to my address—No. 14 Wall Street, New York City.

With Much Respect
Your Obedient Servant
Herman Melville

The novelist, who was soon to begin work on *Moby-Dick* (1851), has been identified by more than one scholar and even by his older brother, Gansevoort, as an inveterate procrastinator.[18] Nonetheless, when he began making plans for his journey in the late summer of 1849, he had immediately set about asking his literary friends for letters of introduction (those informal passports to the inner sanctums of cultural life) to other writers and artists in London and Paris. Through a mutual acquaintance he had even requested a letter from Ralph Waldo Emerson to the Scottish sage, Thomas Carlyle. But Melville had waited until October 1, just a week before he was due to sail on the *Southampton,* to hastily scrawl his passport application letter, even though the novelist planned to stay in Europe for a Grand Tour (of sorts) lasting many months, should an anticipated contract for the British copyright of *White-Jacket* (1850) provide enough funding for the journey.

Melville's general impatience with the application process is also indicated by the rather remarkable "items of personal description" contained in his letter: in addition to his eyes ("Blue"), hair ("Dark brown"), mouth ("Medium"), nose ("Medium prominent"), complexion ("fair"), age ("30 years"), forehead ("Medium"), chin ("ordinary"), face ("oval"), Melville had listed his height at the very precise mark of "5 f. 10 ⅛." Despite the changeability of the human body (and the creativity of the passport applicant), governments across North America and Europe continued to rely on the subjective description of physical characteristics as a means to verify the identity of passport holders for the duration of the century. When Melville next applied for a passport in 1856 (again in preparation for a Grand Tour of Europe), after authoring his ambitious and demanding *Moby-Dick* and then experiencing an all-too-predictable downturn in his commercial successes as writer, his chin had become "round," but more notably (and perhaps more tellingly) his height had been reduced to "5 Feet 8" and some fraction of an inch. We must settle for the vague "and some fraction" because in his apparent haste to post the request Melville had folded the letter before the ink was dry, thus smudging the fraction and rendering it illegible. The actual passport, which Melville filled in by hand sometime later, places his stature at "5 Feet 8 ¾ Inches Eng"—that is, 1 ⅜ inches shorter than just seven years earlier. This odd discrepancy has led to much scholarly speculation about what physical maladies may have afflicted the author during the intervening period, including an expert diagnosis of ankylosing spondylitis, a rare form of arthritis causing a hunched posture.

The height that Melville recorded in 1856 may be an accurate assessment of his diminished physical stature, read faithfully off the body. But it seems almost as likely that these measurements indicate something about his fluctuating self-image as his fortunes in the literary marketplace rose and fell over the course of his career. With no official verification of Melville's physical stature, the measurements offer us a rather dubious empiricism, which amounted to little more than an all-too-biased assessment by the novelist himself. The US Department of State dictated the categories of the physical description to be included in a passport application, but it could do little to determine how the applicant translated his (or, only infrequently, her) physical appearance into those categories. Perhaps, then, this was initially an opportunity to make a more impressive presentation to whomever Melville might display the document on his travels. Or perhaps it was simply a bit of carelessness indicative of his rushed application and his low regard for the document that he nonetheless felt compelled to request, though the precision of the measurement, down to the eighth of an inch, suggests otherwise: every teller of tall tales or fish stories (and was there ever a better one than the author of *Moby-Dick*?) knows the devil, and the credibility, is in the details. In any case, the discrepancy points to problems that have plagued the passport as an identity document for as long as it has aimed to reduce the complexities of personal identity to a standardized list of physical characteristics.

As the example of Mary Diana Dods/Walter Sholto Douglas also teaches us, the status of the passport as an identification document (as much as a travel document) was becoming more and more important during this period. The documentation of individual identity came to be valued as fundamental to recognition and representation in emerging nation-states, where personal encounters and communal ties could no longer be relied upon as a means to establish belonging. This was nowhere more evident during this period than in the United States, where the question of race (and the institution of slavery) meant that the question of citizenship (and movement across the domestic territory) took on a whole new hue. After receiving Melville's letter of application in early October 1849, a clerk in the secretary of state's office responded with a request to provide proof of citizenship, a new requirement for the issuance of a passport. The request resulted in an affidavit, written and signed by Melville's younger brother, Allan, who had recently been called to the bar in New York and now swore that, to the best his knowledge, Herman's claim to citizenship was true. On Thursday, October 4, betraying his growing impatience with the process, the novelist wrote a covering letter for the affidavit (addressed by him to "Hon John M Clayton, Secretary of State, &c &c &c"), which concluded rather bluntly, "I sail on Monday. May I hope to receive the passport by return mail." Of course, the rush was entirely the fault of Melville's own delays, but by some small miracle (in all likelihood, indicative of nothing more than the relatively small number of passport applications submitted to the secretary of state during the period), the great writer and procrastinator was issued passport number 4033 in time to catch his boat.

. . .

The relative ease with which Melville was able establish his citizenship and thus to acquire a passport stands in clear contrast to the experience of his contemporary, Frederick Douglass. Because the US Constitution is largely silent on the topic, citizenship had a rather ad hoc quality in antebellum America, which is to say that it was established only as needed, while the rights and privileges of individuals were more often determined by their age, sex, and race. Sometimes, free people of color—including patent holders, internal passport carriers, and seamen bearing protection certificates—possessed documents that affirmed their citizenship. In this sense, the documentation and registration of identity did not just expose individuals to the gaze of official surveillance, but became a necessity for them to be recognized as citizens in increasingly complex modern societies that could no longer rely on other means of verification. Without such papers and certificates, free people of color were deprived of any community ready and able to guarantee their rights. This crucial role also meant that the documents were often a locus of human ingenuity, turning the mechanisms of state control against themselves in order to forge new forms of identity and to open new spaces of freedom.

Born on Maryland's eastern shore in 1818 under the name Frederick Augustus Washington Bailey, Douglass made his harrowing flight from enslavement in 1838, with the aid of a friend's documents and a sailor's uniform. Even as he became renowned as an editor, orator, and voice of the abolitionist movement, Douglass withheld details about his escape in order to protect those who helped him and those who might follow in his footsteps. But more than forty years later, in "My Escape from Slavery" (1881), he explained the role that borrowed "free papers" played in the liberation of enslaved peoples:

In these papers the name, age, color, height, and form of the freeman were described, together with any scars or other marks upon his person which could assist in his identification. This device in some measure defeated itself—since more than one man could be found to answer the same general description. Hence many slaves could escape by personating the owner of one set of papers; and this was often done as follows: A slave, nearly or sufficiently answering the description set forth in the papers, would borrow or hire them till by means of them he could escape to a free State, and then, by mail or otherwise, would return them to the owner. The operation was a hazardous one for the lender as well as for the borrower. A failure on the part of the fugitive to send back the papers would imperil his benefactor, and the discovery of the papers in possession of the wrong man would imperil both the fugitive and his friend. It was, therefore, an act of supreme trust on the part of a freeman of color thus to put in jeopardy his own liberty that another might be free. It was, however, not unfrequently bravely done, and was seldom discovered.

Because Douglass did not sufficiently resemble anyone he knew with free papers, he resorted to using "a sailor's protection, which answered somewhat the purpose of free papers," even though the person described in the document was not a good match for him either.[19] With the papers in hand, Douglass boarded a northbound train and played the part of a seaman, drawing on his knowledge of sailor slang and ship life, when the conductor came into the car for Black passengers to collect their tickets and examine their documents. Although Douglass became inwardly agitated as he watched this ritual unfold in front of him, he maintained a calm and cool outward appearance while the man worked his way toward the back of the car.

The encounter between the escaped slave and the train conductor provides perhaps the most dramatic episode in all of Douglass's writings, which are crowded with scenes of brutality and struggle, courage and determination, bearing witness to the experience of those who lived and died in bondage:

"I suppose you have your free papers?" [said the conductor.]
To which I answered: "No sir; I never carry my free papers to sea with me."

"But you have something to show that you are a freeman, haven't you?"

"Yes, sir," I answered; "I have a paper with the American Eagle on it, and that will carry me around the world."

With this I drew from my deep sailor's pocket my seaman's protection, as before described. The merest glance at the paper satisfied him, and he took my fare and went on about his business. This moment of time was one of the most anxious I ever experienced. Had the conductor looked closely at the paper, he could not have failed to discover that it called for a very different-looking person from myself, and in that case it would have been his duty to arrest me on the instant, and send me back to Baltimore from the first station . . . Though I was not a murderer fleeing from justice, I felt perhaps quite as miserable as such a criminal.[20]

The parallels with *The Charterhouse of Parma,* written just a few months after these events, are striking—the appropriated passport, the ill-matched physical description, the fears of discovery, even the apparent casualness of the official checking the document—though of course the context and the potential consequences are greatly altered. The fictional Fabrizio was born into a society where he enjoyed wealth and privilege; his flight was a matter of self-expression and his own misdirected striving. Douglass was born into a society where the racialized body was the object of stark oppression; his escape was a matter of self-preservation and pursuing the liberty to engage in self-expression. His personal narrative of emancipation is based precisely on his sense of becoming a person in a society that denies his personhood by relegating him to the status of "bare life"— exploited for his capacity of production and reproduction, while utterly excluded from political representation and citizenship as such. This narrative begins with Douglass appropriating the symbols of state power and asserting his right to freedom of movement.

The borrowed documents helped Douglass to reach New York and then New Bedford, Massachusetts, where he announced himself a freeman and adopted his famous surname, borrowed from a poem by Sir Walter Scott, to affirm his new standing. But for the next nine years, regardless of the renown or influential friends he garnered, Douglas traveled everywhere as a fugitive slave, stolen property, until he was finally able to purchase his freedom and put an end to this constant jeopardy. David W. Blight, author the Pulitzer Prize–winning *Frederick Douglass: Prophet of Freedom,* has recently likened the tenuous condition of the fugitive slave to that of the "illegal" migrant in our own time: "Hope and dread marched on all sides in antebellum America, as they do today in a Jordanian refugee camp, overcrowded boats leaving the Libyan coast, a detention center in Germany, in the border patrol cues at Heathrow Airport, or a customs line at JFK." Even now, the supposedly universal rights of man accrue only to the citizen of the nation-sate, with the proper papers to corroborate that status. Evading the system of "legal" enslavement in the United States, Douglass managed to conduct a two-year-long lecture tour across the Atlantic as he championed the antislavery cause for sympathetic audiences in England, Scotland, and Ireland. His only passport on the journey was his growing reputation as an orator and, later, the success of his memoir–as–abolitionist treatise, *Narrative of the Life of Frederick Douglass* (1845). Yet during this period, as Blight reminds us, "neither fame nor any security guards protected him from potential recapture and return to slavery."[21]

Long after he secured his freedom, Douglass was still unable obtain an official US passport. In 1859, the activist was forced to flee the United States to Canada and then England amid fears of arrest for his role in financing John Brown's raid on Harper's Ferry, even though he had ultimately declined to participate in what he viewed as an ill-conceived revolt. After a brief period in the United Kingdom, he sought to fulfill his "long-cherished desire to visit France," but found himself in need of a passport: after a recent assassination attempt on Napoleon III (by the Italian nationalist Felice Orsini, with the aid of a British passport provided by an English radical) the French government had temporarily instituted stricter enforcement of its passport system.[22] Leaving nothing to chance, the traveler applied for the necessary documentation by writing to the US minister to the United Kingdom. But, as Douglass later recounted, "true to the traditions of the Democratic party, true to the slaveholding policy of his country, true to the decision of the United States Supreme Court, and true, perhaps, to the petty meanness of his own nature, Mr. George M. Dallas, the Democratic American minister, refused to grant me a passport, on the ground that I was not a citizen of the United States."[23]

Two years earlier, in 1857, the Dred Scott case had ruled that African Americans, whether free or enslaved, were "not included, and were not intended to be included, under the word 'citizens' in the Constitution, and [could] therefore claim none of the rights and privileges which that instrument provides for and secures to citizens of the United States." Those rights and privileges, of course, included the possession of a US passport—a decision that Dallas was only too happy to enforce. Refusing to be drawn into a dispute with the US minister, Douglass instead addressed a letter to the French minister to the United Kingdom asking for a permit to visit his country, which was granted without delay (though after learning that his ten-year-old daughter, Annie, had died of a protracted illness at home in the United States, Douglass did not carry on to France in the spring of 1860 as he had planned).

The historical ironies of the passport system—which denied documents to the marginalized and outcast who needed them, while generating inconvenience and annoyance for the privileged who thought they should be able to do without them—became even more apparent as the United States moved toward civil war. Shortly after the Confederate States of America was founded in 1861, the breakaway government established a passport office and instituted an internal passport system that required soldiers and civilians to present documents at a network of sentry posts, rail stations, and entry points across the southern states. "The problem with the wartime passport system," Israeli historian Yael A. Sternhell explains, "was that it resembled the parallel method for governing slaves not only in theory, but also in practice."[24] Enslaved men and women in the South had long been required, on punishment of brutal violence and even death, to carry a written pass from their owners whenever the left their plantations. Now white southerners, like those they considered chattel, were compelled to apply for travel documents – and many complained that the new system represented a vexing intrusion "upon personal liberty," as even the officials in charge had to acknowledge. Moreover, the documents carried by white travelers closely resembled those carried by Blacks moving through the Confederate States, often including not just their name and destination, but also their physical description: height, hair color, eye color, complexion, and scars. Thus, as Sternhell drily observes, "the internal passport system brought into sharp relief the uncomfortable fact that the war had cost Southern masters both their own freedom of movement and the freedom to control the movement of their human property."[25]

It is only fitting to let Frederick Douglass have the last word on the matter. On August 24, 1886, in anticipation of a honeymoon journey with his second wife, the iconic American completed a passport application in Washington, DC, swearing that he was "born in the State of Maryland" and that he was "a Native and Loyal Citizen of the United States . . . about to travel abroad." The description of the traveler was filled in ("Age, 69 years; Stature, 6 feet . . . inches, Eng.; Forehead, medium; Eyes, dark; Nose, prominent; Mouth, medium; Chin, beard; Hair, gray; Complexion, dark; Face, oval") and in the middle of these columns was scrawled "wife" to indicate the identity of his traveling companion (the white abolitionist and suffragist Helen Pitts). The document is twice countersigned by Passport Clerk Newton Benedict, but witness testimony or an affidavit confirming the applicant's citizenship appears to have been unnecessary. It was now nearly two decades since the fourteenth amendment to the United States Constitution had overruled the Dred Scott decision to grant citizenship to all people born in the United States, including former slaves and Native Americans. What is more, the tall, distinguished gentleman standing before the clerk in the Washington, DC, passport office was now well known on both sides of the Atlantic. Douglass had campaigned for the rights of African Americans for nearly half a century, in the process helping to convince Abraham Lincoln that the abolition of slavery should be the aim of the Civil War.

Indeed, as passport enforcement waned across Europe and a golden age of travel commenced in the closing decades of the nineteenth century, Douglass and Pitts could well have undertaken their journey without the bother of a passport. In his travel book *The Innocents Abroad*

(1869), Mark Twain recounts with self-effacing glee his experience of traveling under a borrowed passport with a physical description that was nothing like him: as he approaches Sebastopol harbor in a decommissioned Civil War ship, he is filled with "fear and trembling" at the thought of being found out and summarily executed by Russian officials. On arrival, however, he discovers that "all that time my true passport had been floating gallantly overhead—and behold it was only our flag. They never asked for another."[26] For Douglass, more than a decade and a half later, the document was nonetheless significant. In *The Life and Times of Frederick Douglass* (1892), the great man makes clear that, as he prepared for his honeymoon in Europe, he still agonizingly recalled the occasion many years before when George M. Dallas "refused to give me a passport on the ground that I was not and could not be an American citizen. This man is now dead and generally forgotten, as I shall be; but I have lived to see myself everywhere recognized as an American citizen."[27] The passport he would receive in 1886, the first Douglass ever possessed, was yet another affirmation of that hard-won status.

The fact that the passport was a symbol of citizenship, rather than a necessity for travel, did little to diminish the sense of freedom that it afforded Douglass. After describing the acquisition of his passport, he writes movingly of his long-standing wanderlust: "I had strange dreams of travel even in my boyhood days. I thought I should some day see many of the famous places of which I heard men speak, and of which I read even while a slave."[28] Now, in the company of his new partner, and in possession of the new document, he could finally embark on his Grand Tour. Douglass left empty the blank on the passport application where his destinations were to be indicated, not because the document would go unused, but because his itinerary was open-ended. Again recalling the disappointment he had suffered at the will of the US minister years earlier, he writes:

> my gratification was all the more intense that I was not only permitted to visit France and see something of life in Paris; to walk the streets of that splendid city and spend days and weeks in her charming art

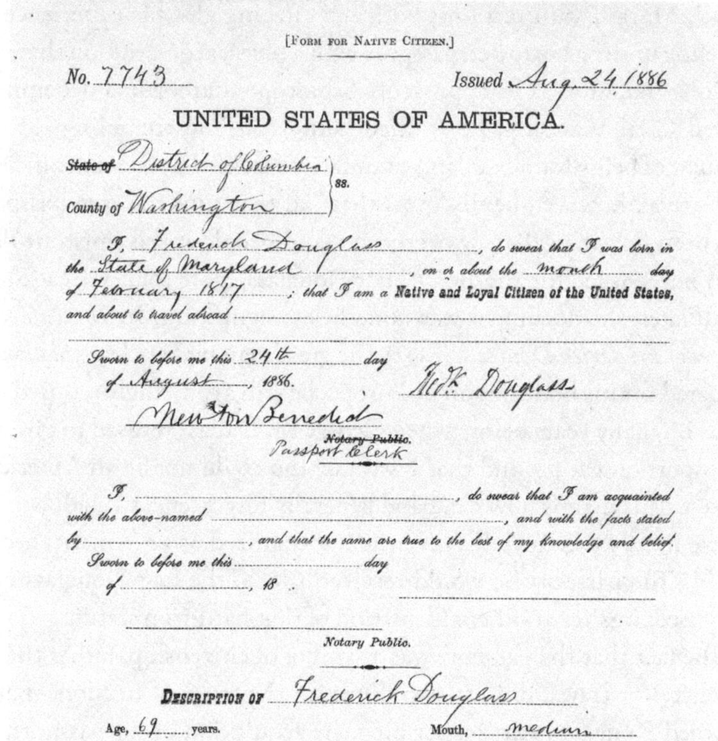

[FORM FOR NATIVE CITIZEN.]

No. 7743   Issued *Aug. 24, 1886*

UNITED STATES OF AMERICA.

State of *District of Columbia*
                                        } ss.
County of *Washington*

I, *Frederick Douglass*, do swear that I was born in the State of *Maryland*, on or about the *month* day of *February 1817*; that I am a **Native and Loyal Citizen of the United States,** and about to travel abroad

Sworn to before me this *24th* day of *August*, 1886.   *Fred. Douglass*

Newton Benedict
~~Notary Public.~~
Passport Clerk

I, _____, do swear that I am acquainted with the above-named _____, and with the facts stated by _____, and that the same are true to the best of my knowledge and belief.

Sworn to before me this _____ day of _____, 18 .   _____

_____
Notary Public.

DESCRIPTION OF *Frederick Douglass*

Age, *69* years.   Mouth, *medium*
Stature, *6* feet _____ inches, Eng.   Chin, *beard*
Forehead, *medium*   Hair, *gray*
Eyes, *dark*   Complexion, *dark*
Nose, *prominent*   Face, *oval*

I, *Frederick Douglass*, do solemnly swear that I will support, protect, and defend the Constitution and Government of the United States against all enemies, whether domestic or foreign; and that I will bear true faith, allegiance, and loyalty to the same, any ordinance, resolution, or law of any State, Convention, or Legislature to the contrary notwithstanding; and further, that I do this with a full determination, pledge, and purpose, without any mental reservation or evasion whatsoever; and further, that I will well and faithfully perform all the duties which may be required of me by law: So help me God.

Fred. Douglass

SWORN to before me this *24th* day of *August*, 1886.

Newton Benedict

Applicant desires passport sent to following address:

_____

_____

FIGURE 8. Frederick Douglass's passport application, 1886. Image courtesy of the National Archives and Records Administration.

galleries, but to extend my tour to other lands and visit other cities; to look upon Egypt; to stand on the summit of its highest Pyramid; to walk among the ruins of old Memphis; to gaze into the dead eyes of Pharaoh; to feel the smoothness of granite tombs polished by Egyptian workmen three thousand years ago.[29]

In between Paris and the pyramids, on a trajectory opposite to the mummified remains of Ramesses II nearly a century later, Douglass passed through Dijon, Lyon, and Avignon with its palace of the Popes, then on to Marseilles and the amphitheater at Arles; he continued east to Nice and Genoa before turning south toward Pisa, with its leaning tower, and then Rome, where he stood in admiration of both the architecture and the practices of the Catholic Church; he saw Vesuvius and Naples, then sailed through the Suez Canal and carried on to Cairo and the land of the Pharaohs, before turning back toward home via Italy, France, and England. His account in *The Life and Times of Frederick Douglass* paints of vivid picture of his travels and their impact on him. He contemplated the cultural geography of modern Europe in the arrangements of its towns, villages, vineyards, and farms; he pondered the conflicts of the past, both spiritual and secular, as evinced in the walled and fortified towns, the ancient monasteries and castles; he observed the changing features and complexions of local populations as he moved southward and eastward; he noted the shared customs of the peoples on both sides of the Mediterranean; he repeatedly compared what he saw in the Old World with what he knew so well of American ideals, values, and aspirations; he reflected on the wonders of ancient Egyptian culture and the religiosity of modern Muslim life. But Douglass never again mentioned his passport.

PART TWO

————

*The Advent of the Passport
as We Know It*

FOUR

Modernists and Militants

TO BEGIN WITH AN ODD detail from a book suffused with odd details, that massive modernist tome *Ulysses* (1922): the novel dedicates more than seven hundred pages to the minute description of that single day in Dublin, June 16, 1904—so if you make it to the final lines (and to be sure, few readers do on the first attempt), you might be surprised to find a colophon that takes you far away from the Irish capital, "Trieste-Zurich-Paris, 1914–1921." There is something deceptively poignant in this brief itinerary, which might otherwise be seen as an advertisement for the cosmopolitan credentials of its author. As he labored on his masterpiece for seven long and tumultuous years, James Joyce was a wanderer much like the Homeric hero of his title, though he would never return home to the Dublin he rendered so obsessively in his novel. The foreign cities listed at the end of *Ulysses* indicate the coordinates where it was composed, as Joyce, the once-willing exile, became an unwilling refugee during the First World War, before finally discovering a new home in the international gathering place that was the French capital.

What is only hinted at in the names and dates at the end of the path-breaking novel is detailed, with the authority of state records and government officials, in the passport that Joyce acquired from the British consulate in Zurich on August 10, 1915, shortly after he fled Trieste with his young family in tow. As foreigners with uncertain allegiances, the Joyces were no longer welcome in the port city, then part of the Austro-Hungarian Empire, after Italy exited the Triple Alliance and entered the

FIGURE 9. The Joyce family passport, 1915. Image courtesy of Sotheby's.

war. In the early weeks of the conflict, nation-states across Europe had reintroduced passport controls in order to better regulate the movements of citizens and noncitizens, nationals and aliens, alike, measures that were posed as a temporary response to a state of emergency. The wartime document belonging to Joyce, Passport No. 557, consists of a double-sided sheet of white and pink paper, measuring approximately thirteen by twenty-one inches (34 × 54 cm) and folded to form ten panels, covered with various visa and renewal stamps in multicolored inks. The passport tells the story not just of his years of restless movement and prolific creativity, his efforts to locate a hospitable site of artistic detachment, but also of the danger and destruction of wartime. With this came the persistent demand to register his family's personal whereabouts and confirm their national identities through assorted processes of bureaucratic management in several countries.

The tension between the autonomy of the individual and the sovereignty of the nation-state is evinced on every panel of the passport. Of course, the document contains the standard "Description of the Bearer," including the now familiar categories of age (33), place and date of birth (Dublin, 2nd Feb. 1882), height (5 feet 10 inches), forehead (regular), eyes (blue), nose (regular), mouth (regular), chin (oval), colour of hair (dark brown), complexion (fair), face (oval). But now, after the passage of the British Nationality and Status of Aliens Act on August 7, 1914 (three days after Britain entered the war), the passport also required a photograph of the holder and any family members traveling under the document's protection. Unlike the strictly standardized photographs in our passports today, these early images still afforded the opportunity for subtle costuming and other forms of self-fashioning or self-authoring. The passport in question bears a black-and-white photograph of Joyce, sporting a pince-nez (under an additional description for "any special peculiarities" he had indicated "wears glasses"), a tidy little moustache, and a blank, if still rather intense, expression. If we see the distinctive features of a dandy in this image of Joyce, his malformed fedora suggests something altogether humbler, more appropriate to the "English teacher" he had indicated under "Profession" in the "Description of the Bearer" (he had kept, or attempted to keep, the household together by giving language lessons in Trieste). Rather than the ambitious author of a highly experimental (and soon to be highly controversial) modernist novel, the hat suggests something more mundane, like his "regular" forehead, nose, and mouth, perhaps all the better to avoid attracting undo attention from consular authorities or border agents.

Whatever we might make of the passport photo of the novelist, the gender politics of the document are all too clear: the husband and father is pictured alone as the head of the family, while his wife and children huddle together in a collective photograph on the opposite panel, as if they were detachable accessories for the traveling man. This collective photograph displays Nora Joyce and her two children, Lucia and Giorgio, each wearing their Sunday-best clothes and fancy hats; the bespectacled boy, with his placid expression, closely mirrors his father in the photo opposite. This patriarchal arrangement is reinforced by the "Passport Regulations" inscribed on the first panel of the document, which indicate that "a married woman is deemed to be a subject of the State to which her husband is for the time being a subject." It was quite unusual during this period for a woman to possess her own passport, and in any case, a married woman could not use the document without her husband present. But the fact that this passport was issued to "Mr James Joyce, and wife Mrs Nora Joyce," suggests something more than this, because the stridently unconventional James and the fiercely loyal Nora were not in fact married (and would not legally marry until 1931, and then only in order to protect her inheritance). Rather than just a concession to social convention, the Joyce family passport was a matter of bureaucratic convenience at a time when securing such travel documents was a chancy business. It also saved the couple, who had been living hand to mouth for years, the expense of 5 shillings for another passport. (This very passport would later sell at a Sotheby's auction in 2011 for some £61,250, or $96,000.)

In 1915, of course, the passport had become more than an affirmation of personal identity or familial hierarchy: it had become an assertion of national affiliation, as the rising tide of nationalism, which had continued to surge since the late nineteenth century, peaked with the outrages of the war. Each side of the conflict saw the other as a threat to their way of life, viewed as civilized, righteous, and beyond reproach. The new passport regime, with its more invasive and expansive means of documentary surveillance, served this age of belligerent "us" and "them" thinking by drawing national borders more sharply than ever before.

Here again, the Joyce document tells a more nuanced story than we might expect from its compact size and standardized format. The novelist attained his passport only by swearing to his status as a "British-born subject" and native of "Dublin." But Irish nationalists had long asserted that British rule was injurious to the interests of the Irish people, and by the summer of 1915 plans were well underway for an armed insurrection centered in Dublin. Extra impetus was given to the planning by fears that the British government would introduce conscription in Ireland, sending young Irishmen to the trenches to fight and die for the British cause. The period covered by the Joyce family passport saw the Easter Rising of 1916, the formation of a secessionist Irish parliament in 1918, and the War of Independence, which ended with the Anglo-Irish Treaty of 1921 and the establishment of the Irish Free State. Indeed, by the time the passport finally expired (after four renewals) in the summer of 1923, "Ireland" (and anyone born in Dublin) could no longer be considered "British."

Joyce had first come to the Continent a decade before he received the passport, largely to escape what he viewed as the social and cultural restrictions imposed on Ireland in the names of both British imperialism and Irish nationalism. In Zurich, he found not just a refuge from the violence raging across Europe, but a community of artistic and political outsiders, one that provided a background hum in tune with the intricate orchestrations of *Ulysses*. This cosmopolitan milieu is captured with irreverent flair in Tom Stoppard's 1974 play *Travesties,* which places Joyce among the "refugees, exiles, spies, anarchists, artists and radicals of all kinds" that had congregated in the city by the lake.[1] In addition to the Irish novelist, the dramatis personae include the Russian political theorist and revolutionary Vladimir Lenin and the Romanian founder of Dadaism Tristan Tzara, though Stoppard omits another important figure, the noted Austrian writer Stefan Zweig, who had once met with Joyce at the iconic Café Odeon. Traveling on a wartime passport from the Austrian government, Zweig was in Zurich for the first production of his vehemently antiwar play *Jeremiah* (1917), which contributed to a kind proxy battle of national cultures taking place on neutral ground. Meanwhile, due to the fact that he held a British passport, Joyce was coming under increasing pressure from the British consulate to register for military service. He soon devised another means to demonstrate his fealty to the cause, albeit one that scarcely placated the foreign service officers in charge of his case and that later provided a source of much mirth in *Travesties:* he would help found a theater company in Zurich ostensibly dedicated to English drama (and pro-British propaganda), though the first production of the Players would be a cunning satire of British society by an Irish playwright, Oscar Wilde's *The Importance of Being Earnest* (1895).

If Joyce had come to Zurich to escape the internecine politics of the war years—to find a state where he could pursue the vocation of an artist "against every state," as he declared in 1918—his fellow exile, Lenin, had arrived in the Swiss city to ready himself for a triumphant return to Russian politics. But their attitudes toward the role of the state and the effects of nationalism were not as dissimilar as one might expect: Joyce had developed socialist sympathies when he was still living in Ireland and he continued to nurse them during his early years on the Continent. Even after he abandoned his nominal interest in socialism, his attitude toward the vicissitudes of Irish history continued to be shaped by socialist ideas for many years. Lenin, meanwhile, had advanced a brand of international socialism that sought to tear down national barriers and eradicate national distinctions (what he called, in a phrase Joyce might well have uttered, "reactionary nationalist philistinism") in favor of a proletarian movement that would bring nations together around a common cause. In Switzerland, he wrote just as feverishly as Joyce did, producing his treatise *Imperialism, the Highest Stage of Capitalism* (1917) and dozens of articles and essays, which critiqued the role of capitalist competition and the bourgeois nation-state in provoking the Great War and perpetuating class domination. Lenin composed these texts and conducted his political career under a pseudonym (he was born Vladimir Ilyich Ulyanov) that many historians have attributed to a passport the revolutionary had in his possession when he first fled Russia in 1900, after three years of exile in eastern Siberia.

In early 1917, after learning that the February Revolution had removed Tsar Nicholas II from power and established the Provisional Government, Lenin wanted anxiously to return to Russia and take up leadership of the Bolsheviks. But the war had closed off all routes for his homecoming from Switzerland. In his desperation, Lenin decided that the best plan of action was to obtain a forged or stolen Swedish passport, which would allow him to travel north through Germany and on to Sweden without attracting unwanted attention. Still, as he spoke no Swedish, he needed a strategy for presenting himself to the guards at the frontier: Lenin thus wrote to a comrade in Stockholm asking him to identify two Swedish deaf-mutes who looked enough like Lenin and his Bolshevik aide-de-camp, Grigory Yevseyevich Zinovyev, to provide them with passports for the journey. Whether this scheme was ultimately deemed impossible or merely absurd, Lenin and a group of other dissidents instead traveled covertly through wartime Germany in a "sealed" train car, bringing them eventually to Finland Station in Petrograd (St. Petersburg). There, the returned exile would deliver a rousing, and soon to be notorious, speech to his Bolshevik supporters, denouncing the Provisional Government as guilty of imperialist aspirations and calling for loyal socialists to initiate an international proletarian revolution.

Lenin would still face the necessity to travel under a false passport, however. In July 1917, after a series of armed demonstrations by soldiers, peasants, and workers, the Provisional Government began a crackdown on the Bolsheviks, including the arrest of many party officials and the publication of allegations against Lenin. Fearing for his life, the Bolshevik leader hurriedly devised a plan to escape arrest: he would sneak through the forest in the middle of night to a small railway station near the Russo-Finnish border; from there, posing as a stoker on a locomotive, he would proceed across the frontier to a safe house. The scheme required a fake passport that would cloak Lenin under the fictitious name "Konstantin Petrovich Ivanov," and a rather inventive disguise: a wig and laborer's cap to conceal his famously bald head, as well as a fresh shave to remove his distinctive Van Dyke beard. The scheme was reminiscent of another he had entertained when plotting his departure from Zurich that spring: Lenin had asked an accomplice to obtain papers for travel to England; then, to complete the ruse, he would put on a wig and take the documents to the consulate in Bern, where he would be photographed for the accompanying image. Now, putting a similar plan into action, Lenin went to a theatrical specialist to secure an appropriate hairpiece, but found that the only one available was a silvery gray model that made the revolutionary look much older. The wigmaker was dismayed by the appearance of his client and reluctant to sell him the wig; Lenin, however, was pleased with the way it concealed his identity (though of course he could not reveal his purpose to the wigmaker). The effect was certainly striking. The passport photo taken of the disguised revolutionary, the only photo of a beardless Lenin in existence, renders him virtually unrecognizable. Rather than the intense and erudite Bolshevik leader, he appears (just this once) as a member of the humble proletariat he had championed so passionately.

· · ·

Photography was meant to make passports an even more powerful tool of state surveillance and control. As noted above, after the outbreak of the war concerns regarding spying, sedition, and sabotage prompted many nations for the first time to require a photograph of the passport holder. The United Kingdom had quickly moved to require photographs on all passports after the apprehension of Carl Hans Lody, a German spy who traveled to England under a US passport pilfered from the American embassy in Berlin. With no photograph for confirmation, the physical description on the document (originally produced for an American citizen named Charles A. Inglis) had matched the spy closely enough to deceive authorities. Photography had been used to identify criminals since the 1840s, shortly after the invention of the technology, and now it was deployed in the war effort because the images were assumed to create a more reliable connection between the passport and the passport holder. Influential media theorists such as Susan Sontag and Friedrich Kittler have emphasized that photographic images once garnered a kind of absolute trust, since they were understood not just to represent the individual, but to *guarantee* that representation: the illuminated body physically imprinted its image on the photographic film. Of course, images like that of Lenin, with his costume and wig, demonstrate how this faith in photography could be manipulated: insofar as his physical person matched the photo on his passport, he would generate little suspicion from the authorities. The integration of photographs into travel documents thus meant that these objects were understood to embody an objective, if not entirely unmistakable, form of identification. They could even be understood as transforming their holder into an *object*, one susceptible to both symbolic and bureaucratic control.

As we well know, the emergency control measures enforced across Europe and North America during the First World War did not disappear after the end of the conflict: they remain with us in much the same form today. To be sure, the passport would quickly become the principal tool for establishing the identity and monitoring the movement of individuals around the globe, whatever the motivation of the state powers involved. Even as postwar treaties were redrawing the map of Europe, Britain and Germany swiftly extended wartime measures controlling entrance to and departure from their territories. Not long before the end of the conflict, the passage of the Wartime Measure Act (also known as the Travel Control Act and the Passport Act) had made it "unlawful for any citizen of the United States to depart from or enter or attempt to depart from or enter the United States unless he bears a valid passport."[2] Shortly after the war, the United States erected new barriers to international labor migration by prolonging wartime passport regulations and expanding the list of nations whose migrants would not be allowed in the country.

The extension of a state of emergency into peacetime thus provided governments across Europe and North America with a new arsenal of powers, and officials did not hesitate in deploying them. For instance, immediately after the armistice in November 1918, organizations such as the National Race Congress and the Universal Negro Improvement Association elected delegates to travel to the Paris Peace Conference in the hope of drawing global attention to the plight of African Americans.[3] But the groups soon became the target of a Military Intelligence Division investigation that led the State Department to refuse passports to all their delegates. Research has since demonstrated that the passports were denied precisely to thwart the organizations from raising "the Negro question" at the conferences, which would have surely humiliated US

President Woodrow Wilson in his role as global peacemaker. Among the thwarted delegates was Ida B. Wells-Barnett, the investigative journalist and civil rights leader, who had once made speaking tours of Great Britain to call attention to lynchings in the United States. At that time, the 1890s, she did not require a passport for overseas travel; now, for want of one, she could not leave her own country. Meanwhile, W. E. B. Du Bois, the author of *The Souls of Black Folk* (1903)—who planned to report on the conferences for *Crisis,* the official magazine of the NAACP—only managed to secure a passport thanks to the last-minute intervention of Emmett Scott, special assistant for Negro affairs to the secretary of war and the highest-ranking African American in the US government.[4]

One of the most significant proposals President Wilson made at the Paris Peace Conference was the foundation of the League of Nations; one of the first acts of the League was to hold the Paris Conference on Passports & Customs Formalities and Through Tickets in October 1920. Although other organizations in Europe had been condemning the persistence of the wartime passport system and calling for a return to freedom of movement, the League of Nations made a strong push to institutionalize the passport system by creating international standards for the documents and their handling. Meanwhile, an informal alliance of modernists complained in their private letters: French novelist André Gide lamented to Austrian poet Rainer Maria Rilke that *"toutes les formalités des passeports"* ("all the passport formalities")[5] had quashed the autonomy that had once allowed the friends to visit each other across national frontiers, while that roving American poet Ezra Pound grumbled that he had had "hell's own time about passports" when he sought to renew his after the war. The ever-opinionated expatriate attributed the difficulties to President Wilson's desire "to tie all serfs to the soil."[6]

Rather than abolishing a system that posed what many saw as vexing inconveniences, not to mention serious threats to the renewal of international relations and the recovery of economic strength, the League ratified a series of regulations for improving its efficiency. Perhaps most significantly, in an effort to ease the burden on border officials faced with passports in a bewildering array of shapes, sizes, and formats, the conference approved general guidelines for a passport booklet for the first time. According to the standards drawn up in 1920 and amended slightly in 1926, a passport should measure 15.5 by 10.5 centimeters and contain thirty-two pages, including twenty-eight pages for visa stamps and four pages for the identifying details of the holder, the issuing place, the origination date, and other official information. All these details should be written in two languages—French and the national language of the issuing country. Finally, the document should be bound in a cardboard cover, displaying the name of the issuing country at the top, the national coat of arms in the center, and the word *passport* at the bottom. "In standardizing the form of the passport," as American literary scholar Bridgette Chalk has pointed out, "the League of Nations effectively dictated the means by which one could inhabit a national identity in a form that would be internationally recognizable" for the next century.[7]

Gide, Rilke, and Pound were joined by many other artists and intellectuals who deeply resented the restrictions on personal freedom they saw manifested in the passport. Associated tensions regarding the designation of both personal and national identities became important, even central, elements of what Paul Fussell calls "the modern sensibility," which had emerged during the war years and only grew in intensity as the new passport system took hold. In the final chapter of his memoir *The World of Yesterday* (1942), Stefan Zweig would write movingly about the sense of loss evoked by these developments:

Before 1914 the earth had belonged to all. People went where they wished and stayed as long as they pleased. There were no permits, no visas, and it always gives me pleasure to astonish the young by telling them that before 1914 I traveled from Europe to India and to America without passport and without ever having seen one. One embarked and alighted without questioning or being questioned, one did not have to fill out a single one of the many papers which are required today. The frontiers which, with their customs officers, police and militia, have become wire barriers thanks to the pathological suspicion of everybody against everybody else, were nothing but symbolic lines which one crossed with as little thought as one crosses the Meridian of Greenwich.

For Zweig, the plague of nationalism had spread only after the war had ended and xenophobia had reached epidemic proportions, as governments around the globe, and their citizens along with them, became progressively more suspicious of outsiders:

> The humiliations which once had been devised with criminals alone in mind now were imposed upon the traveler, before and during every journey. There had to be photographs from right and left, in profile and full face, one's hair had to be cropped sufficiently to make the ears visible; fingerprints were taken, at first only the thumb but later all ten fingers; furthermore, certificates of health, of vaccination, police certificates of good standing, had to be shown; letters of recommendation were required, invitations to visit a country had to be procured; they asked for the addresses of relatives, for moral and financial guarantees, questionnaires, and forms in triplicate and quadruplicate needed to be filled out, and if only one of this sheaf of papers was missing one was lost.[8]

The catalogue of embarrassments and degradations offered by Zweig attests to the exposure of the individual to the forces of state power, which had steadily diminished the agency of self-expression or self-representation. Produced in the context of these rationalized, bureaucratic demands, the passport photo functioned as an official record of identity, as opposed to an aestheticized rendering or artistic interpretation of the individual. And yet the travel documents of cultural and intellectual luminaries, including Joyce, Lenin, and many of their contemporaries, now provide us with a remarkable archive of the modern, or better, *modernist,* sensibility, despite their reluctance to be defined by these official records. If, as Kittler has claimed, "the realm of the dead has the same dimensions as the storage and emission capacities of its culture," then this domain was vastly expanded by the advent of the modern passport, with its requisite photograph, as well as its stamping pages, identifying details, and all the associated documentation that Zweig lists above.[9]

. . .

Even as the modern passport regime placed new pressures and restrictions on the movement of individuals, the documents also bore the stories of those who continued to travel during the interwar period in that cosmopolitan spirit to which Zweig gives testimony. While the web of their crisscrossing journeys is vast, it is undeniable that Paris quickly became one of the most important points of intersection for artists and intellectuals during the era. As his passport attests, Joyce made his way to the city in the summer of 1920, doing so only after Pound convinced him that the French capital would be the best place for the financially strapped novelist to arrange the publication of *Ulysses*. Nonetheless, as the visa stamps on their passport affirm, Joyce and his family planned to stay in Paris (at the "Hôtel Elysée, 9 rue de Beaune, 7th arrondissement") for only a brief period before carrying on to London. Their short stay in the French capital eventually lasted nearly two decades, until the outbreak of the next war compelled the family to abandon their home yet again. During those years, an array of passport-wielding artists and writers congregated in the city looking for cheap accommodations, good wine, and better company with a community of other creatives. Of course, there is much lore about the various salons, coteries, and collectives that formed in Paris during the interwar years. But there is still a history to be written about the passports of these gathered exiles and émigrés, and the questions they raise regarding personal identity, national affiliation, and cosmopolitan feeling. What follows is a small contribution to that narrative. As we will see clearly, though perhaps unexpectedly, even though passports were (and continue to be) deeply implicated in the bureaucratic functioning of the nation-state, these documents can tell us much about the professional ties and intimate relationships of those who carried them.

Take for instance the story of Max Ernst and Paul Éluard. Still reeling from his experience as a soldier on both the Western and Eastern Fronts during the war, Ernst had returned home to continue his artistic career in Cologne, where he founded a short-lived Dada collective and began experimenting with collage. The rebellious young artist first exhibited his collages in the spring of 1921 at Galerie Au Sans Pareil in Paris, but he was unable to attend the opening because, like many other Germans seeking to visit France after the war, he was denied the requisite visa. His work from the fall of that year includes a collage titled *Design for an Exhibition Poster,* which features a passport photo of himself at the bottom of an inverted pyramid made up of photographic reproductions of his works. These images—of sculptures, over-paintings, and other collages—are bounded by pieces of text reading, among other things: "Max Ernst is a liar, legacy-hunter, scandalmonger, horsedealer, slanderer and boxer." Taken together, the composite pieces suggest not the fixed unity of identity promised by a passport, but rather a playful plurality of selves: a series of fictions rather than a singular truth about just who "Max Ernst" might be.

That fall of 1921, Ernst also struck up a lasting friendship with Éluard and his wife, Gala, when the couple visited the artist in Cologne. It was thanks to the French poet, his fellow Dadaist-*cum*-Surrealist, that Ernst finally made his way to Paris (where he longed to join his other artistic allies, Tristan Tzara and André Breton) the following year, after Éluard mailed his own passport to the German painter. Their resemblance was close enough to allow Ernst to pass for Éluard as he crossed the frontier. With the French passport in hand, Ernst added yet another persona to his collection, and indeed, for a period the artist and the poet nearly became doubles. They soon collaborated on an illustrated book, *Misfortunes of the Immortals* (*Les malheurs des immortels,* 1922), pairing their collages and poems; then, for the next two years, Ernst set up house with the Éluards in the Parisian suburb of Saint-Brice and again in the commune of Eaubonne. While the artist spent his days covering the walls of their Eaubonne home with Surrealist murals, he spent his nights in the couple's bed, taking Paul's place there with Gala for a time and establishing a rather cozy ménage à trois.

As we first observed in the revelatory travel document of Joyce and his family, these intimate relations between life and art, passport and artwork, official identity and public persona, are to be found across the modernist canon. Another salient example can be observed in the activities and writings of Gertrude Stein, whose famous salon at 27 rue de

Fleurus, 6th arrondissement, hosted the likes of Pound, T. S. Eliot, Ernest Hemingway, F. Scott Fitzgerald, Richard Wright, Pablo Picasso, Henri Matisse, and Paul Robeson each Saturday evening during much of the interwar period. Stein, along with her partner, Alice B. Toklas, were among a small advanced party of American expatriates who began arriving in Paris shortly after the turn of the century in search of all that was new and exhilarating in the world of arts and letters. Seeking a broader audience (and elusive commercial success) for her writing, Stein would tell the gossipy story of these years in *The Autobiography of Alice B. Toklas* (1933), a book that was far more conventional in approach than the experimental verbal portraits she had previously produced. But the "autobiography" is nonetheless a playful ruse, adopting the verbal mannerisms and quirky sensibility of Toklas to present Stein as a great genius among lesser geniuses. Consequently, the book can be read as an extended, if rather ironic, exercise in reputation building, drolly lampooning the established conventions of life writing, which generally promises to tell us, in so many words, who the subject of the biography really is.

In all its playfulness, *The Autobiography* also addresses the interwar milieu in Europe in a highly unconventional manner. One way it mocks the notion of authentic identities is through a constant reliance on national labels (always written in lower case) to characterize Stein, Toklas, and just about everyone who passes through their salon: "many hungarians, quite a number of germans, quite a few mixed nationalities, a very thin sprinkling of americans and practically no english," and so on.[10] Just as her Dada counterparts had done in the immediate postwar years, Stein draws attention to the absurdities of nationalism, which had turned the accident of being born within a particular set of borders into a reason to kill and die for the "homeland." Perhaps nothing made this seem more absurd than the postwar treaties that demarcated new nation-states across the remains of the former German, Russian, Ottoman, and Austro-Hungarian empires.

Stein also highlights the arbitrariness of all this by drawing attention to the recent rise of the passport regime: the ease with which she and

Toklas moved about before the war—"we had no papers, nobody had any papers in those days"—contrasted with the bureaucratic charades the two faced while traveling during the war.[11] For example, *The Autobiography* details an encounter with the American consul in Madrid, as the pair attempt to return to Paris after an extended holiday in Mallorca: "He looked at our passports, he measured them, weighed them, looked at them upside down and finally said that he supposed they were alright but how could he tell." Given his uncertainty, the American consul defers authority to his assistant, who in turn defers authority to another nation-state altogether by sending Stein and Toklas off to see the French consul: "since you are going to France and you live in Paris and if the french consul says they are alright, why the consul will sign."[12] At the time, the travelers were infuriated with the American consul for his derogation of duty. But narrating these events years later, Stein-as-Toklas suggests that his conduct may well have been part of an unofficial international agreement, allowing the French consul to determine whether a given passport holder was welcome in his country.

With its idiosyncratic approach to life writing, *The Autobiography* serves as a remarkable counterpoint to the images of Stein and Toklas presented in their actual travel documentation. As one might expect, the book begins with details regarding the origins of its eponymous figure: "I was born in San Francisco, California. . . . My father came of polish patriotic stock."[13] Reviewing the multiple passport applications that Toklas (always in the company of Stein) filled out during and shortly after the war, one is struck by how closely they mirror this mode of self-presentation. Case in point, her 1921 application: "I solemnly swear that I was born at *San Francisco* . . . in the State of *Calif.* on *April* 30, 1877, that my father *Ferdinand Toklas* was born in *Kempen, Poland* . . . " Together, the official versions of Toklas and Stein presented to the US Department of State provide a kind of précis of *The Autobiography,* albeit one rendered almost exclusively in terms of places of birth, residence, travel, and the associated dates, along with details about their physical appearance. We might also compare the passport photographs in the files, with their mugshot qualities, to the famous portrait of Stein painted by Picasso before the war or, better, the famous photograph of the writer sitting before the portrait in her Parisian apartment. These widely circulated likenesses helped Stein to promote an image of herself as the eccentric modernist mastermind. The passport applications, by contrast, document an identity that is not so much an inner essence or personal expression as a verbal and visual construct managed by bureaucratic conventions and imposed by state authority.

Even so, as we learned from the Joyce family passport, these official documents betray at least the fleeting possibility of an individual intervening to manage or manipulate the construction of his or her identity. At the same time, the documents can be seen as far more personal than the broadly distributed images and narratives that Stein deployed to promote her career, precisely because they offer versions of herself that she did not intend us to see. No doubt this strange sense of intimacy gives them their appeal. For instance, compelled to provide an "AFFIDA VIT TO EXPLAIN PROTRACTED FOREIGN RESIDENCE AND TO OVERCOME PRESUMPTION OF EXPATRIATION," Stein testified that:

> I came to France to complete my litterary [sic] studies and to collect materials for my books. In November 1917 I took up war relief work, with the American Fund for French Wounded. I drove my automobile for them till July 1919. I was decorated by the French Government with the medal "Reconnaissance Francaise." Since July 1919 I have taken up my writing of books again.

This brief memoir, emphasizing her service to the Allied cause (and conveniently leaving out her propensity to consort with avant-garde artists and other suspicious types), seems to have been effective in pleasing its audience of one, M. L. Sevre, American Vice-Consul, who offered his "OPINION OF THE OFFICER TAKING THE AFFIDAVIT" as a kind of bureaucratic literary critic: "I believe that the facts recited are sufficient under the established rules to entitle her to protection as an American citizen."

But readers of *The Autobiography*, with its far less cautious approach, would later learn that Stein and Toklas had joined the American Fund for French Wounded on a whim after spotting one of the cars used by the group on the Rue des pyramides in Paris. They would also find out that Stein, genius though she may have been, experienced repeated mishaps as she learned to drive a car for the organization, including running out of gas and causing a scene on the Champs-Élysées. But perhaps the most remarkable discovery related to these passport applications—and the bureaucratic form of life writing that they contain—is simply the amount of space they occupy in the archive. During a period when very few women held their own passports, these extraordinary expatriates were amassing their own sizable passport collections: the National Archives hold no fewer than eight US passport applications for Toklas, dating between 1907 and 1921, and eight for Stein dating all the way back to her first trip abroad in 1896, when she was still a student at Radcliffe College in Cambridge, Massachusetts. Each application offers a chapter in their shared bureaucratic biography.

The so-called Lost Generation—that collective of damaged and disoriented, though mostly young and ambitious, American writers who gathered in Paris after the war—could not have gotten "lost" without their passports. When a newly married Ernest Hemingway sailed for Paris on December 8, 1921, seeking to transform himself from a cub reporter (he identified himself as a "journalist" in his passport) into not just an international correspondent for the *Toronto Star Weekly* but what he conceived of as a "real" writer, he traveled on a passport issued to him, "accompanied by his wife." Kept in the John F. Kennedy Library, along with many of other Hemingway papers (the president was a big fan of the novelist), the document bears a picture of the confident young man with a rather puzzling look on his face, somehow indignant, stern, and yet boyish and naïve, though there is no picture (not even a place for one) of his bride. Elizabeth Hadley Hemingway (née Richardson) receives little more than brief mention in his biographical details, even though her ability to travel abroad to Europe or return home to the United States depended entirely on this document (and thus on the whims of her all-too-mercurial groom).

Arriving in Paris that winter, Ernest set himself to writing fiction and to meeting those who could advance his career (or at least share a drink while discussing his work); he was soon in the company of Stein, Pound, Joyce, and the rest of the passport-toting literati, though Hadley was not always welcome along. In the fall of 1922, Ernest went off to Constantinople to report on the Greco-Turkish War and then to Switzerland to cover the Lausanne Peace Conference, but it was only later that, feeling a bit lonely and remote, he mailed the joint passport to Hadley so that she could join him in Romandie.[14] It was at the very outset of her fateful journey, even before she left the train station in Paris, that Hadley lost a suitcase containing the manuscripts (and carbon copies) of all the fiction Ernest had written during their time in France. The couple survived the mishap for a time, and their next passport, from December 1923, pithily chronicles the family history of "Ernest Miller Hemingway," now identified as a "writer," "accompanied by wife, Hadley and minor son, John H.——." This time the document, as archived, also includes a loose photograph of Mrs. Hemingway, wearing a rather pursed, if not pained, smile. Lamentably, when Ernest applied for his next passport in early 1926, the document was just for himself (although it was later amended to include his son), because Hadley had recently discovered his affair with her friend and confidante, Pauline Marie Pfeiffer. Although Hadley disappears from the archive of Hemingway travel documents at this point, the Kennedy Library also holds the passport of Ms. Pfeiffer, issued December 10, 1926, just a few months before she would become the second Mrs. Hemingway.

Several years later, through a rather delightful clerical error, Hemingway himself would discover just how it felt to be constrained, misrepresented, even stripped of his authorial authority by his passport. Filling out an application in 1931, he apparently scrawled his answers a bit too quickly and messily, so that the clerk processing the form, failing to recognize the now-famous "writer" Ernest Miller Hemingway, mistook his occupation as "waiter." The proud author of *The Sun Also Rises* (1926) and *A Farewell to Arms* (1929) felt compelled to correct the error: writing to the passport office, he protested that it would cause him "serious inconvenience when traveling" if he were identified as a humble restaurant employee. With a keen awareness of his public image (and the powerful role that passports had come to play in fixing the identity of their holders), he loftily affirmed: "My true occupation is that of WRITER or AUTHOR."[15]

When F. Scott Fitzgerald relocated his young family to France in 1924, pursuing his own literary glory and, in the age of Prohibition, freely flowing booze, the updated US passport format called for pictures of the entire family: from top to bottom on the picture page we see Scott, with his wild hair and wilder eyes; Zelda, with her flapper hairstyle and slightly stunned expression; and Frances Scott ("Scottie"), their two-year-old daughter, with her Dutch-boy bob and quizzical smile. Thanks to the success of his early novels *This Side of Paradise* (1920) and *The Beautiful and the Damned* (1922), the latter based on their lives together in New York café society, Scott and Zelda were already becoming youthful icons of the Jazz Age when they arrived in France. The passport photos capture them at a moment when the world lay open to them, when everything still seemed possible, as they moved on to conqueror Parisian café society, with the "author" (as inscribed in the "occupation" blank) and patriarch perched at the top of the family totem pole, prepared to compose the next chapter in their lives. Of course, Scott would seek to sustain their dashing public image as they capered and caroused across Europe. But just few years later, as the Roaring Twenties neared their disappointing finale, his next passport shows a man who had matured, if not mellowed, with the trials and tribulations of the intervening period written clearly on his visage—now fuller, the eyes more placid, the lips clamped firmly together. Below him, in separate images, the faces of Zelda and Scottie smile easily. But the photos were cross-hatched with an ink pen at some point, just a few years later, to indicate that mother and daughter now carried their own documents and were no longer compelled to travel in the company of Mr. Fitzgerald.

This was not exactly a liberation. In the summer of 1930, with her marriage and her mental health both reaching a point of crisis, Zelda traveled from France to Switzerland, where she entered the Prangins Clinic, near Geneva, for psychiatric treatments that would last more than a year. Unable to visit her for most of this period, Scott spent much of his time wandering through nearby towns and writing imploring, often manipulative, letters to his wife and her doctors. For her part, Zelda had left him a poignant memento, presumably derived from her new, personal travel document, which Scott described in a letter at the time:

> When I saw the sadness of your face in that passport picture I felt as you can imagine. But after going through what you can imagine I did then and looking at it and looking at it, I saw that it was the face I knew and loved and not the metallic superimposition of our last two years in France. . . . The photograph is all I have: it is with me from the morning when I wake up with a frantic half dream about you to the last moment when I think of you and of death at night.[16]

Here was an image of Zelda that he could not craft or recast in his fiction, as he would later attempt to do in *Tender Is the Night* (1932), but only seek to make sense of through his letters. The photograph was a reminder of their strained relationship, the pain it had caused both of them, and also of her newfound autonomy, however tenuous it may have been at the time. Grasping it, holding it close from dawn to dusk, Scott sought to embrace her in a way that he no longer could in their lives together.

Passport photos, then, could possess both a remarkable intimacy and an exaggerated personal importance, despite their bureaucratic function and increasingly standardized form. A fiercely private person, Willa Cather destroyed or had destroyed many of her personal papers and photographs, so that there is now only one known picture of the novelist together with her companion of almost forty years, Edith Lewis. Yet their passport documentation provides an affecting record of their long partnership. In the spring of 1920, as the positive reception of *My Ántonia* (1918) continued to expand her fame, Cather made plans for an extended trip to Europe with Lewis: the writer would visit the battle-fields of the Western Front (and the gravesite of her cousin, G. P. Cather, who had been killed there) as she completed her novel of the Great War, *One of Ours* (1922). Within a week of one another, Cather and Lewis applied for passports in New York City, where they had lived together since the fall of 1912; and each woman indicated the same destinations and the same purposes: "France (Name of country), Magazine work (Object of visit), Italy (Name of country), Magazine work (Object of visit)." Cather's application is accompanied by a sworn affidavit with Lewis's signature, attesting that she has "known Willa Sibert Cather for twenty years" and that the writer was "was born of American parents near Winchester, Virginia." During the review process, a clerk (the same clerk, judging by the handwriting) scrawled "single" across the top of each document to indicate that the female applicants were free to submit the paperwork on their own and need not be identified as "wife of . . ." on their travel documents.

More strikingly, at a time when the official criteria for passport photographs still allowed for considerable variation, the images of Cather and Lewis tacitly affirm their bond across separate files in the archive: each woman is lit from her left, so that dramatic shadows are cast across the right side of her face; each is framed with a vignette from just below her neckline, so that the edges of the photograph fade to white around an oval image. The two portraits, that is, are quite evidently the work of the same photographic studio, likely on the same day. The general effect of the photographs is almost classical, like a marble bust, their shared features drawing them together in an implicit, if detached, portrait of the couple. Perhaps this connection, along with the flattering effect of the lighting and framing, has something to do with the fact that, as demands for publicity grew, Cather had many copies of her passport photograph printed for distribution. The passport photographs of Stein, Hemingway, and Fitzgerald would not be widely circulated until after their deaths, when the images began to appear on book covers and, even later, on various websites, providing us with a glimpse of the modernist icons at the mercy of the bureaucratic gaze. With an odd twist, however, Cather was quite pleased with the portrait in her passport and even told her niece, Helen Louise Cather, that it was her favorite photograph of herself. Indeed, Cather liked the image so much that, regardless of official expectations, she used it again when she applied for her next passport in March 1923, this time to visit her friends Isabelle and Jan Hambourg just outside Paris.

. . .

If the passport evoked difficult questions regarding personal identity for those travelers and expatriates who left home relatively secure in their national belonging, the document's capacity to induce doubts about that communal affiliation was perhaps even stronger. It could also be suggested that, for those marginalized by their societies, the question of national identity is never more pressing than when they are on the move, far beyond the boundaries of their homelands. Langston Hughes acquired his first passport in July 1920, when he was just eighteen years old, in order to visit his father in Mexico, where the older Hughes had relocated in an effort to escape the pervasive racism he had experienced in the United States. Decades after Frederick Douglass had been denied a passport by George M. Dallas, it was still not easy for a Black man or woman in a segregationist America to attain such a document. Hughes's application required two affidavits, including one signed by his mother's hand swearing that her son was a "native citizen" of the United States by virtue of his birth in Joplin, Missouri. (As was often the case, the attending physician had failed to provide a birth certificate at the time and the city records did not contain documentation for the Black child.) The passport application also contains a striking photograph of the youthful Hughes in a confident head-on pose, dressed in a dark suit and tie, suggestive of his ambition to enroll at Columbia University upon his return to the US. Before that, however, Hughes would compose his first major poem, "The Negro Speaks of Rivers," inspired by the view from his train car on his trip south that summer.

The journey to Mexico only stoked his wanderlust, and after Hughes left university early to escape the racism of the faculty and his classmates, he searched for work as a crewman on a merchant ship. Eventually he

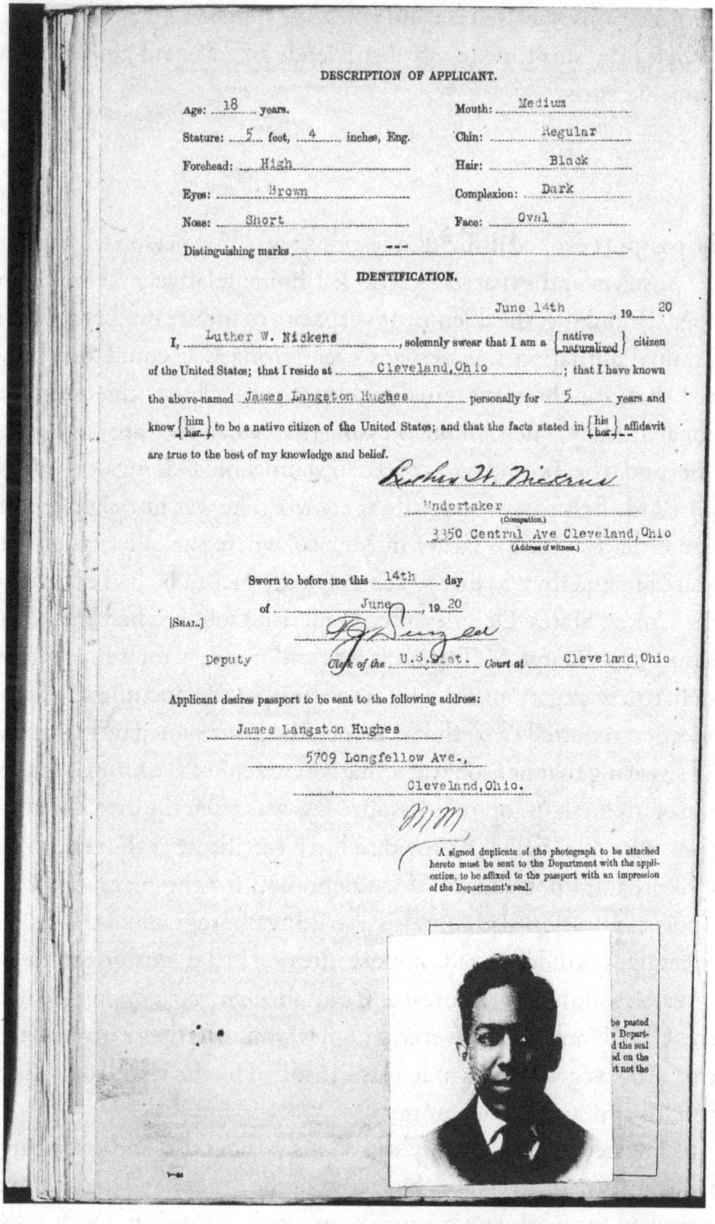

DESCRIPTION OF APPLICANT.

Age: 18 years.   Mouth: Medium

Stature: 5 foot, 4 inches, Eng.   Chin: Regular

Forehead: High   Hair: Black

Eyes: Brown   Complexion: Dark

Nose: Short   Face: Oval

Distinguishing marks ___

IDENTIFICATION.

June 14th, 19 20

I, Luther W. Nickens, solemnly swear that I am a {native / naturalized} citizen of the United States; that I reside at Cleveland, Ohio; that I have known the above-named James Langston Hughes personally for 5 years and know {him / her} to be a native citizen of the United States; and that the facts stated in {his / her} affidavit are true to the best of my knowledge and belief.

Luther H. Nickens

Undertaker
(Occupation.)

2350 Central Ave Cleveland, Ohio
(Address of witness.)

Sworn to before me this 14th day

of June, 19 20

[Seal.]

Deputy   Clerk of the U.S. Dist. Court at Cleveland, Ohio

Applicant desires passport to be sent to the following address:

James Langston Hughes

5709 Longfellow Ave.,

Cleveland, Ohio.

A signed duplicate of the photograph to be attached hereto must be sent to the Department with the application, to be affixed to the passport with an impression of the Department's seal.

be pasted
a Depart-
d the seal
ed on the
t not the

FIGURE 10. Langston Hughes's passport application, 1920. Image courtesy of the National Archives and Records Administration.

signed on with an old freighter called the S.S. *Malone* and, after unceremoniously ditching most of his books in waters off Sandy Hook, departed for a six-month voyage up and down the west coast of Africa. Then, in the spring of 1924, he endured a harrowing crossing from New York to Rotterdam, where he jumped ship and caught a train to Paris, realizing his long-time dream of visiting the city. Soon he found a job in a Montmartre night club and, despite the challenges of living abroad without much money or many contacts, began enjoying the charms of a culture still reemerging after the devastation of the war.

Many other promising young African American writers and artists, Claude McKay and Gwendolyn Bennett among them, began arriving in Paris during this period. Hughes would have an auspicious encounter in the city with Alain Locke, who was just then preparing to launch the Harlem Renaissance with the publication of his dazzling anthology of African American writing, *The New Negro: An Interpretation* (1925). That two of the movement's leading figures met for the first time in Paris, rather than in Harlem, suggests something of its cosmopolitan ambitions. Locke, the first African American to be awarded a Rhodes scholarship to study at Oxford University, had also studied in Berlin, and he was now in Europe, on leave from his position at Howard University, to conduct research, revive old contacts, and initiate new ones. His passport for the journey is emblematic of his cosmopolitan ethos, picturing the urbane scholar in a three-piece suit, with a bow tie and wingtip collar, as if poised to visit a symphony performance or gallery opening. After exchanging letters with Hughes for nearly a year, Locke had come to see the young poet in Paris so that they might discuss his anthology project—and perhaps strike up an intimate relationship. The well-connected professor invited the young poet to the Manon Opéra Comique, facilitated a meeting with the wealthy art collector Albert C. Barnes, and arranged a viewing of a collection of African sculptures owned by Paul Guillaume. Locke would later develop the metaphorical notion of a "passport of color," which connected people around the world through a shared experience of Black and Brown life. In the late summer of 1924 he rendezvoused with Hughes in northern

Italy, where they took in the sights of Verona and Venice like the Grand Tourists of previous generations, the older scholar sharing his vast knowledge of Renaissance art and architecture with his precocious companion.

Even within these transnational cultural contexts, the story of Hughes and his passport emphasizes the ever more prominent role that the documents came to play in affirming national affiliation, and sustaining national feeling, during the postwar years. If Joyce's passport had registered his cosmopolitan detachment from the perceived restrictions of Irish social and cultural life, as well as an almost tragic severance of communal ties on the eve of national independence, then Hughes's document could be said to generate an even more complex assemblage of emotions, an even more strained sense of ambivalence.

In his autobiography, *The Big Sea* (1940), Hughes recounts how, traveling by train back across northern Italy with Locke that September years before, he had pinned his valuables inside his coat pocket, as his grandmother had taught him to do when he was a child. But after the exhausted traveler fell asleep in his crowded third-class carriage, Hughes awoke to find that he had been robbed of both his money and his passport. Without the travel document, he could not reenter France, so he exited the train in Genoa and made a visit to the American consul, who told him kindly but too casually that there was nothing he could do for the young man. So Hughes found himself marooned in the birthplace of Christopher Columbus. Growing hungry and desperate, he determined that his only option was to make himself a presence in the busy port of Genoa until he could get hired on a ship heading back to the United States. But as the days dragged on, Hughes witnessed white sailors getting hired on with ease, while he was repeatedly turned away or overlooked.

It was in these circumstances—stranded far from home, deprived of his passport, denied a way back due to the color of his skin—that Hughes wrote one of his most enduring poems, "I, Too." The brief verse rails against his exclusion from the banquet of American plenty, from the trappings of the American dream, but ends with a powerful, tormented assertion of his American identity in the face of segregation and discrimination:

> Tomorrow,
> I'll be at the table
> When company comes.
> Nobody'll dare
> Say to me,
> "Eat in the kitchen,"
> Then.
> Besides,
> They'll see how beautiful I am
> And be ashamed—
> I, too, am America.

PART THREE

The Passport as We Know It

FIVE

Expelled and Stateless

THE TITLE OF MARC CHAGALL'S black-and-white etching *A Man without a Passport before the Captain of the Rural Police* (*L'homme sans passeport devant le Capitaine-Ispravnik*, 1923) describes its subject matter clearly enough: In the foreground, the police captain stands with his back to us, his hands clasped waist-level behind his military-style coat (a sign of his authority over the other man), his head oriented so that we can only see the back of his cap. Before him stands the passport-less man, his shoulders slumped in his ill-fitting tunic (tied awkwardly at the waist with an old piece of string), his face downcast, though we can just discern his blank stare and the dark smudge of his mouth, slightly agape as if muttering something to the captain. All this is illustrated in Chagall's signature mode of expressive awkwardness, entirely apposite to the coarse subject matter. The scene in fact derives from Nikolai Gogol's picaresque satire of Russian provincial life, *Dead Souls* (1842), though it is not part of the story's action; rather, it comes from a hypothetical scenario described in comically convoluted fashion by the book's protagonist, Pavel Ivanovich Chichikov, as he attempts to put fear into a group of escaped serfs. The guiding conceit of Gogol's narrative is that, due to a quirk of Russian tax law, serfs (or "souls") could be just as valuable dead as alive to the likes of the scheming Chichikov: their mistreatment at his hands becomes emblematic of the failings of Russian society before the Emancipation Edict of 1861.

The internal passport system played a significant role in this state of affairs. Like American slaves, Russian serfs were effectively the private

FIGURE 11. *A Man without a Passport before the Captain of the Rural Police* (*L'homme sans passeport devant le Capitaine-Ispravnik*), by Marc Chagall, 1923. Image courtesy of Wikiart .org.

property of the landowners whose fields they worked; and like their American counterparts they could be bought, sold, or mortgaged like chattel, excluded from political participation even as they were exploited for their productive and reproductive capacities. Similar to the slave passes and free papers employed in the United States during the same period, the internal passports used in Russia testified to the personal identity and proper location of the holder: without an official document listing their name, ethnic group, marital status, address, and criminal record, Russian laborers had no legal status. Runaway serfs, then, were akin to escaped slaves or illegal migrants, in constant peril of arrest and abuse. As Chichikov cruelly reminds his audience of fugitives, whenever they stray beyond the domain of their landlords, serfs are required to present their documents to police officials on demand. Indeed, even after emancipation, tsarist Russia continued to impose an internal passport system on its peasants in order to regulate their movement and restrict seasonal migration. Anyone caught without the necessary papers was regarded as a fugitive or vagrant and subjected to harsh punishments, including forced resettlement to Siberia or the painful branding of their right forearm with the letter B—the initial for both "fugitive" (бродяга, or *brodyaga*) and "vagrant" (беглец, or *beglets*) in Russian—their status thereby rendered indelible on the surface of their bodies.

In 1923, as he worked on his illustrated edition of *Dead Souls,* Chagall himself was in danger (once again) of becoming a man without a passport. Born Moishe Shagal to a Belarussian Jewish family of tradespeople in 1887, he had escaped his provincial upbringing to study art in Vitebsk and, later, St. Petersburg. Because Jews were not allowed in the Russian capital unless they possessed an internal passport—"that famous permit," as Chagall called it in his memoir, *My Life* (1923)—he only succeeded in attending the prestigious Imperial Society for the Protection of Fine Arts by borrowing a passport from a friend in Vitebsk.[1] In 1910, to pursue his artistic career in freer surroundings, he relocated to Paris, where he rubbed shoulders with Fauvists and Cubists even as he continued to explore Eastern European Jewish motifs in his painting. It was in the French capital that Chagall took the name he is known by, and it was there that he developed his signature style: the blue cattle, the red horses, the airborne figures, the green fiddlers on the roof, all rendered in a manner reminiscent of the folkloric traditions he had grown up with. After several years of mounting success, Chagall returned to Vitebsk in 1914 to marry his sweetheart, Bella Rosenfeld, but the couple was then trapped in Russia by the outbreak of the First World War and the closing of the frontier. When officials rejected Marc's appeal for a passport to return to Paris with his new bride, the Chagalls were compelled to wait out the

European war, as well as the Russian Revolution and Civil War that followed, in St. Petersburg and later Moscow. Eventually, the painter fell into a series of aesthetic and ideological disputes with the Soviet artistic committees, which did not appreciate the unique admixture of Jewish folk culture and modernist innovation in his art. The couple suffered more and more from personal financial difficulties, as well as the general food shortages in Russia, so that by the early twenties the painter and his wife were living in near destitution.

Chagall desperately desired to return to Paris, where he might again pursue his art in less distressing circumstances. But he had to wait until 1922 to acquire a passport, and then only with the help of a high-ranking ally—the People's Commissar for Enlightenment, Anatoly Lunacharsky—as the Soviet regime began to strictly limit emigration. Subsequently, traveling back to Paris through Berlin in 1923, Chagall discovered that he required a French visa, which the French consulate in the city initially refused to grant. It was only after the painter produced a certificate from the Paris Police Prefecture dating back to his time in the French capital before the war that he was acknowledged as a legal resident and his passport was stamped. This would be the last trip the migrant artist ever took as a Russian citizen: by returning to France, Marc, Bella, and their young daughter, Ida, effectively passed into statelessness.

In this regard, the painter and his family joined more than one and a half million other Russians who fled the country during the era of civil war and famine and who scattered across Europe and around the globe in the years that followed. As Agamben points out, the period saw the "first appearance of refugees as a mass phenomenon" in world history.[2] During the postwar years, following the breakup of the Russian, Austro-Hungarian, and Ottoman empires, hundreds of thousands of White Russians, Armenians, Bulgarians, Greeks, Germans, Hungarians, and Romanians were also displaced from their home countries, many of them without valid passports. At the same time, the demand for state sovereignty resulted in new measures to denaturalize and denationalize those who had left, effectively severing the tie between nativity and nationality that had been taken for granted for so long. In the newly founded Russian Soviet Republic, even as the Bolshevik government was restricting emigration, the All-Russian Central Executive Committee issued a decree in December 1921 depriving the right of citizenship to exiles and émigrés, except in certain special cases. As the international system of passport controls solidified in the aftermath of the war, it also confirmed the status of stateless peoples, whose legal ties with their country of origin were often severed when their travel documents were denied or nullified.

Looking back on these events after her own prolonged experience of statelessness, German Jewish philosopher Hannah Arendt would argue (in a manner that has deeply influenced Agamben and other contemporary political thinkers) that the breaking of the birth-nation link represented a profound crisis for the rights of man, because the stateless suddenly found themselves without recognized legal or political status. No longer could the convenient fiction that all men belonged to the "family of nations" maintain a tacit balance between the universal rights of the individual and the sovereign claims of the state: "The Rights of Man, after all, had been defined as 'inalienable,'" Arendt later wrote, "because they were supposed to be independent of all governments; but it turned out that the moment human beings lacked their own government and had to fall back upon their minimum rights, no authority was left to protect them and no institution was willing to guarantee them."[3] The fate of millions of stateless people in the twentieth century would hinge not on their status as sovereign individuals, but on their belonging to some kind of political community capable of restoring their legal status. It was never more important to possess official papers and certificates, to keep them close and secure, in order to make a claim to one's basic rights.

An early effort to address these concerns in the international community came in the form of the so-called Nansen passport, which was actually a whole series of identification and travel documents issued to stateless persons during the interwar period. During these years, nearly half a million of the passports were issued by the fifty-three governments that had ratified the effort, each of which had its own version of the document, related to others only by the "Nansen stamp" that made them all official. The passports were named for Fridtjof Nansen, the Norwegian zoologist, oceanographer, explorer, historian, and university professor turned humanitarian and statesmen, who proposed the idea of a supranational passport shortly after he assumed his position of High Commissioner for Refugees at the League of Nations in 1921. The adventurous Nansen had conducted a series of harrowing Artic expeditions in the 1890s, and later participated in several oceanographic voyages in the northern Atlantic, exploring possible trade routes that brought him into close contact with the Russian people of the Siberian interior. For his efforts on behalf of stateless Russians and other refugees across Europe he would receive the Nobel Peace Prize in 1922. The travel documents named for him offered a lifeline to those who had been cut loose by the new nation-states emerging after the war; the form of intergovernmental cooperation embodied in the passports initiated what many scholars and journalists have identified as the emergence of international refugee law.

Thanks to the Nansen program, many expatriate Russian artists, composers, and writers were allowed to continue their careers between the wars, despite the persistent trials of statelessness. Like Chagall, Igor Stravinsky had made a name for himself in the artistic circles of Paris before the war, especially with the premiere of his radically avant-garde ballet *The Rite of Spring* in 1913. But unlike the painter, the composer came from a well-connected artistic family, which had enjoyed a prominent place in the cultural life of St. Petersburg; also unlike the painter, he had waited out the war abroad, spending much of the period near Lake Geneva in Switzerland, where he continued to develop his intricate style of dissonance and rhythm. Stravinsky, again in contrast to Chagall, could be classed as an estranged tsarist sympathizer, so that the outbreak of the Russian Revolution in 1917 meant that he was both unable and unwilling to return to his homeland. With the triumph of the Bolsheviks, the loss of the homeland he loved was all but complete. In 1922, the same year that he received a Nansen passport, Stravinsky became convinced that he should also abandon his identity as a Russian composer, to "scuttle the limited tradition of my birthright," and instead pursue the composition of "pure music," detached from any national affiliation.[4] Living once again in France, his new passport was crucial to this phase of his career as he embarked on his first concert tours, conducting and playing piano in Belgium, Denmark, Germany, Italy, Poland, the United States, and elsewhere. Opportunely for the dallying composer, life on tour with his Nansen passport also allowed him to carry on a long-term affair with his mistress, Vera de Bosset, while his wife remained at home with their family in Biarritz.

Not all Nansen passport holders found the documents quite so advantageous. In the fall of 1917, long before he gained international celebrity with the publication of *Lolita* (1955), a young Vladimir Nabokov and his family (of an old aristocratic lineage) fled St. Petersburg for the estate of friends in Crimea as revolutionary rioting encroached on their lives in the city. In the spring of 1919, taking flight again ahead of the advancing Red Army, the Nabokovs resettled in England, where Vladimir and his brother, Sergei, enrolled at Cambridge University. The following year, the rest of the family relocated once more, this time to Berlin, where they became part of a large community of Russian émigrés. It was during this period that the Soviet government set into motion the denaturalization process for large portions of the expatriate population, including the Nabokovs. Vladimir visited his family in Germany during school holidays and eventually relocated there after completing his degree in 1922. Among his fellow expatriates, in what he later called an environment of "material indigence and intellectual luxury," the youthful writer began to publish his first poems and stories, under the pen name V. Sirin to avoid being confused with his influential father.[5] Yet the situation of the family became even more tenuous when the older Nabokov was killed by right-wing assassins as he attempted to protect the exiled leader of the Constitutional Democratic Party, Pavel Milyukov.

The combined losses of his motherland and father were devastating for Vladimir. As he moved about with his family after the revolution, his "utter physical dependence on this or that nation, which had coldly granted us political refuge, became painfully evident when some trashy

'visa,' some diabolical 'identity card' had to be obtained or prolonged."
In 1925, the writer married Vera Yevseyevna Slonim, a Russian émigré of
Jewish descent, and the stateless couple commenced their life together
by applying for Nansen passports, which they hoped, despite warranted
fears to the contrary, might make possible a finer future for them. In his
first novel, *Mary* (1926), Nabokov includes a scene that conveys traces
of these emotions: having decided to leave Berlin for what he believes to
be a better life in Paris, an elderly Russian poet struggles through the
bureaucratic ritual of queues, crowds, and foul smells to attain the requisite passport, only to lose the document before the day is over.

For the young Russian novelist, the possession of a Nansen passport—
which he referred to as "a very inferior document of a sickly green hue" in
his autobiography, *Speak, Memory* (1951)—was hardly a boon. "Its holder,"
Nabokov reflected, "was little better than a criminal on parole and had to
go through most hideous ordeals every time he wished to travel from one
country to another, and the smaller the countries the worse the fuss they
made." For the passport was a constant reminder, to the novelist and anyone who inspected it, that he was stateless: reliant on the conditional
hospitality of reluctant host nations and subject to an "avid bureaucratic
hell" that would close in around him whenever he was required to present
the document.[6] No doubt there was good reason for this angst regarding
the passport. Even as the League of Nations and the international community that it represented sought protections for the stateless, they also
asserted a global monopoly on the legitimate definition of statelessness
and citizenship, on the determination of exclusion and inclusion, and
on the management of those deemed to exist outside the system of
nation-states.

Yet despite these troublesome restrictions, things would get much
worse for the Nabokovs after Adolf Hitler became German chancellor
in January 1933. As the couple fashioned a life together in Berlin, Véra
had become a muse, trusty amanuensis, and personal literary critic for
Vladimir, not to mention his primary source of financial support for
many years. But with the rise of the Nazi regime, her livelihood as a
stenographer and translator was in ever-increasing jeopardy.

The new government quickly introduced a series of anti-Semitic measures, including the establishment of the first concentration camp in March, the organization of a boycott of Jewish businesses in April, and the administration of a special census to identify German Jews and monitor their movement in June. Sophisticated administrative techniques of intimidation and control rapidly extended to other segments of the German population considered threats to the German Reich: gypsies, Blacks, homosexuals, and the disabled, as well as many artists, writers, and intellectuals whose work was deemed to be dissenting or, worse, "degenerate" (*entartet*). Soon, with anti-Semitism becoming official state policy, the books of Stefan Zweig were burned, the paintings of Marc Chagall were banned, and prospects of an academic career for the young Hannah Arendt were extinguished, while thousands queued up outside foreign consulates in the hope of attaining visas and immigration documents.

It was against this backdrop that the Nazi Party undertook additional measures to marginalize Jews living in Germany. Crucially, these included the "Law on the Retraction of Naturalizations and the Derecognition of German Citizenship," which enabled the government to strip German citizenship from anyone who had acquired it since the end of the First World War. By September 1935, the party would issue two more infamous decrees on the matter, known together as the Nuremberg Race Laws, which excluded German-born Jews from citizenship in the name of protecting "German Blood and German Honor." The totalitarian regime, as Arendt would later emphasize, had so corrupted the principle of sovereignty that it could assert the "right" to ban those who were deemed "other" to the "pure" race or nation. In depriving these groups of citizenship, the laws put in place by the Nazi government effectively severed the bond between man and citizen, nativity and nationality, and opened the way to sending former citizens to concentration camps, where they were consigned to the realm of "bare life," bereft of all the legal protections provided by the "normal" juridical order. A state of exception became the rule.

In 1936, the increasingly hostile environment in Berlin resulted in the revocation of Véra's work permit on ethnic grounds and ultimately led the Nabokovs, now including their young son Dimitri, to relocate to France with their Nansen passports the following year. After living an itinerate existence in Cannes, Menton, Moulinet, and Cap d'Antibes, the family finally settled into the Russian émigré community of Paris, where they found some modicum of financial security and physical safety, at least for a time. Indeed, the period saw yet another wave of artists and intellectuals flood into the French capital, as they sought refuge from the malignant policies of the Nazi regime.

Everything began to change, however, when France declared war on Germany in September 1939. After eight months of the so-called Phony War, the German invasion and the installation of the Vichy government in the summer of 1940 would abruptly transform the status of Russian émigrés into that of *prestataires,* that is, people in service of and owing a debt to the state. In *VN: The Life and Art of Vladimir Nabokov,* Andrew Field explains the new situation this way:

> No one could understand the decree, though its potential dangers were clear to all. The Nansen passport had been exceedingly annoying (one had to lodge application to travel abroad at least three weeks prior to travel, and the passport did not automatically include permission to work), but the Nansen was not subject to cancellation, nor were its holders deported in ordinary circumstances. Now denunciations were being made and people were being arrested. Russians were called before committees of émigré Fascists and reactionaries for questioning about possible Jewish blood.[7]

Anticipating what such developments would mean for his wife and son, Nabokov frantically made arrangements to escape France ahead of the advancing German army, though the family had little money for travel and only their troublesome Nansen passports to secure exits and entries. Fortunately, an offer to teach Russian literature at Stanford University allowed the writer to secure US entry visas for the family, and a Jewish rescue organization run by a friend of Nabokov's late father stepped in to offer them trans-Atlantic passage—though they still had to negotiate the intransigent French bureaucracy to procure *visas de sortie* (exit visas). No form of documentation was more crucial at the time. It took months of entreaties at one government office after another before a well-placed bribe to "the last rat in the last rathole" finally had the desired effect.[8] In early May 1940, just days before Hitler took Paris, Nabokov, his wife, and their young son sailed for New York. His brother, Sergei, chose to stay in Europe with his partner, Hermann Thieme, despite the dangers faced by homosexuals under the Nazi regime; Sergei was later arrested and transported to Neuengamme, a concentration camp in northern Germany, where Nazi scientists carried out horrific medical experiments on the inmates. He died there in January 1945.

. . .

The experience of being stateless and on the run, bereft of rights, dependent on the hospitality, not to say the whims, of foreign governments was a pervasive feature of the 1930s and '40s for many. Perhaps no writer articulated this set of circumstances more poignantly than Stefan Zweig, who would also end up in New York by 1940. Like Nabokov, he was one of the most extraordinary writers of the twentieth century; also like Nabokov, he lived a life that was in some sense entirely typical of the era, at least with regard to its many upheavals. In his own words, as "an Austrian, a Jew, an author, a humanist, and a pacifist," Zweig "always stood at the exact point where these earthquakes were the most violent."[9] In 1934, after his books were burned in Berlin—"reduced to ashes in huge bonfires to the accompaniment of patriotic sentiments"—and the Austrian Republic was transformed into the Austrofascist Ständestaat (precipitating the forcible search of his home), Zweig left Salzburg for an extended stay in London.[10] For a time, he could inhabit the city quite contentedly as a place where politics felt "far away."[11] But with the annexation of Austria by Nazi Germany and the expiration of his passport imminent in 1938, Zweig was compelled to apply to the British authorities for an emergency "white paper," another "passport for the stateless."

Initially, Zweig saw this new necessity as a mere formality, even something to be celebrated, for in his "cosmopolitan reveries" he had often "imagined how beautiful it would be, how truly in accord with my inmost thoughts, to be stateless, obligated to no one country and for that reason undifferentiatedly attached to all."[12] And yet as he waited on the petitioner's bench in some bureaucratic anteroom to exchange his passport for an alien's certificate, he began to feel otherwise:

> An Austrian passport was a symbol of my rights. Every Austrian consul or officer or police officer was duty bound to issue one to me on demand as a citizen in good standing. But I had to solicit the English certificate. It was a favour that I had to ask for, and what is more, a favour that could be withdrawn at any moment. Overnight I found myself one rung lower. Only yesterday, still a visitor from abroad and, so to speak, a gentleman who was spending his international income and paying his taxes, now I had become an immigrant, a "refugee."

Zweig had entered into the plight of the stateless, becoming one of those Arendt describes so affectingly as nonpersons, possessing no inalienable legal rights or political status. Henceforth, he would have to resort to special pleading for each foreign visa on his new travel document; as "one of the outlaws, of the men without a country," he encountered suspicion and intolerance at every turn—for if he overstayed his welcome, there was nowhere to deport him to, no homeland obligated to receive him. In these circumstances, Zweig continually recalled what a Russian exile (like Chagall, Stravinsky, or Nabokov) had told him years earlier: "Formerly man had only a body and a soul. Now he needs a passport as well for without it he will not be treated like a human being."[13] As he relinquished his citizenship and became entirely dependent on the hospitality of host nation-states, Zweig also became keenly aware of how "human beings were made to feel that they were objects and not subjects, that nothing was their right but everything merely a favour by official grace."[14]

Something of this pathos is captured in Wes Anderson's 2014 film *The Grand Budapest Hotel,* which was "inspired by the writings of Stefan Zweig," as the closing credits tell us. Tempering Anderson's usual whimsy with moments of heartbreaking desperation and shocking violence, the film is set in a fictional central European country, the Republic of Zubrowka, on the eve of war in the 1930s. Artfully designed Zubrowkan currency, police forms, postage stamps, and travel documents all contribute to the cinematic illusion. Meanwhile, the architecture of the eponymous inn, drawn from midcentury Hollywood films and Photochrom prints of alpine resorts, offers a cosmopolitan fantasy of an urbane and inviting world that never quite existed. Beyond the *Jugendstil* lobby of the Grand Budapest Hotel, however, looms the menace of a rising fascist regime and an impending global conflict.

These threats become evident about fifteen minutes into the film: the dapper concierge of the hotel, Monsieur Gustav (Ralph Fiennes), and his "Lobby Boy," Zero Moustafa (Tony Revolori), hurriedly leave their familiar confines to board a train, where they are accosted by a company of gray-uniformed soldiers from the police militia. An intertitle has just indicated, rather enigmatically, "19th October / The Closing of the Frontier," but now the situation comes into focus as one of the soldiers, Franz, demands to see the documents of the two travelers. A bit of jovial banter sees M. Gustave through the passport ritual quickly, but the soldier lingers much longer over the tattered document produced by Zero. Sensing the delicacy, even danger, of the circumstances, M. Gustave intervenes nonchalantly: "That's a Migratory Visa with Stage Three Worker Status, Franz darling. He's with me." Nevertheless, the confrontation soon escalates and the soldiers roughly apprehend the travelers, evoking a fierce exclamation from the previously unflappable Mr. Gustave: "You filthy, goddamn, pock-marked, fascist assholes! Take your hands off my Lobby Boy!" The situation is only saved when the commanding officer, Henckels (Edward Norton), arrives on the scene and recognizes M. Gustave, who "was very kind to [him]" years before when the officer was "a lonely little boy" staying at the Grand Budapest Hotel. After shooing away his soldiers, Henckels writes out a ticket granting Zero temporary freedom of movement and then informs M. Gustave: "Your colleague is stateless. He'll need to apply for a revised Special Transit Permit, which, honestly, at this point may be very difficult to acquire." To the genteel concierge, the intervention suggests that "there are still faint glimmers of civilization left in this barbaric slaughterhouse that was once known as humanity," although his hasty and uncharacteristically vulgar conclusion—"Oh, fuck it."—lets us know he cannot quite bring himself to believe what he has just said.

With the coming of war (the "Start of the Lutz Blitz," as the intertitle tells us) later in the film, this tenuous illusion can no longer be sustained. Now, invading forces take the alpine town and penetrate the inner sanctum of the hotel, turning the lobby into a crowded meeting place for the enemy high command and festooning its walls with SS-style banners. As the narrative moves toward its finale "on the 21st day of the occupation, the morning that the Independent State of Zubrowka officially ceased to exist," M. Gustave and Zero (along with his new bride, Agatha) again board a train and again are accosted by menacing soldiers, now dressed in even more menacing SS-style uniforms. As before, M. Gustav attempts to defuse the tense circumstances with some lighthearted, if darkly comic, remarks: "You're the first of the official death squads to whom we've been formally introduced. How do you do? . . . *Plus ça change,* am I right?" But on this occasion, when the Lobby Boy's papers raise suspicion and tensions escalate, no "civilized" police inspector arrives to set things right. Instead, we witness a soldier bash Zero's head with his rifle as M. Gustave struggles with the other uniformed men. Voiceover narration delivered by a much older Zero (F. Murray Abraham)—now the owner of the Grand Budapest Hotel, looking back on these unfortunate events many years hence—tells us wistfully, "There are still faint glimmers of civilization left in this barbaric slaughterhouse that was once known as humanity . . . he was one of them." But we also learn from Zero that M. Gustave was later shot by the occupying forces, snuffing out that glimmer entirely.[15]

The plight that Anderson depicts in his make-believe version of European history became all too real for those, like Nabokov and Zweig, who were in a panic to get their papers in order during the early days of World War Two. James Joyce had lamented, only half-jokingly, that the German invasion of Czechoslovakia in March 1939 threatened to distract the attention of the world from the imminent publication of his *Finnegans Wake* (1939), a novel more than seventeen years (that is, nearly the entire interwar period) in the making. The writer, however, would soon have more to worry about than his new book as the brutal realities of war steadily encroached on his life. With the German invasion of France in May 1940, Joyce suddenly became an "enemy alien" thanks to the British passport he still held; meanwhile, his son, Giorgio, was at risk of either internment by the Germans or conscription by the French, because he had lately reached military age.

The family had already left Paris for the small village of Saint-Gérand-le-Puy the previous year, as fears of war mounted and their friends began abandoning the city one by one. Now, with Nazi soldiers patrolling the streets of the 7th arrondissement where the Irish novelist had once strolled, Joyce began a series of urgent efforts to return the family to Zurich in neutral Switzerland, where they could wait out the present conflict as they had the First World War. But crossing the border into the Alpine country was not as easy as it had been a quarter century earlier; and this time Joyce also had his daughter, Lucia, understood to be suffering from schizophrenia, to worry about. He applied to the Swiss consulate in Lyon for visas but was rejected because, as he learned through a friend, he was identified as a Jew—apparently, such was his literary reputation that Joyce had been confused, by some consular official or other, with the protagonist of his *Ulysses,* Leopold Bloom. A second application was accepted, but only after the novelist rallied an assortment of Swiss dignitaries to vouch for him, offered a substantial financial guarantee (to be paid by a friend in Zurich), and penned a persuasive, if rather dubious, declaration of his additional assets.

Meanwhile, Joyce also solicited the assistance of influential friends in France—including novelist Jean Giraudoux, art historian Louis Gillet, and Armand Petitjean, the founder of Lancôme Cosmetics, who was now an official in the Vichy government—to secure his family's visa de sortie. After considerable effort, he did obtain permission to depart for himself, Nora, and Lucia, though authorization was still lacking for the military-aged Giorgio. With time running out on the exit visa, the young man managed to have his passport stamped by an understanding official in the nearby township of Lapalisse, where he cycled frantically one day in December 1940, despite being subject to arrest should he be caught outside of Saint-Gérand-le-Puy. All this was necessitated by the fact that his father had summarily refused an offer of Irish passports—the passports of a neutral country—which would have allowed the family to depart France without difficulty. The novelist's reasoning amounted to a principled, though nearly perverse, assertion of his personal sovereignty and artistic autonomy: "he should not accept in wartime something he did not desire in peacetime."[16]

. . .

While the Joyces were holding their ground, others were seeking any means available to leave France behind. As the stories that follow demonstrate time and again, everything depended on having the right travel documents, which provided the only means to run the gauntlet of wartime Europe and find safety across the Atlantic—the only means, moreover, to surmount the many perils of statelessness and gain access to the rough hospitality of the nation-state. In September 1939, shortly after France had declared war on Germany, Max Ernst was apprehended by French authorities in Paris as a "citizen of the German Reich" (and holder of Deutsches Reich Reisepass no. 003185, issued in Paris on October 17, 1936). In the state of emergency brought on by the conflict, the French government had set up internment camps where the rule of law was effectively suspended on the pretext of defending "national security." The hospitality of the nation-state was no longer extended to its guest after the appearance of this threat: freedom of movement within the host country was immediately revoked. Ernst was quickly sent off to Aix-en-Provence and interned at the notorious Camp des Milles, a former tile factory where he occupied a cramped cell alongside hundreds of other German artists and intellectuals.

Again, as he had done some twenty years earlier, Paul Éluard came to the aid of Ernst, this time writing a beautifully worded letter to French president Albert-Pierre Sarraut on behalf of the artist. But before release papers could be secured, Ernst escaped from confinement and was rearrested—only to escape again. While on the run, he somehow managed to begin work on his masterpiece *Europe after the Rain* (1942), a Surrealist landscape that provides a glimpse of an apocalyptic world to come. After the German invasion of France, with the rule of law now effectively suspended across the entire country, the painter found himself in even greater danger, hunted by the Gestapo as a degenerate artist and traitor to the Reich.

Ernst would thus have to rely on the remarkable exploits of another ally. Sometimes referred to as the "American Schindler," Varian Fry was an unlikely hero: he had studied classics at Harvard, where he also founded a literary periodical, *Hound and Horn*, before going on to serve as a foreign correspondent for a popular magazine, *The Living Age*. On assignment for the publication in the summer of 1935, he witnessed firsthand an anti-Jewish riot in Berlin, which led him to pursue fundraising efforts for anti-Nazi organizations. Following the German offensive on France, he resolved to take more direct action. By late June 1940, Fry and a group of more than two hundred prominent cultural figures in New York had established the Emergency Rescue Committee, which soon acquired a number of emergency US entry visas with help from First Lady Eleanor Roosevelt. By early August, he had embarked on his covert rescue mission, arriving in Marseille with $3,000 in cash (strapped to his leg for safekeeping) and a list of notable refugees, mostly artists and intellectuals of Jewish origin, who were then in immediate danger of capture by the Gestapo.

Once on the ground in France, Fry quickly realized the need to assemble a team and set up a cover organization: the American Relief Center or ARC (in French: Centre américain de secours), ostensibly dispensing humanitarian "relief" (*secours*) in order to protect its actual mission of offering "rescue" (also *secours*) to those in jeopardy by helping them to escape the Nazi threat in Europe. In addition to coordinating with a not-always-cooperative US State Department to acquire visas, Fry undertook a range of clandestine activities to help his refugee clientele. With the aid of a German expatriate (and noted economist), Albert Otto Hirschman, he bought forged passports and other papers, including overseas visas acquired from foreign consulates (Chile, Cuba, China, Panama, and others), which would in turn allow refugees to obtain crucial Spanish and Portuguese transit visas. Ultimately, he hired his own forger, a young Jewish political cartoonist named Wilhelm Spira, who had fled his native Austria and now went by the name of Bill Freier. In order to safeguard his clientele, Fry also rented the Villa Air-Bel, a rather neglected château just outside of Marseille, where he could provide temporary residence for those on the run. Word quickly spread about the American who was working to get people out of France, and as the situation in Europe continued to worsen, hundreds of writers, artists, musicians, deposed government officials, and others desperate to reach safety began to pour into his office or send letters pleading for his assistance.

One of them was Ernst, who headed to the Villa Air-Bel shortly after his second escape from French custody—bringing many of his paintings with him. While staying at the château, Ernst initiated a romance with the American heiress and art patroness Peggy Guggenheim, who had come to Marseille to speak with Fry about the activities of the ARC. Meanwhile, Fry helped the painter to obtain a US Emergency Visitor's Visa. The process was facilitated by Ernst's connections in the United States, including his son, Jimmy (formerly Ulrich), who worked at the Museum of Modern Art in New York and appealed to his boss for assistance. But Fry was unable to attain the elusive visa de sortie for his charge. Fearing that the document would never arrive, he urged Ernst to take the considerable risk of traveling without it to Lisbon, where he would rendezvous with Guggenheim and board a clipper for New York. Alarmingly, when the painter attempted to exit France across the Spanish frontier, a place of heightened surveillance and extreme danger, he was waylaid by an inspector because his papers were not in order. But after Ernst allowed the inspector to view a few of the paintings he was carrying, the official had a change of heart: while telling Ernst he must return to France, the inspector simultaneously pointed toward the train to Madrid, intimating that the painter should get on board. Several weeks later, Ernst was safe in New York with Guggenheim.

The stakes for possessing the right documents could not have been higher, though that was not evident to some on Fry's list until it was almost too late. After many years of residence in France, Marc Chagall and his family had finally become naturalized French citizens in 1937. The artist, however, continued to have difficulties with his passport, since the French officials, who for years had issued his identification documents under the name of "Marc (called Moïse) Chagall," had, as he noted in a letter, recently "omitted 'Marc'" for some mysterious reason. This meant that the famous painter, known to the world as Marc Chagall, could no longer travel under that name and risked losing the legal protections associated with that identity. Of course, in the context of the Nazi menace and widespread anti-Semitism, it also meant that his documents now worryingly emphasized his Jewish heritage. He appealed to the French friends who had recently helped him obtain citizenship for more assistance: "I will be especially grateful to you if you could intervene with the authorities to settle this little matter which has grown into a detective novel."[17]

Yet even after the German occupation began in the late spring of 1940, Chagall and his family stayed on in Vichy France, heedless of the fact that anti-Semitic laws were being instituted and French Jews were being rounded up by Gestapo agents. At this very time, his works were being torn from the walls of German museums and burned in public ceremonies. Well aware of the dangers facing Chagall, Fry's organization made a series of entreaties to the painter, who was on the American's original roll of imperiled artists and intellectuals. In the fall of 1940, Fry even arranged an invitation (and the requisite US entry visa) for Chagall to visit an exhibition at the Museum of Modern Art, but the painter hesitated to accept the offer, apparently because he feared forfeiting his newly acquired French citizenship.

In any case, Chagall was soon to be deprived of his citizenship under the new anti-Semitic laws in Vichy France. In March 1941, Fry and Harry Bingham, the American consul general in Marseille, spent a weekend with Chagall at his studio in Gordes and managed to convince the painter to leave France for America. In anticipation of their departure,

Chagall and his wife took a hotel room in Marseille, only for the painter to be arrested and taken into custody during a police raid of the premises. Fearing the worst, Bella wisely requested assistance from Fry, who immediately phoned the prefecture and threatened to embarrass the police force and the entire Vichy government by reporting the detention of the renowned artist to the *New York Times*. The ploy worked and Chagall was released, but now the severity of the situation was undeniable. In early April, the Vichy government instituted further legislation to remove French Jews from public and academic posts and then began to divest them of citizenship status and property rights as well. Even as they sought a way out of the country, Chagall and his wife lost their French citizenship and were rendered stateless for the second time in their lives— though now they were also in imminent danger of being sent to the camps. In these increasingly dire circumstances, Fry was unable to secure exit visas for the couple, but he did arrange for their clandestine transport across the Spanish border and passage across the Atlantic from Portugal. The Chagalls arrived in Lisbon in May 1941 and, a little more than a month later, disembarked in New York, safe from the war at last.

. . .

All told, Fry and the ARC helped to rescue as many as four thousand people from the Nazi regime; but in the face of global war, abrupt revocations of citizenship, and the many perils of statelessness, the organization could only do so much. The pervasive sense of vulnerability, which could be temporality overcome or permanently exacerbated by a little book, meant the emergence of a radically different kind of politics (beyond the collapsing notions of "man" and "citizen"), which Hannah Arendt was among the first to articulate. After the burning of the Reichstag in February 1933, she felt compelled to abandon Germany due to her outspoken criticism of the Nazi Party and her clandestine work with a Zionist group. Arendt fled the country without the benefit of a passport or other travel documents; she would spend the rest of the decade and more as a stateless person, first in Prague and Geneva and then

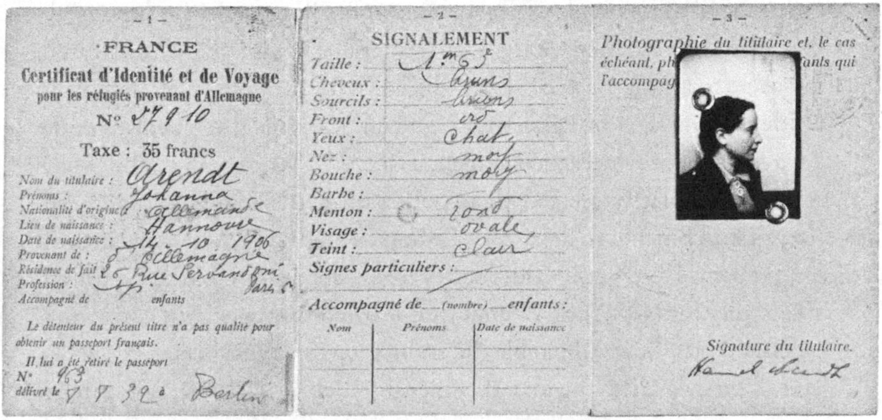
– 1 –

FRANCE

Certificat d'Identité et de Voyage
pour les réfugiés provenant d'Allemagne

Nº 27910

Taxe : 35 francs

Nom du titulaire : Arendt
Prénoms : Johanna
Nationalité d'origine : allemande
Lieu de naissance : Hannover
Date de naissance : 14 10 1906
Provenant de : Allemagne
Résidence de fait
Profession :
Accompagné de enfants

Le détenteur du présent titre n'a pas qualité pour obtenir un passeport français.

Il lui a été retiré le passeport
Nº 963
délivré le à Berlin

– 2 –

SIGNALEMENT

Taille :
Cheveux :
Sourcils :
Front :
Yeux :
Nez :
Bouche :
Barbe :
Menton :
Visage : ovale
Teint : clair
Signes particuliers :

Accompagné de (nombre) enfants :

Nom	Prénoms	Date de naissance

– 3 –

Photographie du titulaire et, le cas échéant, ph[...] [...]fants qui l'accompag[...]

Signature du titulaire.

FIGURE 12. Identity and Travel Certificate for Refugees from Germany (*Certificat d'identité et de voyage pour les réfugiés provenant d'Allemagne*), issued to Hannah Arendt, 1938. Image courtesy of the Library of Congress.

in Paris, where she worked for several Jewish refugee organizations. After the outbreak of the war, she was interned as an "enemy alien" at the Gurs camp in southern France, though in the confusion of the French defeat she managed to escape into the Vichy region. Many of those who did not flee were later moved to extermination centers in Germany. During this tumultuous period, Arendt began to compose bits and pieces of what would eventually become her first major treatise, *The Origins of Totalitarianism,* even while she reflected on the ironies of the current situation: "[We are] a new kind of human beings," she wrote in 1943, "the kind that are put in concentration camps by their foes and in internment camps by their friends."[18]

Like so many others, Arendt and her husband, the poet Heinrich Blücher, made their way to Marseille in pursuit of visas to America. In October 1940 they arrived at Fry's door looking for help, but they were then little-known writers and appeared nowhere on the American's all-important list, which contained few names that were not already considered distinguished or well known. It was only through the intervention of Fry's fixer, Hirschman—who knew Blücher personally

and attested that Arendt was "a woman who will someday be famous"—
that the ARC defied State Department directives and dedicated
resources to attain the necessary documents for the couple: an "Affidavit
of Identity in Lieu of Passport," a French "Certificat d' Identité et de
Voyage," and an American emergency visa.[19] In January 1941, the Vichy
government briefly relaxed their policy on exit permits and allowed
Arendt and Blücher to depart for Lisbon by train; with the assistance of
the Hebrew Immigrant Aid Society, they were later able to board an
ocean liner for New York. Arendt thus learned from her own harrowing
experience just how vulnerable the anonymous stateless person could be,
later observing that "the loss of citizenship deprived people not only of
protection, but also of all clearly established, officially recognized identity." In this situation, "only fame"—"the degree of distinction that will
rescue a man from the huge and nameless crowd"—could help restore
safety: "It is true that the chances of the famous refugee are improved
just as a dog with a name has a better chance to survive than a stray dog
who is just a dog in general."[20]

Many lesser-known refugees did not manage to escape like Arendt
and Blücher. Walter Benjamin was a prodigious writer and thinker—a
cultural theorist, sociologist, philosopher, and Jewish mystic, whose
work has found its way into many corners of the humanities and social
sciences over the last eighty years. He was a close friend of Bertolt Brecht
and an honorary member of the Frankfurt School, along with the likes
of Theodor Adorno and Max Horkheimer, who sponsored his work in
the 1930s. He was also a close friend of Arendt in Paris and, like her, had
fled Nazi Germany and had his citizenship revoked at the request of the
Gestapo; like her too, Benjamin lived a tenuous existence in Paris and
was later interned in a French camp for a time. But he was not yet famous
and he did not manage to arrive on Fry's doorstep with the right references. By the time of the German invasion, he had spent seven years
living in exile, moving from one part of Europe to another, with no fewer
than twenty-eight address changes. So it is little wonder that he insisted
on staying in Paris—a place that meant so much to him, both personally
and professionally—through early June 1940, abandoning the French

capital only a day before German troops marched down the Champs-Élysées. After a series of delays, he too made his way to Marseille, that city of refugees, where he met with Arendt long enough to hand off the typescript of his "Theses on the Philosophy of History"; she was to deliver it to Adorno and Horkheimer, who had already abandoned Europe several years earlier and set up operations at the New School of Social Research in New York (the graduate faculty of which was originally known as the University in Exile).

Of course, in order to reach safety and join his colleagues in America, Benjamin would require a whole cache of official documents: a French residence permit, a French exit visa, a transit visa to cross Spain into Portugal, and then, of course, another visa to enter the United States. With the help of friends, he was also able to collect an emergency visa from the American consulate, but as was the case with so many of his fellow refugees, he was unable to attain the almost-unattainable visa de sortie. Without it, the other documents would do him little good. But to request such a visa from the French authorities would have alerted them to his status as a German refugee and in turn drawn unwanted attention from the Gestapo.

In September 1940, fearing that the exit visa would never materialize, Benjamin took the fateful decision to leave France clandestinely with a small group of other refugees, who would try to travel on foot through the Pyrenees to Portbou in Spain. The crossing would be no easy stroll, for it included a 550-meter mountain pass and more than sixteen kilometers of uneven terrain. Many of the refugees who were to attempt the journey during the war suffered from poor health after long stays in internment camps or months of living in hiding from the Gestapo without regular room and board. Benjamin, that man of letters, not a man of action, had been in fragile health for most of his adult life and, after years of exile, now complained of asthma and heart palpitations. In late September, he nonetheless attempted to cross the frontier in the company of another rescue activist, Lisa Fittko, and two refugees Benjamin had met in Marseille. Falling behind on several occasions, he struggled through the whole journey, even more so because he insisted on carrying a heavy black suitcase containing his own portable archive: a passport issued by the American Foreign Service, six passport photos to be used for supplementary documents, and a number of additional papers, including an unidentified manuscript that Benjamin seemed to value more than his own life, according to Fittko.

Despite the difficulties of the crossing, Benjamin and the rest of the group succeeded in reaching Portbou on September 26, only to learn that the border had been closed just a day earlier to anyone without a French exit visa. Benjamin was already exhausted from the arduous journey and now he succumbed to acute despair, for he believed that being sent back into France very probably meant falling into the hands of the Germans. Later that evening, in a small hotel room on the French side of the border, the writer took his own life with a handful of morphine tablets, which he had carried with him since abandoning Paris several months before. The subsequent police report tells us that the suitcase holding his passport and manuscript were left in the room, though the items were soon lost to history. In the cruelest of ironies, the very day after Benjamin committed suicide, the Spanish authorities reopened the crossing to the rest of his group, who were allowed to continue on toward Portugal and safety.

That a refugee was able to escape from the dangers of wartime Europe had almost nothing to do with their human rights or the protections of a benevolent government. Instead, it far too often depended on happenstance: one might be waved onto a train by a capricious official; another might be watched over by a dedicated benefactor; still another might receive grudging assistance from that benefactor. But one might also be barred from escape by the whims of a government agency or border guard. With no nation-state to protect them, what inalienable rights did the stateless retain?

A decade later, after reaching safety in America, Arendt would publish her account of the conditions that had led to all this. In one of the central chapters of *The Origins of Totalitarianism,* she reflects on what her experience as a refugee had taught her about the status of the stateless, that new class of human beings who could no longer claim to be citizens of any sovereign nation-state. Regrettably, the refugees who should have enjoyed the "inalienable" rights of man instead embodied a radical crisis for that concept. Those who lost their citizenship simultaneously lost their rights to employment, education, and freedom of movement—even that most basic human right, the right to live. Arendt summed up this situation in a pithy, but poignant, formulation: the stateless had been denied "the right to have rights."[21] This phrase echoes through the refugee crisis brought on by the Nazi regime and the catastrophe of the Second World War, just as it continues to ring through the refugee crises that have defined the geopolitics of the present century. We continue to abide by the same dire logic.

Christian Petzold's 2018 film *Transit* captures the persistence of these issues through a telling use of anachronism. Based on Anna Seghers's 1944 novel of the same name, the film tells the story of a German refugee, Georg (Franz Rogowski), who narrowly avoids capture in Paris and then makes his way south to Marseille. His hopes of leaving the country depend on posing as a recently deceased writer, Weidel, whose papers he has appropriated. Many of the novel's details are based on Seghers's own experience in the early 1940s as she and her husband attempted to escape from France via the port city, just like the many refugees described above. But the film translates these details into a contemporary setting: a France in the late 2010s overrun by German soldiers and desperate Europeans trying to flee the dangers of war. In keeping with this time shift, the film also contains allusions to more contemporary refugee crises: arriving in Marseille, Georg encounters the wife of one of his fallen friends, Melissa (Maryam Zaree), and her son, Driss (Lilien Batman), Middle Eastern migrants living illegally in the city. Much of the action involves Georg's efforts to secure an exit visa at various crowded consular offices with the use of the dead writer's identification papers. Along the way, he has several chance encounters with the writer's estranged widow, who has come to the city with the same purpose. Eventually, Georg offers her his passage out of France, only to learn, shortly after her departure, that her ship has been sunk by an enemy torpedo and all aboard have perished. The confusion of identities, the escape offered to Georg, the tragic outcome of his generosity, all speak to the role of accident in the refugee situation and the contingencies of a world ordered by passports and visas. Meanwhile, the present-day setting and the presence of Melissa and Driss remind us that this situation has remained with us long after the end of the Second World War.

SIX

Migrants and Marxists

ABOUT AN HOUR INTO AI WEIWEI'S award-winning documentary on the global refugee crisis, *Human Flow* (2017), there is an extraordinary example of the passport control ritual. Up to this point, the film has shown us flotillas of rubber lifeboats, overflowing with passengers as they drift slowly toward the coast of Lesvos; views from high above a refugee camp in the barren desert of Iraq, captured with a camera on a hovering drone; crowds of refugees filing into an enormous ferry bound for the European mainland; endless lines of migrants stretched across the landscape as they trek westward toward the Hungarian frontier; a massive refugee camp in the desolate no-man's land at the Syrian-Jordanian border—all these images providing a sense of the massive scope of a refugee crisis that, at the time the documentary was filmed, had resulted in the displacement of more than sixty-five million people worldwide, forced from their homes by famine, climate change, and war. The images offer us detachment, quiet observation, even aestheticization, in order to document a crisis almost too vast and too tragic to properly comprehend. Yet these expansive tableaus are intercut with more intimate scenes, including interviews (often conducted by Ai himself) with UN workers, Amnesty International Human Rights Observers, government officials, Princess Dana Firas of Jordan, and a number of migrants, who reflect on their status as outcasts, unsafe at home, unwanted elsewhere.

At the halfway point of the film, the Chinese dissident artist-turned-documentarian enters a refugee encampment in Idomeni on the

Greek-Macedonian border, where his camera observes the daily rituals of physical survival: men ducking out of the rain into small nylon tents; mothers and children huddling together to stay warm; inhabitants of the camp cooking over a makeshift campfire; others gathering firewood and wild root vegetables from near the fence line. His microphones capture the sounds of feet trudging through the mud mixed with rapid conversations in Arabic and the rasping coughs of those suffering in the rain, mist, and cold. Ai wanders through the camp, making conversation and filming other quotidian activities. Then the shot cuts to the grinning face of a migrant man, who is surrounded by a crowd of other migrants, hooded against the rain, some smiling broadly, some simply bemused. The man begins to unzip his heavy coat, as we hear Ai from offscreen:

AI: I'll show you my Chinese passport. I also have a passport.

MAHMOUD: Yes, we're exchanging passports.

AI: I'll become a Syrian and you become a Chinese, right?

MAHMOUD: Yeah, I hope.

AI: Where's my passport? Oh, here's my passport. So you go to China and I'll come to . . .

MAHMOUD: . . . to Syria

AI: Yeah, yeah, yeah. [They show the passports to each other and to the camera.] You take this, I'll take that.

MAHMOUD: Thank you very much!

AI: What's my new name?

MAHMOUD: Mahmoud

AI: Mahmoud?

MAHMOUD: Yes.

AI: [reading from the biodata page of the passport] Mahmoud. Abdullah Mahmoud.

MAHMOUD: I'll give you my tent.

AI: My name is Ai Weiwei. So, next time you're Ai Weiwei. And I'm . . .

MAHMOUD: Mahmoud. Nice to meet you. If you want to take my tent. It's . . .

AI: [pretending to pocket the passport] Take your tent, too? Then you have to take my studio in Berlin. I have a studio in Berlin.

MAHMOUD: [handing the passport back] Thank you. Really, thank you.

AI: I respect you. I respect . . .

MAHMOUD: We have to respect . . .

AI: . . . the passport and I respect you.

The exchange amounts to a devastating parody of the passport control ritual: here, rather than inspecting the document and interrogating the holder in order to assess his threat to the host nation-state, Ai offers a gesture of radical hospitality in the form of his own passport, his own identity, his own citizenship. Of course, we cannot ignore the setting in which the parodic scene takes place: a refugee camp. As Agamben observes, even facilities run by humanitarian organizations can be complicit with oppressive state power insofar as they treat refugees as sacred or "bare life," clothing and feeding them, rather than recognizing their political existence and taking political action on their part. In this sense, the camp is a site where the state of exception has become a permanent arrangement, meaning that whatever protections the passport may offer elsewhere have no bearing, no force, here: Mahmoud and the other migrants find themselves in a space where they have been abandoned by the law. They have been orphaned, disowned by the "family of nations," and now appear destined to inhabit one camp after another, surviving day by day, until some nation-state deigns to invite them in, if this happens at all.

The camp setting thus contributes a plaintive, nearly tragic, tone to the scene played out by Ai and Mahmoud: if only one's identity, one's belonging, and one's status before the law could be so easily transferred from one's body to that of another; if only the world-famous artist could take the place of the desperate migrant; if only the accident of their birth in China or Syria could be reversed, undone; if only the fictions of borders and nations that circumscribe the lives of migrants could be recast into another fiction—"So, next time you're Ai Weiwei. And I'm . . .

FIGURE 13. A smiling Abdullah Mahmoud (*left*) exchanges his passport with Ai Weiwei in *Human Flow* (2017). Participant Media.

Mahmoud."[1] I'll take your worthless passport; you take the one that grants you recognition, mobility, and a future beyond the fate of a discarded migrant, an unwanted refugee.

It would be easy—and perhaps even reasonable—to see in the little ruse that Ai performs for the camera a kind of callous disregard for the condition of the migrant and the status of his Syrian passport. But this would be to misread the situation. To be sure, the scene clearly highlights the brutal contingencies of the current refugee crisis: as in Europe during the Second World War, one's fate is closely tied to what kind of passport one holds. It might land one person in a refugee camp on the Greek-Macedonian border; it might find another person in a massive art and production studio in Berlin. (Indeed, many of the inhabitants of the camp have identified Germany as their destination and place of asylum, a grimly ironic reversal of the human flow witnessed in the 1930s and '40s). But the very fact that Ai has his artistic base in Berlin speaks to another history of displacements, of state control, of the generalized state of exception that has come to dominate modernity. In press interviews for *Human Flow*, when asked about his connection to the migrants and refugees he documents, Ai repeatedly asserted his identification with them—and his desire to use his voice, as a celebrated artist, to give them a voice on the global stage; he repeatedly called on his audiences—and governments around the world—to consider the ethical stakes of the migrant crisis: "to think of humanity as one," so that when anyone's rights are violated, everyone's welfare is at stake.

During these interviews, Ai also evoked the story of his own childhood living as a political exile. In 1958, when he was just a year old, the Anti-Rightist Campaign purged his father, the famed poet Ai Qing, from the Chinese Communist Party and interned his entire family at State Farm 853, a labor camp in Heilongjiang province. Three years later, party authorities exiled the family to a small desert village in the distant province of Xinjiang, near the Kazakh and Mongolian frontiers. Qing was branded an "enemy of the people" and forced to do hard labor, cleaning the communal toilets in the village day after day, year after year. Weiwei has described his youth as taking place in conditions of constant discrimination and humiliation. The future artist and his family were forced to live under these circumstances for nearly two decades, until the death of Chairman Mao Zedong in 1976 finally brought an end to their persecution and allowed for their return to Beijing. Ai thus shares with the migrants in his film an experience of the camp as a site where human existence is reduced to bare life, driven to the very margins of society and denied the rights enjoyed by citizens of the state. He shares their experience of being banished to a space of exception outside the normal juridical order, deprived of any sense of agency over their own lives. For this reason, he could claim that it was "natural to approach those people" while filming *Human Flow*, "because I am part of them, I understand them so well, speak the same language, there is no boundary between us."[2]

Ai has dedicated much of his career to criticizing the current regime in Beijing, earning him both worldwide attention as the most exhilarating Chinese artist of his generation and unwanted scrutiny from the Chinese government for his relentless candor. He gained notice from both audiences in 2009 with an installation piece called *Remembering*, which honored the more than eighty thousand Chinese who died in the

2008 Sichuan earthquake, including more than five thousand children who perished when their shoddily constructed school buildings collapsed. Part of a one-man show at the Munich Haus der Kunst, the installation used more than nine thousand backpacks like those found in the buildings after the earthquake to spell out a message (in Mandarin) across the façade of the museum: "She lived happily for seven years in this world." While the Chinese authorities sought to suppress information about the tragedy, Ai attempted to identify the names of the children who were lost and then list their names on social media and in other exhibitions. Another art piece, a thirty-eight-ton sculpture called *Straight* (2012), is composed of once-mangled rebar recovered from collapsed buildings in Sichuan, straightened with the help of a team of craftsmen, and laid out in undulating rows on a gallery floor. Yet another piece, more direct in its assault but still playfully evasive, features a photograph of a leaping Ai, nude but for a plush toy of an alpaca species called a *cǎonímǎ* held over his genitals. The title of the image, 草泥马挡中央 (*Cǎonímǎ dǎng zhōngyāng*), means literally "a Grass Mud Horse covering the center," but because *cǎonímǎ* is a homophone for the Mandarin *cào nǐ mā*, the title can also be interpreted as "fuck your mother, Communist Party Central Committee."

The Chinese government responded harshly to these artistic protests. In the spring of 2011, Ai was at Beijing Capitol International Airport about to board a flight for Hong Kong when state security agents placed him under custody and, covering his head with a black hood, took him to a prison facility at an undisclosed location. The agents also confiscated his passport. The Chinese media initially reported that the artist was detained because "his departure procedures where incomplete," but the Ministry of Foreign Affairs later claimed that he was being investigated for tax evasion. Although the state authorities never formally arrested or charged Ai, and acknowledged that they had no "legal basis" for holding him in custody, they also claimed that they could do as they wanted with him. This included confining him twenty-four hours a day in a four-meter-by-four-meter cell, where two uniformed military police sergeants watched over him at all times. Ai would later create a stunning series of small-scale dioramas depicting his circumstances in the secret prison. Even after his release on "probation" eighty-one days later, the government maintained its hold over him by confiscating his passport with no legal justification or promise of return. Thus, despite an international outcry and his own repeated requests, Ai remained suspended in a state of bureaucratic perdition: under house arrest at his Beijing studio, FAKE Design; under constant surveillance; and unable to travel to his exhibitions and other engagements abroad.

During this period, Ai turned his growing despair into another piece of protest art titled *With Flowers:* every morning, he placed an ample bouquet in the basket of a bicycle outside the large steel doors of his studio, a mordant gesture of hospitality to the government agents that monitored his every move. As the days of his confinement dragged on, he marked each with a fresh bunch of blossoms and documented the ritual on Flickr.

In the end, Ai would have to wait more than four years for the return of his passport. On July 21, 2015, he posted a picture of himself on Instagram holding up the maroon document for the camera, with the simple caption, "Today, I got my passport" ("今天, 我拿到了护照"). The Chinese government never provided a reason for returning the document, but this did not lessen his satisfaction. "When I got it back I felt my heart was at peace," he told the *Guardian.* "I feel pleased. This was something that needed to be done." He added: "I was quite frustrated when my right to travel was taken away, but now I feel much more positive about my condition."[3]

At the same moment, however, the Chinese government was waging an offensive on Chinese human rights lawyers and activists, who disappeared into police custody and in some cases have remained in detention. It was not long until Ai moved to Berlin, which had recently become a destination for many of the nearly five million Syrians who were fleeing war in their homeland. There he set up his massive studio operation and began a new phase in his artistic production, with broader attention to the issues of human rights and the worldwide migrant crisis. In doing so, Ai also began distancing himself from his identity as a "Chinese" artist:

"Why do I have to be labeled? I'm not a car seller. Nothing can replace freedom, and that's a challenge, and I'm ready for that."[4]

We might, then, see his playful exchange with Abdullah Mahmoud in this light: rather than callous or exploitative, it was a heartfelt gesture from someone who has had his own painful experience with camps and passports. The artist does not feign his respect for the refugee. As his art became more cosmopolitan, more global, more inclusive, as he has left behind a China that had limited his freedom of movement from his earliest years, Ai has embraced the challenge of fashioning an identity for himself as what he calls "a person with no nationality."[5]

· · ·

Ai Weiwei's story is only a recent installment in a much longer narrative, which has regarded the passport as a tool for both the abuse of state power and the assertion of personal and political dissent. We can locate another notable episode in the story of Lev Davidovich Bronstein, better known to the world as Leon Trotsky, a name he acquired from the forged British passport he used to escape from Siberian exile in 1902. The name Trotsky was borrowed from one of his jailors in an Odessa prison, where he was held for his revolutionary activity on behalf of the farmers and peasants of tsarist Russia. In the years that followed, the Russian dissident was truly a man without a country: he worked as a writer and journalist in London, St. Petersburg (before a second exile to Siberia), Vienna, Geneva, Munich, Paris (before deportation to Spain), Madrid (before deportation to the United States), and New York City. After the outbreak of the revolution in early 1917, he again returned to Russia, where he quickly rose through the ranks of the Bolshevik Party and commanded the Red Army during the civil war. After the death of Lenin in 1924, however, Trotsky would be expelled from the Politburo and Communist Party as Joseph Stalin outmaneuvered him to fill the leadership void left by their predecessor. His rivalry with Stalin eventually led to his exile to Kazakhstan in 1928, and then his complete ejection from the newly formed Soviet Union in 1929. Trotsky would never return to his native land. In the early 1930s, finding refuge first in Turkey and then in France, Trotsky published some of his most important works, including his autobiography, *My Life* (1930), and his three-volume *History of the Russian Revolution* (1930), even as he attempted to form a new Marxist Fourth International to overthrow both Stalinism and global capitalism.

The revolutionary would nonetheless remain dependent on the hospitality of host nations. In the spring of 1935, the French government deported him due to increasing pressure from the Nazi Party, which viewed his influence on German communists as a threat; Norway then offered Trotsky and his family asylum, that protection from one sovereign authority offered by another, though mounting demands from the Soviet Union soon compelled the Norwegian government to place him under house arrest in the summer of 1936. After Stalin had orchestrated his conviction and death sentence at the so-called Moscow Trials, Trotsky effectively became a modern embodiment of *homo sacer,* a man cast out from the protections of his national community, who could be murdered (but not sacrificed) without penalty or consequence for his killer.

Help came from a rather improbable source when the renowned muralist and former member of the Mexican Communist Party Diego Rivera managed to convince Mexican president Lázaro Cárdenas to grant asylum to the notorious Russian exile. To enable his departure from Norway, Mexican authorities issued a passport to Trotsky and his wife, Natalia, on December 15, 1936. The hastily arranged document, listing his occupation as *escritor* (writer), utilizes two unrelated snapshots of the couple, hand-trimmed into appropriately sized ovals in order to repurpose them as passport photos: each would-be traveler appears in a casual near-profile pose, Leon with windblown hair and Natalia donning a small cap. Once affixed to the document, the photos were stamped with an official seal to indicate their authenticity, but the passport contains no visa stamps, because none were necessary for the Mexican passport holders to travel to Mexico. The document ultimately brought the Trotskys to the Coyoacán neighborhood of Mexico City, where Rivera

FIGURE 14. Photo page of Leon and Natalia Trotsky's passport, 1936. Image courtesy of Bonhams.

and his partner, Frida Kahlo, took them in as guests at their famed Blue House. When Leon and Frida began an affair in close proximity to their spouses and were found out, the Trotskys moved a few blocks away to a house on Avenida Viena, which they gradually transformed into a kind of urban fortress—complete with barricades and turrets, as threats from Stalinist sympathizers became ever more insistent.

Ultimately, these fortifications proved no defense against the dashing young Ramón Mercader. The Spanish communist and Soviet secret agent arrived in Mexico and infiltrated the Trotsky inner circle by posing as "Jacques Mornard," a Belgian playboy and diplomat, with the aid of a forged Canadian passport. Curiously, stolen, faked, and forged Canadian passports have a long and checkered history of involvement in espionage and assassination, including the document that allowed James Earl Ray to escape to Europe after he assassinated Martin Luther King Jr. Mercader struck down Trotsky with an ice pick to the back of the skull on August 20, 1940. The assassin was immediately captured and spent nearly twenty years in a Mexican prison, before traveling via Havana to Moscow, where he received the highest distinction awarded by the Soviet state, Hero of the Soviet Union, in 1961.

During the Cold War years, geopolitical interests also led to new restrictions on movement for citizens of the West, the United States in particular, through the denial, revocation, or nonrenewal of passports—strategies that harked back to those of the Wilson administration in the aftermath of the First World War. Undoubtedly, the most prominent target of these efforts was the legendary singer, actor, political activist, and global civil rights leader Paul Robeson. An All-American football player at Rutgers University and law graduate from Columbia University, Robeson began his career as an entertainer during the height of the Harlem Renaissance in the 1920s and before long brought his powerful presence to stage and screen in productions such as *The Emperor Jones, Showboat,* and *Othello.* But his mounting disgust with American segregation and discrimination led this son of a formerly enslaved person to spend more and more time abroad. During this period, Robeson also grew more enamored with the Soviet Union due to its apparent disavowal of racism: "Here I am not a Negro," he reflected, "but a human being. . . . Here, for the first time in my life I walk in full human dignity."[6]

His experiences abroad made Robeson increasingly determined to fight for "common people" everywhere, and he began to employ his mastery of languages and his rumbling baritone voice to advocate for a range of causes: from labor reform for coal miners in South Wales to political support for the independence of African nations. His voice would come to amplify the efforts of millions engaged in struggles around the world. In the 1930s, Robeson used his concert performances to champion the socialist experiment in the Soviet Union and the Republican cause in the Spanish Civil War, even singing for wounded soldiers and visiting the battle front to boost morale. With the outbreak of the Second World War, and the alliance between America and Russia against the Nazi regime, Robeson also volunteered to perform for US troops deployed around the globe.

After the war, he became a central figure in the World Peace movement, working tirelessly to avert armed conflict between the United States and the Soviet Union. In April 1949, as the Cold War continued to intensify, he delivered a speech at the World Congress of Partisans for Peace in Paris, addressing both the plight of Black people in the United States and the pressing need for international understanding to avoid another global conflict. The address was received with enthusiasm by the likes of Pablo Picasso, Paul Éluard, and Louis Aragon, but the Associated Press misquoted Robeson to the effect that it was "unthinkable" for African Americans to participate in any hostility toward the Soviet Union. He was immediately branded a traitor in the US media.

The bad press soon resulted in his blacklisting and the cancellation of more than eighty of his concerts in the United States, though the most damaging repercussion for the singer-activist was to come the following year with the loss of his passport. Despite the consequences of his speech in Paris, Robeson continued to speak out on the issues of civil rights, colonial independence, and international peace in interviews and other public forums, including a Civil Rights Congress rally held in late June 1950 at Madison Square Garden. There he castigated President Truman for his recent decision to enter the Korean War and his staunch determination to stop the spread of communism, even as the rights of African Americans continued to be denied at home. Unable to perform on US soil, the singer-activist had plans to take his message overseas in a series of concerts and peace assemblies later that summer, but the US government had very different ideas for him. In July, acting in coordination with the State Department, FBI director J. Edgar Hoover sent his agents to locate Robeson in New York City and confiscate his passport. When the singer-activist declined to surrender the document, the State Department notified immigration and custom officials that the passport had been canceled and that they were "to endeavor to prevent his departure from the [United States]," for any reason.

Although his attorney, Nathan Witt, wrote to Secretary of State Dean Acheson requesting an explanation, Robeson received only the vaguest response from the State Department: allowing him to travel abroad would be "contrary to the best interests of the United States." The singer and his lawyer immediately protested that this was not "a sufficient answer": it offered a conclusion with no justification. Eventually, in a meeting that August, passport officials from the State Department told Robeson that "his frequent criticism of the treatment of blacks in the United States should not be aired in foreign countries"—because it was a "family affair," apparently.[7] The parallels with the story of Ai Weiwei—on the other side of the globe, some sixty years later—are striking. Robeson had not broken any laws, he had not been arrested, he had not been found guilty, and yet his government had deemed it necessary to prevent him, the most famous Black man in the world, from traveling abroad to express his views on world peace and civil rights. His freedom of movement was essentially revoked, his resonant voice effectively silenced, at least for a time.

The Robeson case would play out over the course of many years and attract considerable international support for the singer-activist, even as he was largely isolated at home by the combined efforts of the US government and the mainstream press to portray him as "an enemy of the people." In their dismaying August 1950 meeting with passport officials, Robeson and his attorney were also told that unless he signed an affidavit stating he was not a member of the Communist Party and pledged not to give any speeches overseas, the State Department would refuse him a new passport. Since Robeson would not bow to these extraordinary demands, his only recourse was to take the matter to court. In December, his team of lawyers initiated a civil complaint against Secretary Acheson "in his representative capacity" as the head of the US State Department, so that the singer-activist could return to his foreign commitments. Insisting that Robeson was a "loyal, native born American citizen," the complaint argued that the actions of the State Department had not only prevented him from practicing his profession, they had deprived him of his constitutional rights to freedom of speech, thought, assembly, and travel. Meanwhile, Robeson continued to receive numerous invitations to perform around the world, as well as many requests to speak at peace conferences and political rallies. As the court cases associated with his passport dragged on and on, messages of encouragement arrived from concerned parties abroad, such as peace organizations in Uruguay, South Africa, and Iraq, and from famous admirers everywhere, including Charlie Chaplin, Ivor Montagu, Sylvia Townsend Warner, and future Nobel laureate Pablo Neruda.

The celebrated Chilean poet, an artist-activist of comparable stature to Robeson, had suffered similar treatment from his own government due to his criticism of President Gabriel González Videla. Following his election in 1946, the former Radical Party presidential candidate had turned against the members of his own Communist Party, including Neruda, who had been elected as a senator the previous year. The poet grew increasingly troubled as Videla first expelled his former Communist allies from his cabinet and then banned them from the country altogether with his *Ley de Defensa Permanente de la Democracia* (Law of Permanent Defense of Democracy). After Videla ordered the forceful suppression of a miners' strike organized by Communist leaders in October 1947, Neruda delivered a caustic indictment of the president's actions on the floor of the Chilean senate. The speech, which listed the names of mineworkers detained at the Pisagua internment camp, later became known by the Zolaesque title "Yo acuso" ("I accuse"). As it earned more attention for his concerns, the speech also resulted in threats of reprisal against Neruda and obliged him to retreat to southern Chile, before fleeing over the Andes to Argentina in March 1949.

Under the constant threat of arrest and extradition, Neruda quickly borrowed the passport of an old friend in Buenos Aires, the Guatemalan novelist Miguel Ángel Asturias, who bore a distinct resemblance to the Chilean poet. The document allowed Neruda to board a flight to Paris, where he received unexpected assistance from none other than Pablo Picasso, who had long admired Neruda and now stepped in to help him navigate the labyrinth of French bureaucracy. Ultimately, however, the poet's own reputation proved more useful. At the behest of the Chilean ambassador, the Parisian chief of police ordered Neruda to relinquish his diplomatic passport, which meant that he would be in immediate danger of deportation. When the poet insisted that he did not have a diplomatic passport, only a standard one he considered to be his private property, the police official—acknowledging his admiration for Neruda—called the ambassador and refused to confiscate the document. After hanging up the phone, he declared to the poet with great hospitality, "You can stay in France as long as you wish."[8]

As chance would have it, Neruda had arrived in Paris just in time to attend the World Congress of Partisans for Peace, where he heard Robeson deliver his infamous speech on world peace and US race relations. The poet later made a surprise appearance at the concluding session of the conference: Picasso presented him to the assembled delegates, who were astonished to see him there, many believing that he had been killed by Videla's agents. Still very much alive, but now cast into exile, the poet spent the next three years traveling through Europe, India, China, Mexico, and the Soviet Union on his personal passport. He finally returned to his homeland in August 1952 so that he could lend support to the presidential campaign of Salvador Allende, the nominee of the Chilean Socialist Party. With Videla's coalition losing its grip on power, Neruda reclaimed his prominent role in Chilean cultural and political life in the years that followed. In the summer of 1955, the poet and statesman would write to Robeson to tell him, "I am speaking about you and your case in a great meeting for public freedom here in Santiago" to "be attended by delegates of all Latin American countries . . . I have remembered many times the promise you [made] to me long ago: to sing for the Chilean people who admire and love you"; "we are prepared to pay your voyage and return," he ended optimistically.[9]

Unfortunately, Robeson remained trapped in the United States, despite the best efforts of his friends and admirers abroad and his team of dedicated lawyers at home. For nearly a decade, the State Department held firm as his attorneys filed appeal after appeal, asserting that the right to a passport should not depend on political attitudes, which should be protected under the right to free speech. For want of a travel document, Robeson continued to turn down invitations to speak and perform around the world: London, Tel Aviv, Prague, Moscow, and on and on. At about the time that Neruda was writing to the singer-activist, the leader of the American Communist Party, John Williamson (who had been deported in 1949), launched a political pressure campaign in England with the slogan "Let Robeson Sing." The effort gained momentum as the decade wore on. But as long as Robeson refused to provide an affidavit testifying to his relationship with the Communist Party, the State Department declined to even consider his application for a new passport. The US attorney also reaffirmed that it wished to suppress his vocal support of colonial independence overseas and equal rights for African Americans at home, which had frequently been aired during his "concert tours of foreign countries." Meanwhile, Hoover and the FBI continued to hound the singer-activist, the mainstream press persisted in scandalizing his name, and the House Committee on Un-American Activities brought him in to testify on his political views and personal associations.

Robeson never backed down from his principles. When questioned by the House Committee in 1956 about his refusal to submit a "non-Communist affidavit," he proclaimed that "under no conditions would I think of signing any such affidavit, . . . it is a complete contradiction of the rights of American citizens."[10] Two years later, still without a passport, Robeson published his memoir-as-manifesto, *Here I Stand,* where he reflects at length on the civil rights of African Americans in relation to the freedom of movement. He recalls that when Frederick Douglass traveled abroad to arouse antislavery sentiment in Europe, he was "bitterly denounced" by powerful members of both the US government and the newspaper industry as a "glib-tongued scoundrel."[11] Robeson also reminds his readers that in 1951 W. E. B. Dubois, the "great humanitarian, teacher and leader," had been indicted as a "foreign agent" and had his passport confiscated as a result of his efforts to publicize the Stockholm Peace Appeal against nuclear weapons. How can we be silent, Robeson asks, until such an exemplary American has his right to travel restored? Private citizens, whether Black or white, were not servants of the State Department, but rather the State Department was a servant of the American people. "Hence," he argues, "no job-holder in Washington has the legal or moral right to demand that any American traveler advocate the viewpoint of that official in order to get a passport."[12] But while he held firmly to his convictions, Robeson paid an immense financial and psychological price as his appeals were repeatedly denied and his hopes of ever again traveling abroad were gradually destroyed.

It was not until June 1958 that another court case, *Kent vs. Dulles*, finally brought justice: in a 5–4 split decision, the US Supreme Court ruled that the State Department had violated the civil rights of painter Rockwell Kent when it revoked his passport as a consequence of his involvement with the Stockholm Appeal and the World Peace Council. The court had confirmed, at last, that the US government had no right to refuse a passport to a US citizen based on his or her political beliefs (or, for that matter, to demand that an applicant provide an affidavit regarding his or her relationship with a political group). The State Department "immediately capitulated" in its denial of Robeson's passport application, conceding that the ruling applied to his case as well. The singer-activist soon left for engagements in London and returned to the international stage, but the personal and professional damage had been done: although he performed for a few more years, he struggled with depression and ill-health during the period, eventually retiring from public life in 1963.

.   .   .

Ticking off the days, the months, the years, hoping for the arrival of a document that never seems to come: this has become a common theme in both reporting and fiction on the modern passport. Consider Herta Müller's *The Passport* (the English translation of her 1986 novella *Der Mensch ist ein großer Fasan auf der Welt*), which was quickly rushed back into print after the German-Romanian writer won the Nobel Prize for Literature in 2009. The book opens with a description of its protagonist, a miller named Windisch, cycling past a war memorial adorned with slowly wilting roses on his way to the mill each morning; as he rides along, Windisch marks the days since he first decided to emigrate from Romania to West Germany. A member of the ethnic German minority living under Nicolae Ceaușescu's Romanian regime, the miller never seems quite at home in the midst of the poverty and pessimism of his small village, which has become a mire of joyless sexuality, rampant superstition, and casual violence. Yet he has remained there for want of a passport. Rendered in Müller's spare prose, this benighted world takes on a Kafkaesque quality as the miller tries repeatedly, with small bribes and other inducements, to convince the mayor and other Communist officials to expedite Windisch's application for the travel document. In the end, it is only through the sacrifice of his daughter's innocence that his family's escape is finally secured, after the poor girl consents to provide sexual favors for the village priest and a local militiaman in exchange for the precious passport.

The revolutions of 1989, which led to the end of Communist rule across Central and Eastern Europe, brought with them a radical rethinking of the nation-state and its sovereign authority, especially in the context of authoritarian and autocratic rule. The Ceaușescu police state, built on a series of purges targeting "enemies of the state" for deportation, internment, and even extrajudicial killing, was toppled in the violence of the Romanian revolution of December 1989. Across the western border in the Socialist Federal Republic of Yugoslavia, political tensions had been escalating ever since the death of Communist leader Josip Broz Tito in May 1980: within a few years, for instance, Slovenian leaders had commenced a program of gradual liberalization, which generated increasing friction within the League of Communists of Yugoslavia. Another sign of liberalization could be seen in the formation of a political art collective known as NSK or *Neue Slowenische Kunst* (a German phrase meaning "New Slovenian Art" and evoking the complex relationship between Slovenia and Germany) in 1984. Reappropriating symbols from totalitarian and fascist movements, along with elements of Dada and kitsch aesthetics, the collective sought to play a prominent role in the "pluralization" of Slovenian culture and society during the eighties, as demands for reform, democratization, and independence grew louder and louder.

In the aftermath of the Ten-Day War (the Slovenian War of Independence) and the declaration of an independent Slovenia in 1991, the NSK proclaimed the foundation of the sovereign *NSK Država v času* (NSK State in Time), an art project "conceived as a utopian formation which has no physical territory and which is not to be identified with any existing national state." Initially, the project was an overtly fictional rejoinder to the ideology of the new Republic of Slovenia, which had asserted a narrow view of national identity, based on the assumption of exclusively "Slovene" traits. To confirm its "temporal space," the NSK State soon began to issue its own passports, which, according to the collective, grant "the right to NSK citizenship . . . to thousands around the world, to people of different religions, races, nationalities, sexes and beliefs."[13] Aspiring NSK citizens need merely to navigate to the NSK website, print out a passport application, complete and sign it, and then send it off to the NSK Information Center in Ljubljana, along with a €32 application fee. In parodying the design of "real" or "official" travel documents, the fantasy passport seeks to connect identity not to a national territory or community, but to an artistic collective and its imagined community of NSK citizens. By reappropriating this familiar instrument of state authority, by playing with the signs of nationality, belonging, and mobility, the passport works to provoke reflection on the attachments we have to territorial states and, more importantly, on the possibility of reconceiving or even remaking those affiliations.

The documents thus offer participation, however indirect, in a new form of art-activism for whomever becomes a holder of these mass-produced *objets d'art* and thereby becomes a "member" of this collective-of-choice. Undoubtedly, the most widely recognized citizen of the NSK State is Slavoj Žižek, the prolific Marxist philosopher, Lacanian critic, and all-around controversialist (as well as former Slovenian presidential candidate), who has defended "the mythology of the state" against claims that it is "the original source of Evil, as a living dead sponging off the body of the community." In other words, Žižek challenges thinkers like Agamben who seek the abolition of the state (or its subordination to the community) as the first step in breaking its ideological machinery and its "process of supervising and maintaining discipline." In reflecting on the NSK State, after witnessing the breakup of Yugoslavia and the ensuing lawlessness in Bosnia and Serbia, Žižek has advocated an alternative, perhaps paradoxical, position:

> Today the concept of utopia has made an about-face turn—utopian energy is no longer directed towards a stateless community, but towards a state without a nation, a state which would no longer be founded on an ethnic community and its territory, therefore simultaneously towards a state without territory, towards a purely artificial structure of principles and authority which will have severed the umbilical cords of ethnic origin, indigenousness and rootedness.[14]

The NSK State can be viewed as just such a project (or at least an artistic gesture toward such a project), given its definition "as an abstract body whose borders are in a state of constant flux, depending on the activities of its physical and symbolic body, and whose territory is situated in the consciousness of its 'members.'"[15] In this regard, the concept of utopia should not prevent us from critiquing the state, but rather rule out all pragmatic or political constraints to transforming its future. To give its abstract body a physical presence, the NSK State has set up consulates— some of them temporary, some of them less so—in Moscow, Ghent, Berlin, Florence, Graz, Sarajevo, and New York, often connected with an exhibition in the city. Meanwhile, the NSK State has issued more than 15,000 of its fantasy passports, produced by the same printing firm that makes the "official" passports of the Republic of Slovenia—and word has circulated that NSK passport holders have managed to cross "real" borders using the document.

Unfortunately, the success of the project has also generated confusion among groups of potential migrants desiring access to Europe. Beginning in 2004 and accelerating through 2007, the NSK headquarters in Ljubljana received thousands of passport applications from Nigerians imagining that the NSK State was an actual territorial state ready to accept new citizens. The utopian project, that is, had come to be seen as a tangible opportunity to leave behind poverty, to escape ethnic violence, to pursue a new life in better circumstances. With applications pouring in from Africa, the Slovenian government took notice and demanded the art collective post disclaimers on its website: "NSK citizenship does not equal Slovenian citizenship"; the "NSK passport does not allow its holder to enter the Schengen zone."[16] In 2010, as representatives of the NSK State grew more and more uneasy with the expectations attached to the document, three of them, Borut Vogelnik, Miran Mohar, and Inke Arns, even traveled to Nigeria for an event at the Centre of Contemporary Art (CCA) in Lagos, where they sought to clarify the intent of the documents and to dispel any false hopes. For the fantasy document, meant primarily to prompt reflection on the status of the nation-state and citizenship in the age of globalization, no longer maintained its ironic function in these rather unforeseen circumstances. Perhaps it could no longer be viewed as an art object at all.

As the European migrant crisis intensified over the decade that followed, the NSK continued to pose the question of what nation-state citizenship should mean, while promoting the construction of new collectivities and new forms of collective identity. One manifestation of this ongoing project was the NSK State pavilion at the 2017 Venice Biennale, which took its place alongside the many "actual" national pavilions at the arts exhibition. The NSK contribution included an installation piece by Ramesch Daha and Anna Jermolaewa—"an open archive of experiences, ideas, and hopes," including reflections on the promise of "Europe" written by a hundred migrants from the global South and the former Eastern bloc—as well as a temporary NSK State passport office. The Slovenian art collective was not alone at the Biennale in presenting work that interrogated traditional conceptions of the nation-state and document-dependent movement: Tunisia presented a "dispersed" installation piece on the grounds of the Biennale, with three kiosks staffed by migrants and refugees who issued "freesas" (i.e., "free visas"), fantasy "Universal Travel Documents" that mischievously claimed to authorize "freedom of movement without the need for arbitrary state-based sanction." Both exhibitions thus sought to call attention to the maltreatment of "undocumented" and "paperless" people in the current world order, which denies them legitimacy for want of a passport or proper visas. By now, this is an all-too-familiar logic.

With the assistance of several Italian NGOs, the NSK State Pavilion was also staffed by asylum seekers and stateless migrants, who guided visitors across the exhibition hall and through a curtain into the passport office. The temporary office mimicked the bureaucratic obstacles that migrants face on arrival to Europe: with a passport desk sitting atop a high platform, the installation compelled exhibition visitors either to roll a large steel staircase to the platform or to jump on a small trampoline to launch themselves to the necessary height. The desk itself was supervised by four officers—newly arrived refugees from India, Ghana, and Nigeria—employed by the NSK to process the pavilion visitors and manage their passport applications. While the participation of the migrants added an undeniable immediacy, even urgency, to the installation, it simultaneously raised uncomfortable concerns regarding their exploitation for the purposes of an art exhibition. Yet at the same time, the procedures in the faux passport office also placed visitors to the Biennale in the uncomfortable position of having to navigate bureaucratic processes like those that confront nearly every aspirant for a new passport: listing personal information, including sex, blood type, eye color, hair color, height, and profession, as well as consenting to have this information stored in a state register and pledging "to support the integrity of the NSK State to the best of his or her ability." The issue, then, is much like that raised by the passport scene in Ai Weiwei's *Human Flow* described at the beginning of this chapter: whether this parody of the passport ritual is effective in producing a useful or politically significant kind of empathy, in generating a new understanding of or at least a more sustained attention to the migrant crisis, including the demand to submit oneself to the invasive procedures of the state—or whether it is mere spectacle.

Some insight into the matter can be gained from the defense of the NSK State offered by Žižek, who opened the Venice Biennale exhibition (and its redux in Vienna a few months later) with a keynote lecture on, among other things (in his inimitably digressive style), the larger project undertaken by the art collective. As he told Benjamin Ramm of the BBC shortly before the lecture, "The uniqueness of NSK is this idea of the 'stateless state.' It is not, as some leftists think, just a parody. They are not mocking the state, and this assumption reveals a typical liberal fear: what if some people take it seriously and are seduced? But they are to be taken seriously!"[17] A year earlier, Žižek had stirred up controversy with the publication of his treatise *Refugees, Terror, and the Trouble with Neighbors* (2016), which critiques *both* the rise of anti-immigrant populist movements across Europe *and* the liberal ideal of open borders and multicultural harmony. The philosopher identifies what he sees as an intractable problem in leftist humanitarianism that refuses to recognize both cultural differences and the seemingly inevitable tensions arising from the competition for employment and resources. Empathy is not enough. But Žižek rejects the "open our hearts" approach not for the reasons associated with the political right—that is, out of fear or hatred of the other—but because, he claims, the approach too often distracts from the political action necessary to break the grip of the neocolonial relations and geopolitical machinations that have created the problems migrants flee from at home.

In his opening lecture for the Vienna exhibition, later published in his book *Like a Thief in Broad Daylight* (2018), Žižek challenged what he calls the "bourgeois notion of human rights" by evoking the work of Jean-Claude Milner and his "reactivation" of the distinction that Hannah Arendt had once stressed: between human rights and the rights of the citizen. For Milner, the "human" has nothing to do with some eternal nature or universal essence, but instead can be considered natural only to the degree that it is *subtracted* from a particular polis or community. This is exemplified for Žižek and Milner in the so-called Calais jungle, a refugee camp in northern France where, they both contend, one can witness a radical deprivation of rights for those who are precisely *not* citizens: "those who are assembled there from 2000 are not guilty of anything, they are not accused of anything, they do not infringe upon any part of the law; they are simply there and they live; the proof that they live is that sometimes they die."[18] The stateless inhabitants of the camp, without a home, without documentation that entitles them to the rights of citizenship, have been reduced to bare life, the material body threatened with the deprivation of its material needs: water, food, hygiene, a minimal space of privacy. They have become reminders of this status, diminished to the function of the *homo sacer* that "render[s] visible in a negative way the real of the rights of man/woman."[19] In light of this, Žižek suggests, the NSK State passport also stands as a reminder of the unavoidable difference between human rights and the rights of the citizen: a critical gesture toward the privileges that accrue to EU passport holders at present; a material prompt to recognize that the rights we enjoy depend on the passports we hold; a signal that utopian thinking must take into account, and not simply abandon, the role of the state and its sovereign authority.

SEVEN

Alien and Indigenous

THE PASSPORT, AS WE HAVE SEEN, occupies a place in some of our most avid fantasies. Nicholas Roeg's 1976 film *The Man Who Fell to Earth* opens with a montage of spacefaring imagery: a rocket thruster coming to life, a broad skyline streaked with stratocumulus clouds, the rocket-powered spacecraft exiting an atmosphere, another skyline lumped with distant mesas, a space capsule entering the atmosphere, followed shortly by a point-of-view shot plunging toward a lake in the high desert of the southwestern United States and then a final cut to an enormous splash in the water. (These last shots were filmed at Fenton Lake in the Jemez Mountains, home to various Pueblo Indian tribes long before European settlers arrived in the region now known as New Mexico.) Then, silhouetted against a hillside, a solitary figure in a long, hooded coat is seen stepping carefully as he makes his way past an abandoned mining operation. We have just witnessed an intergalactic journey with none of the familiar hassles of air travel—no customs and immigration checkpoints, no border guards or passport officials—though as the individual reaches the valley below the mine, we see that he is being watched carefully by a stern-faced man in a dark suit. Eventually, not unlike a high-plains drifter from a Hollywood western, the lone figure wanders to the outskirts of a small town—"Haneyville, Village Limit, Elcv. 2850," the sign tells us—where he rather disconsolately throws back his hood to reveal a mane of unnaturally red hair, surrounding a pale, thin, almost-aquiline visage.

Yes, now we can clearly see that the intergalactic traveler is David Bowie, nearly as out of place in Haneyville, New Mexico, as an actual alien from outer space might be. Indeed, the place itself is rather strange. We soon cut to the unexpected image of a clown-faced bounce-house, threatening to break its tethers in the wind, as a nearby carnival worker belches loudly and then beckons to our protagonist: "Hey fella, come here, come here!" Obviously weary from his long voyage, the space traveler instead crosses the street and splays himself on a wooden bench in front of a "buy-sell" store to rest for a few moments. It quickly becomes evident that, despite being so clearly out of place, this stranger in a strange land knows quite well how to navigate his new surroundings. When the elderly proprietress arrives to open the store for the day, the traveler revives himself and follows her inside. Visibly concerned by his presence, she asks with suspicion in her voice, "Can I help?"; his answer comes in a soft South London accent—"Yes, I'm sorry. I'd like to sell this"—as he gently hands her a small golden hoop. The experienced proprietress then asks, even more suspiciously, "Where'd you get this ring?" Hesitating only slightly, he replies, "It's mine . . . my wife gave it to me—look, the initials are on the inside." With the aid of a magnifying glass, she reads off the letters—"T . . . J . . . N"—and then immediately follows with another question: "Do you have your ID?" As the stranger reaches toward the breast of pocket of his black jumpsuit, he replies, "I'm British. I have a passport," before handing the document over to her. Taking hold of the passport and peering through the cutout in its cover, she reads the name on the document aloud, "Thomas Jerome Newton," while he silently mouths the syllables, as if rehearsing them yet again to commit the name, his earthly identity, to memory.

Cut to a tight shot of the document: as the proprietress opens it, the camera zooms in on the picture page displaying a black-and-white photograph of a serious but serene Bowie, with finely quaffed hair and wide-collared shirt. If you freeze the frame just right, you can make out the details on the personal description page—Occupation: Salesman; Place of Birth: Henfield, Sussex; Date of Birth: 8–1-46; Country of Residence: England; Height: 5 feet 10 inches—though the shallow depth of field used in the shot has blurred perhaps the most interesting details, Colour of Eyes, Colour of Hair, and Special Peculiarities. Significantly, for the

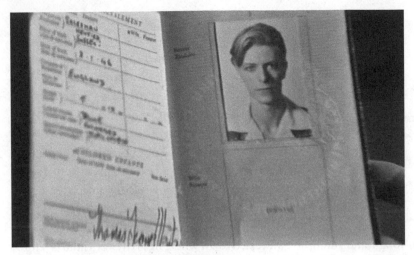

FIGURE 15.   Photo page of Thomas Jerome Newton's passport from *The Man Who Fell to Earth* (1976). British Lion Films.

lone traveler who has left his family far behind, the sections describing his wife and children have been left blank. Cut back to a close-up of Bowie as Newton, who quickly brushes his longer, darker hair to the side of his face in an attempt to appear more like the image in the passport. Apparently convinced of the document's authenticity, the proprietress perfunctorily mutters, "This is not a pawn shop . . . If I buy this ring now, you can't redeem it later, understand."[1]

There was something alien about Bowie long before he splashed down in the New Mexico highlands. Thomas Jerome Newton may have been his first role in a feature film, but the rock star-turned-movie star had already been creating and recreating personae for nearly a decade as he transitioned from the prosaic David Jones born in Brixton to the stage guise of David Bowie (deriving from the Bowie knife and its American pioneer inventor) and on to the androgynous sci-fi extremes of Ziggy Stardust in the early 1970s. Bowie had brought his alter ego and his backing group, the Spiders from Mars, on a concert tour of the United States in the fall of 1972, crisscrossing the country for more than six months with his elaborate stage show, which featured such space-travel-inspired songs as "Space Oddity," "Life on Mars?," "Starman," and of course, "Ziggy Stardust." At the center of all this was his rail-thin figure adorned with garish kabuki-like makeup, a crest of shocking red hair, and a wardrobe of outlandish costumes that accentuated his otherworldly appearance. By the time he was cast as Thomas Jerome Newton in *The Man Who Fell to Earth*, Bowie was already transitioning to a less extravagant new persona, the Thin White Duke, whose neatly groomed hair and cabaret-style wardrobe closely resembled the passport photograph in the film. But Bowie's casting in Roeg's film was an extension of the rock star's otherworldly stage persona, emphasizing his nearly emaciated limbs, milky-white skin, slightly effete mannerisms, and aloof, distracted gaze.

In this guise, Bowie embodies something entirely foreign to the rough-and-tumble New Mexico town where he arrives as Thomas Jerome Newton. His passport, when any form of identification would do, helps to explain his strangeness: he is one of those Brits with their funny accents and uppity ways (there is a bit of sly humor in this, then). David Bowie or Ziggy Stardust or the Thin White Duke, and their associations with avant-garde rock music and globalized popular culture—they are, yes, almost as unexpected in this small town as a man from Mars (thus another layer to the subtle joke). Yet the document also affords his presence, as strange as it is, with a certain legitimacy: he is here with the proper papers (even if we know what the proprietress does not: the document cannot possibly be authentic).

Bowie as Newton is a passport-bearing emissary of the outlandish new cultural movement of pop music and celebrity that had emerged in the 1960s; *The Man Who Fell to Earth* is, in an important sense, a film about our perception of Bowie and his many personae. Fundamentally, it is also a film about our perception of the "alien," perhaps even more so than Bowie or Roeg realized at the time. Thomas Jerome Newton is called an "alien" just once in the film, though the label is followed immediately by a pressing question: "Do you know what would happen if they found out your visa had expired?" (another knowing joke, surely). Alien—in the sense of "of, belonging to, or relating to an (intelligent) being or beings from another planet; designating such a being; extraterrestrial"—is a term that derives from science fiction and first emerged from the genre in the late 1920s.[2] *Alien* in the sense used in the film—"born in, or owing allegiance to, a foreign country; esp. designating a foreigner who is not a naturalized citizen of the country where he or she is living"—can be traced to fourteenth-century France, and the etymology of the term goes all the way back to ancient Rome, with its highly nuanced ideas about citizenship.[3] The current meaning of "illegal alien," however, also gained currency in the United States during the late 1920s, when the first mass deportation of Mexicans and Mexican Americans began, though use of the term increased greatly in the 1970s as immigrant communities grew to form a much larger percentage of the US population. No longer were newcomers considered prospective citizens. Instead, the term became popular among those on the political right who saw the violation of immigration law as an existential threat to the sovereignty of the United States as an independent nation-state, subject to constitutional constraints and governed by the rule of law.

Yet the United States was already inhabited by at least one native-born "alien" at the time: Sun Ra (aka Le Sony'r Ra, born Herman Poole Blount in Birmingham, Alabama) lived out the persona of the spaceman even more boldly than David Bowie. As a college student in the 1930s, Ra had a visionary experience that shaped the rest of his life: "I landed on a planet that I identified as Saturn ... they teleported me and I was down on [a] stage with them. They wanted to talk with me. They had one little antenna on each ear. They told me ... I would speak [through music], and the world would listen."[4] No doubt these beings from another planet offered a more inviting destiny than the white southerners who dominated economic and political life in Jim Crow–era Alabama. Beginning his career as a gifted young piano player in Birmingham, Ra went on to become the leader of an "interplanetary" band that generated a prolific output of experimental jazz into the 1990s. Over the course of his long career, he would develop his youthful vision into a personal mythos of cosmic travel and an early version of Afrofuturism, radically reimagining the place of Black culture in midcentury American society. In 1952, he legally changed his name to Le Sony'r Ra, which ultimately transformed into Sun Ra, evoking (twice over) the Egyptian God of the Sun; shortly afterward, he founded a musical collective known as the Arkestra (aka the Myth Science Arkestra, both names playing on *orchestra* and *ark of the covenant*), whose concerts featured ornate costumes combining elements of ancient Egyptian regalia and space-travel-inspired chic. In 1960, Ra and his Arkestra recorded their landmark "We Travel the Spaceways"—a cacophonous jazz dirge, including the apt refrain "interplanetary music"—and they soon began to perform against extraterrestrial backdrops.

But "Sun Ra" was not just a stage persona. Readying for his first European tour in 1970, the musician went to a passport office in New York City to apply for his first travel document—and, to affirm his adopted identity, he did so as Sun Ra from Saturn. As John F. Szwed recounts the events in his biography of Ra, the otherworldly musician, dressed in "street clothes" that were still quite "far out," completed the requisite forms and handed them to the passport clerk only to be told: "Sir, you're going to have to give us better information than this. We need your parents' names, your birth date . . ." Standing his ground, Ra retorted, "That *is* the correct information." Faced with this unusual situation, the bewildered clerk deferred to his supervisor, who, after a brief conversation with Ra, suggested that he come back a few hours later to recommence the application process. When the musician returned later that day, he was met by another employee of the passport office who was apparently less bothered by protocol than his colleagues: "We'll just give you the passport," he swiftly conceded. Surely, a mere government functionary could not be expected to resist the visionary zeal of an interplanetary superstar. The passport became a key component of the Sun Ra persona: official recognition of the identity that he had created for himself, rather than the one that the vexing history of American racial politics had imposed upon him. Travel documents, as we know, have long been handy for this kind of thing.

In the years that followed, as Szwed's biography reports, the passport acquired "talismanic" significance among Ra's fellow musicians, precisely because it was an official document that registered his rejection of mainstream American social and cultural life, along with its pervasive (and predominantly white) government bureaucracies. The passport, moreover, gave the wild fantasy of his cosmic identity a kind of authoritative manifestation and material grounding. As Talvin Singh, the London-based producer, composer, DJ, and tabla player, later commented: "His philosophy was that either you be part of society or you don't. And he wasn't part of it. He created his own. I mean, I actually saw his passport and there was some weird shit on it. It had some different stuff."[5] For one thing, the document confirmed his birthplace as "Saturn," but indicated no birthdate.

Not everyone was so impressed by the passport, however. In December 1970, as their European concert tour drew to a close in Copenhagen, Ra and his Arkestra made a spontaneous decision to fly to Egypt, having made no prior arrangements for transportation or lodging. The impromptu journey soon hit a snag when the musicians were waylaid by customs and immigration officials at the Cairo airport. If it was suspicious that an entire jazz band would arrive in Egypt as tourists, it was even more suspicious that its leader should have the name of an ancient Egyptian deity on his passport. But Ra had a response for that: the officials should call the curator of the Museum of Egyptian Antiquities, so that his name could be evaluated in the context of Egyptology. Met with Ra's opposition, the officials soon relented, although they impounded most of band's instruments, apparently to guarantee their timely return to the airport and departure from the country. Fortunately, an Egyptian admirer quickly came to the aid of Ra and his Arkestra: Salah Ragab, a jazz drummer, who happened to be a brigadier general and band leader for the Egyptian army, managed to secure replacement instruments for the group. Although he was later disciplined for his intervention, Ragab made several recordings with Ra and his Arkestra, and the collective would complete a concert tour of the country before the musicians retrieved their own instruments and flew back to the United States. The trip to Egypt, like the ancient Egyptian-inspired regalia worn by the band, would become an important element of their Afrofuturist vision, situating them as it did between a glorious African past and the promise of a magnificent interplanetary tomorrow.

This mythos found its fullest expression in Ra's 1974 feature film *Space Is the Place,* which, as the title suggests, envisions the new opportunities for Black Americans not in a return to Africa but in a move off planet, a journey that will require no passport. The result is a kind of blaxploitation sci-fi fantasy: think *Shaft* meets 2001: *A Space Odyssey.* The movie opens with Ra, dressed in his elaborate Egyptian-inspired costume, humming a tune and then entering into a monologue, apparently directed at a hooded, mirror-faced inhabitant of a distant jungle planet:

> The music is different here. The vibrations are different. Not like planet earth. Planet earth . . . sound of guns, anger and frustration. There was no one to talk to on planet earth who would understand. We set up a colony for black people here. See what they could do on a planet all their own, without any white people there. They could drink in the beauty of this planet. It would affect their vibrations, for the better of course . . . We'll bring them here through either isotope teleportation, transmolecularization, or better still, teleport the whole planet here through music.

We begin, then, with a grand plan to extend the African diaspora to the distant reaches of the galaxy and to establish a harmonious anticolonial colony, beyond the grasp of the violence, materialism, and racism that have plagued our world. The ensuing plot, interspersed with the polyrhythmic free jazz of Ra and his Arkestra, verges on incoherence at times. But for the most part, it follows the musician in his attempts to fulfill this interplanetary mission, even as he must vie with a demonic pimp known as the Overseer (Raymond Johnson) to "win" the African American community with his vision of the future.

Soon, the voyager arrives in Oakland, where he introduces himself to a group of "Black youths of the planet earth" as "Sun Ra, ambassador from the intergalactic regions of the Council of Outer Space." Returning after many years off planet, he is now an alien, an outsider, but also a potential savior, who offers them an escape to a faraway future, if the youths first recognize their own treatment as aliens in the United States.

Inevitably, he encounters disbelief and even mockery at his attempts to recruit travelers to his utopian space community. To promote his message, Ra soon enters into an arrangement with an agent of the Overseer who claims to have "his finger on the impulse of the entire communications network in this country, every TV, radio, movie house, newspapers, magazines, you name it." As word of his mission begins to spread, Ra also attracts the attention of a team of virulently racist NASA scientists, who capture him and threaten him with bodily harm if he does not reveal the secret of transmolecularization and his other technologies. The "alien," like other "illegal" visitors, inhabits a space in American society at the very threshold between violence and right. Ra escapes in time to play a concert in Oakland, and then, as government agents and the Overseer close in on him, he begins waving his hands in the air and teleporting Black youths from across city onto his spaceship. The film ends with the vessel hurtling away as the debris of an exploding planet tumbles through space—a judgment on the racial injustice that has put the African American community "out of tune with the universe."[6]

Space Is the Place offers a striking counterpoint to the vision offered in The Man Who Fell to Earth. Thomas Jerome Newton did not come to earth to save its inhabitants, or any particular community, but rather to acquire enough water to save the population of his own drought-stricken planet. In a series of flashbacks, which amount to a troubled migrant's memories of home, we get glimpses of Newton and his family wandering the desert expanses of his dying world somewhere far away, as he prepares to leave on his rescue mission. He thus embodies a threat closely associated with both sci-fi fantasies and the fear of illegal aliens: that the visitor will exploit his new country, sapping it of resources, which will be sent back to his homeland with little thought of the toll exacted. But there is something for the alien to fear too: that he will be stranded in this new world and corrupted by its culture, increasingly drawn in by America's materialism, its excesses of sex and alcohol, and its teeming media landscape. Some of the most striking scenes in the film involve Newton sitting before a bank of television sets as he is bombarded by an entirely unreconcilable maelstrom of imagery and information.

Roeg's film also taps into another iteration of the immigrant story, especially in America: founding a business empire by patenting a range of new technologies, Newton builds a personal fortune to rival that of any native-born entrepreneur. In his strange way, he embodies the American Dream. His success, moreover, makes him a media sensation, though this newfound fame means that he is soon hounded by the press, not unlike David Bowie the rock star. Newton intends to accumulate enough wealth to build a new spaceship and return home with the water necessary to save his planet. But in the process, like Sun Ra in *Space Is the Place*, he attracts the unwanted attention of government agents, who capture him and carry out a series of experiments on his gaunt body. Passport or no, he is abruptly reduced to bare life; passport or no, he is doomed never to return home.

· · ·

If interpreting *The Man Who Fell to Earth* as an (admittedly, rather strange and estranging) immigrant narrative seems ever more plausible, even unavoidable, as we move well into the twenty-first century, this is due to the fact that certain features of the story have been reinforced in the American imaginary over the last half century. We might even point to the mythos that has developed around one particular immigrant to the United States, namely Elon Musk. Here is another outsider who has come to the country with seemingly otherworldly talents, who has amassed an enormous fortune with his technological prowess, and who now longs for nothing more than to leave earth in a rocket ship of his own design, with the objective of bringing life to a seemingly uninhabitable planet. The producers of *The Simpsons* picked up on these striking parallels, translating them into a 2015 episode titled "The Musk Who Fell to Earth." As the episode opens, a rocket descends into the family's backyard in Springfield and the door swings open to reveal Musk (voiced by the billionaire himself, in his robotic monotone), "the greatest living inventor." The visitor goes on to translate Homer's bumbling human musings into a series of dazzling new inventions aimed at improving the town and, in the process, showing "the planet how to save itself" (though Musk also manages to bankrupt Springfield in the process, leading Homer to lament, "Of all the planets in the Universe, why did he have to come to this one!").[7]

The actual story of Elon Musk, like many immigrant narratives, hinges on a passport. Growing up in South Africa in the 1970s and '80s and ingesting a steady diet of comic books and technology magazines, he came to believe in another mythos: "It always seemed like when there was cool technology or things happening, it was kinda of in the United States. So, my goal as a kid was to get to get to America basically."[8] The young man took additional inspiration from his reading of Douglas Adams's *The Hitchhiker's Guide to the Galaxy* (1979), the comedic sci-fi novel that highlighted for him "an important point, which is that a lot of times the question is harder than the answer. . . . So, to the degree that we can better understand the universe, then we can better know what questions to ask."[9] It was during these childhood reveries that Musk started to dream of colonizing Mars.

First, however, he would have to come to America. For years, Musk tried to persuade his parents to move to the United States, but he could not quite convince them; nor could the young South African just show up in the country alone and unannounced. Instead, at age seventeen, he discovered another path: his mother, Maye, was born in Canada, which meant that she could apply for a Canadian passport, even though she had spent almost her entire life in South Africa. Through her, Elon could get one too. Just three weeks after receiving his new passport, Musk was on a plane to North America. Canadian citizenship helped the young man enroll at Queen's University in Kingston, Ontario, and later, with a US student visa, transfer to the Wharton School of the University of Pennsylvania. Musk would then enroll at Stanford University to pursue a PhD in Energy Physics and Material Science, studying ultracapacitors for application in electric cars. But he left the program just a few days into his first term to launch his first startup, a web software company called Zip2; he was able to stay in the US with an H-1B visa, for foreign workers in "specialty occupations," because he had already completed an undergraduate degree. The entrepreneur would go on to start a half dozen more companies over the next two decades.

Musk made headlines in June 2020, amid the Covid-19 pandemic, when he posted on Twitter in response to news that his fellow Wharton graduate, President Donald J. Trump, had suspended the issuance of temporary work visas, including the H-1B: "Very much disagree with this action. In my experience, these skillsets are net job creators. Visa reform makes sense, but this is too broad."[10] Earlier, during the 2016 presidential campaign, a meme attributed to the billionaire entrepreneur had circulated widely on social media, claiming: "I am Elon Musk. I was an ILLEGAL immigrant and if Mr. Trump and some of you had it your way, I would've been kicked out of the USA and never founded Zip2, PayPal, Tesla Motors, SpaceX, Solar City. I wouldn't have changed the world and employed thousands of Americans and grown your economy."[11] While Musk did not, in fact, write these words, and he never was an illegal immigrant, his experience as a resident alien contributed to his repeated criticism of the restrictive immigration policies enacted under the Trump administration. In January 2017, a week after he was sworn into office, Trump signed his infamous executive order restricting immigration from seven predominantly Muslim countries, which relied on section 212(f) of the Immigration and Nationality Act. The act permitted the president to "suspend the entry of all aliens or any class of aliens as immigrants or nonimmigrants, or impose on the entry of aliens any restrictions he may deem to be appropriate," whenever the president finds such entry "to be detrimental to the interests of the United States." In short, this was a blunt exertion of sovereign authority. Musk was quick to condemn the ban, stressing that it would affect those who had done nothing wrong and "don't deserve to be rejected" (he subsequently deleted harsher criticisms from his Twitter feed). Much like those who protested at airports across the United States, the unlikely human rights advocate was speaking out for a world where everyone, regardless of national origin, can claim their legitimate right to freedom of movement.[12]

Musk also remarked on the restrictions that stopped him from hiring foreign workers to design rockets, preventing the employment of many talented engineers at SpaceX. The H-1B visa suspension by the Trump administration only compounded the problem for a company founded with the audacious purpose of colonizing Mars, so that the human species might survive an ecological disaster or nuclear holocaust. But one must assume that space travelers will someday need a passport and a special visa to disembark on the Red Planet.

The futurist fantasy of Martian colonies is perhaps more plausible than the cosmopolitan dream of a world without national borders—and therefore without the "illegal" aliens and international strife that might necessitate a planetary escape plan. Consider the passport story of Yasiin Bey, the artist formerly known as Mos Def (also Dante Beze, Flaco, El-Bey the Moor, Blante Dante). Born Dante Terrell Smith in Brooklyn, New York, the rapper, actor, entrepreneur, and activist has had an astonishingly eclectic career: from founding (with Talib Kweli) the influential rap duo Black Star (named for the shipping line established by Marcus Garvey to facilitate African American migration to Liberia); to playing Ford Prefect, the quirky but amiable alien field researcher "from a small planet somewhere in the vicinity of Betelgeuse" in the 2005 film adaptation of *The Hitchhiker's Guide to the Galaxy;* to proclaiming his retirement at age forty-three (on Kanye West's website), only to open the Compound, an art gallery in the South Bronx, which mixes fine art exhibitions with hip hop music, and to start a podcast, *The Midnight Miracle,* with Kweli and Dave Chappelle. Bey is also a human rights activist who has been likened, on more than one occasion, to a twenty-first-century Paul Robeson. As if swapping places with Musk, the artist and his young family took up residence in Cape Town, South Africa, in 2013 (not long after retiring the name Mos Def) to enjoy the vibrant art and music scene in the city, but also, like Sun Ra before him, to leave behind the systemic racism and police violence of the United States: "For a guy like me," Bey said in an interview at the time, "who had five or six generations not just in America but in one town in America, to leave America, things gotta be not so good with America."[13]

As a means of protesting the state of the nation, Bey stopped using his US passport shortly after moving to Cape Town. In January 2016, on his way to a music festival in Ethiopia, he attempted to board a flight from South Africa using a so-called World Passport, issued not by any nation-state but by a nonprofit organization in Washington, DC, called the World Service Authority or WSA (an organization founded precisely to pursue the creation of "a world without national borders"). But because South Africa does not acknowledge the World Passport as a valid travel document, Bey was arrested at Cape Town International Airport, taken into custody, and charged with contravening the provisions of the South African Passports and Travel Documents Act No. 4 of 1994 and the Immigration Act No. 13 of 2002. Only six countries formally recognize the World Passport, although dozens, including South Africa, have accepted them and stamped them with visas on at least one occasion. Shortly after his arrest, Bey conceded that "South Africa might call the World Passport fictional," but he went on to assert that nation-states themselves are grounded on nothing more than collective agreement: "Really South Africa is fictional."[14]

In this respect, Bey echoes the thinking of Garry Davis, the devoted peace campaigner behind the World Passport. In 1948, Davis renounced his US citizenship and declared himself a "world citizen," although in doing so he immediately become a man without a country, an alien to all recognized nation-states. Once a budding Broadway star, he had served in the US Army during the Second World War, flying dozens of bombing missions over Germany, including one over Brandenburg that resulted in thousands of civilian deaths. Following the war, Davis gradually became convinced that nationalism was the root cause of its horrors and concluded that the world would be a far better place if it were not divided, more or less arbitrarily, into distinct nations. He would attempt to convert his private fantasy into a shared reality. After surrendering his citizenship at the US embassy on the Place de la Concorde in Paris, Davis claimed sanctuary at the nearby Palais de Chaillot, which had been designated "international territory" during the United Nations General Assembly session just getting underway there. He spent weeks at the palace in a kind of diplomatic limbo, camping out on the grounds and loitering in the official UN restaurant, where he held court with journalists, intellectuals, and other activists. His story soon made headlines around the world, though the idealistic young man was generally dismissed as impossibly naïve, even a bit ridiculous.

Despite his many detractors, Davis garnered the attention of several prominent French intellectuals, including Albert Camus, André Breton, and André Gide (that longtime critic of the passport), who set up the "Garry Davis Council of Solidarity" to support his cause. Convinced that the United Nations was doing nothing to end state sovereignty, members of the new council helped to engineer a protest at the General Assembly meeting on November 19, 1948. During a lull in the proceedings, Davis rushed to the podium and declared, "Mr. Chairman and delegates, I interrupt in the name of the people of the world not represented here.... Pass the world to the people! One government for one world."[15] Before he could say more, security officers appeared and escorted him from the hall.

Davis would soon establish his own idiosyncratic (and mostly ineffectual) counterpart to the United Nations, the World Government of World Citizens and its administrative arm, the World Service Authority, which quickly began to issue "world citizen" documents, including birth certificates, marriage certificates, and, of course, passports. Rather ironically, Davis drew his mandate for the travel documents from the Universal Declaration of Human Rights (article 13.2), adopted by UN General Assembly Resolution 217A (III) of December 10, 1948: "Everyone has the right to leave any country, including one's own, and to return to one's country." Hannah Arendt would point out the paradox that the declaration required nation-states to protect the "universal" rights of human beings, even as nation-states continued to affirm their own legal and territorial sovereignty. By creating the World Passport, Davis sought a way beyond this paradox. By 2020, the WSA could claim that there were some 750,000 World Passport holders around the globe, many of them refugees and stateless people lacking official travel documents from recognized nation-states. Although some of these passport holders have managed to cross borders or prove their identity using the documents, the function of the World Passport remains largely symbolic: to remind us of the fictional status of nation-states and the borders they rely upon. The documents assert that all human beings belong to a single family, which has been divided up by man-made boundaries and historical circumstances; moreover, they affirm, even if they cannot guarantee, the sacred and inalienable rights of man, separate and distinct from the rights of the citizens of nation-states.

This emblematic quality has been the most meaningful legacy of the World Passport. When asked why Yasiin Bey had chosen to travel from South Africa with such a document, his official representative told *Okay Africa* that the artist-activist "considers himself a world citizen and wanted to use his World Passport in support of the United Nations Declaration of Human Rights." The representative went on to suggest that, in the United States, "various state and local law enforcement bodies have violated the most fundamental human right—that is the right to life of several young, unarmed, black men."[16]

Not long before he moved to Cape Town in 2013, Bey had performed an even more radical protest against human rights violations by the US government: in a short film produced by the nonprofit organization Reprieve, the artist consented to be force-fed through his nose with a rubber tube, the same brutal procedure used against hunger strikers in the Guantanamo Bay detention camp. Reminiscent of scenes in both *The Man Who Fell to Earth* and *Space Is the Place,* the graphic video simulates the experience of detainees reduced to the status of bare life, nothing more than corporeal being, deprived of their rights and subject to the violence of a sovereign power. In this way, it served to raise awareness of the previously secret practice, which the UN Human Rights Commission later identified as a form of state-sponsored torture; indeed, the film can be viewed as drawing attention to many of the same ethical and political concerns about the nation-state embodied in the World Passport. In another short video, filmed just prior to his arrest in South Africa and later included in a documentary on the life of Garry Davis, Bey sums up his motivation for acquiring the document: "My country is called earth. This whole thing belongs to everyone who's on it. And if there's anything I can do with my career, it's to hopefully encourage the generations around me and after me to have that worldview."[17]

Predictably, South African authorities did not share this vision: a court ruled that, "for violating local immigration laws," Bey had fourteen days to leave the country—and he would no longer be allowed the same visa-free travel to South Africa that US passport holders enjoy.

• • •

This is the type of treatment that "world citizens," whatever their cosmopolitan aspirations or human rights commitments, and other holders of fantasy travel documents have come to expect from nation-states around the globe. Not long before he passed away in 2013, Garry Davis sent World Passports to two well-known fugitives who had been rendered effectively stateless by their antistatist activism: Australian Wikileaks founder Julian Assange and American NSA whistleblower Edward Snowden. (Rather incongruously, a World Passport has also reportedly been issued to former US president Barack Obama.) At the time the documents were processed, Assange had recently entered the Ecuadorian embassy in central London to seek asylum, while Snowden was stranded in his own diplomatic limbo at Terminal F of the Moscow Sheremetyevo International Airport. Ultimately, the boyish, bespectacled whistleblower was held in a windowless room at the airport for over a month, after Secretary of State John Kerry and the US Department of State revoked his passport. It seems that, at the time of the revocation, Snowden was in midair between Hong Kong and Moscow (although other reports claim that his passport had already been canceled when he was allowed to board his flight by authorities in Hong Kong) as he sought to flee capture via Havana, Cuba, and Caracas, Venezuela, en route to Quito, Ecuador, where he expected to receive political asylum. Davis, in one of his final public acts, released a statement on the Snowden affair: "This unprecedented situation reveals dramatically the power of one individual versus the nation-state system, while highlighting individual sovereignty. The fact that Snowden is immobilized in a Moscow Airport Transit Lounge further exposes the fiction of nation-state frontiers."[18] The efforts to bring the whistleblower to justice had led his own government to effectively cancel the protections of his citizenship and imprison him in a foreign country with no means of escape.

In his own statement issued on July 1, 2013, Snowden claimed that "although I am convicted of nothing, [the US government] has unilaterally revoked my passport, leaving me a stateless person. Without any judicial order, the administration now seeks to stop me exercising a basic right. A right that belongs to everybody. The right to seek asylum."[19] The World Passport would not help him in these circumstances, abandoned as he was by the legal protections of the nation-state; in fact, neither Assange nor Snowden tried to put the document to use, although Assange did attempt, unsuccessfully, to help Snowden escape Russia for Ecuador. The WSA would later report that they had issued "more than 10,000 free World Passports to refugees residing in camps throughout the world," though the vast majority of those documents have proven useless.[20] Meanwhile, the US Department of State's *Foreign Affairs Manual* has singled out the documents for special attention: "World Service Authority Passports are *not* acceptable as 'passports' for visa issuing purposes. The World Service Authority is a private organization and not a 'competent authority' . . . The document is a 40-page, passport-size document with a bright blue cover with gold lettering."[21]

The World Passport is also found on the "Non-Exhaustive List of Known Fantasy and Camouflage Passports," published by the European Union (EU) and based on information received from its member states. Generally speaking, the list contains documents "to which a visa may not be affixed," while it defines fantasy passports specifically as "'passports' issued by minorities, sects, and population groups and identity documents, etc., issued by private organizations and individuals."[22] The documents can be viewed as so many attempts to circumvent the sovereign authority of the nation-state (and its interstate collectives), although their presence on this list (and their status as exceptions) provides a basis on which to frame that authority. They are incorporated into the juridical order of the EU precisely via their incommensurability with EU law. In addition to the World Passport and the NSK State passport, the EU list includes more than one hundred different travel documents that have this function in common, such as passports from the Association d'entraide humanitaire internationale, Byzantine Empire, Confederate States of America, Hare Krishna Sect, Hawaiian Kingdom, Principality of Sealand, and Republic of San Cristóbal, as well as a so-called Planetary Passport from Canada.

The EU list of "fantasy" passports also includes a number of documents that make strong claims to legitimacy in the international community, such as the "Aboriginal Nation[s] Passport" and the "Ha[u] denosaunee (Native American passports)." In 1987, Tasmanian lawyer and activist Michael Mansell began issuing Aboriginal passports as an alternative to Australian passports and a prelude to the founding of the Aboriginal Provisional Government (APG) in 1990. The passports were first used for international travel in March 1988, when Mansell and an Aboriginal delegation traveled to Libya at the invitation of Colonel Muammar Gaddafi, who recognized the documents in the wake of convening a Conference on Peace and Revolution in the Pacific the previous year. Yet when members of the delegation returned to Australia, immigration authorities refused to stamp their Aboriginal passports and barred their reentry until Australian documents were produced. In the decades since this trial run, the APG has continued to offer passports to any Aboriginal person "who provides all of the necessary documentation and details," despite the fact that they can expect "some form of harassment from officials" whenever they pass through Australian customs.[23]

The documents have nonetheless taken on heightened significance in recent years. Aboriginal activist groups, such as the Indigenous Social Justice Association (ISJA), have presented symbolic Aboriginal passports to asylum seekers and other non-Aboriginals "arriving in Australia without state authorization . . . as an act of welcome and solidarity across different forms of state exclusion." In September 2012, for instance, the association held a brief ceremony on the land of the Gadigal and Wangal people of the Eora Nation (in what is now known as Sydney, New South

Wales) to present an Aboriginal passport to Julian Assange, who had only just sought political asylum at the Ecuadorian embassy in London (his father, John Shipton, accepted the document in his place). In a coauthored statement, the ISJA in association with the WikiLeaks Coalition and Support Assange, asserted that the gesture was in response to "the total lack of support by our Federal Government to assist Julian . . . for informing the world's people of the absolute lies that all governments continue to tell their people." The presentation of the passport by the ISJA acknowledged that Assange's Australian passport had been "completely worthless to him" during his search for asylum, even as their gesture demanded that Australian officials recognize the Aboriginal passport.[24]

Documents like the Aboriginal passport have become a means for indigenous peoples around the world to assert their sovereignty and reject the territorial and jurisdictional claims of settler colonial states. At the same time, as Australian legal scholar Sarah Dehm has pointed out, the documents have provided an opportunity for indigenous nations to circumvent the efforts of these states to monopolize the "legitimate means of movement" in the modern world.[25] For instance, Aboriginal activist Callum Clayton-Dixon has asserted the right of his people to use the Aboriginal Nations passport, instead of an Australian passport (which he has called "a foreign and colonial travel document"), as "an act of Aboriginal sovereignty."[26] The APG has since formalized this stance on its website:

> The Aboriginal passport is a document issued by the APG as part of its policy of acting sovereignty. The act of presenting an Aboriginal passport on arriving in other countries and when re-entering Australia shows you are committed to the principle that the Aboriginal nation is separate from the Australian nation. Aboriginal people have inherent independent rights, including having a separate passport.[27]

Again, the United Nations is cited as the authority on the matter, in its affirmation of "the fundamental importance of the right to self-determination of all peoples, by virtue of which they freely determine their political status and freely pursue their economic, social and cultural development."[28] This status should be understood in the context of a history that had long denied citizenship to indigenous peoples in both the United States (until 1924) and Australia (until 1971) and continued to deny them the franchise even after granting citizenship.

The colonial settler project (of those original immigrants) in both the United States and Australia works to make the indigenous "alien" and the settler "native," insofar as the settler and the settler state become "naturalized." Even as the project struggles to incorporate indigenous peoples within its territorial and jurisdictional claims, it nonetheless continues to assert that these peoples exist within the boundaries of the sovereign settler state. US-based scholar and theorist Mark Rifkin has likened this situation to the state of exception defined by Agamben: in this regard, the sovereignty of the settler state is dependent on the presence of indigenous peoples, since the state is founded precisely on the basis of what is excluded at its threshold. Indigenous peoples, in other words, are "incorporated via their incommensurability," insofar as the settler state can invoke its sovereignty to cast them as exceptional, aberrant, alien in relation to the "normal" operation of its political order.[29] In contrast, indigenous sovereignty projects reassert the inherent authority of native peoples to govern themselves within the borders of modern nation-states: they thus disrupt "the tradition of Westphalian territorial sovereignty, imagining a single sovereign absolutely controlling a defined territory and its associated population, rather than conceptualizing ambiguous spaces, neither entirely foreign nor domestic."[30] Indigenous sovereignty therefore entails the full right and authority of indigenous groups to govern themselves, to enact legislation, and to establish law enforcement systems, although the extension of that authority to the issuance of passports has been denied consistently by other nation-states.

Like the Aboriginal passport, the Haudenosaunee passport provides both a form of identification and a means to underscore the sovereignty of indigenous peoples, in this case the Six Nations Haudenosaunee, also known as the Iroquois Confederacy (composed of Mohawks, Oneidas,

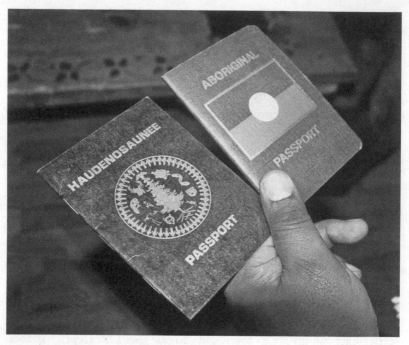

FIGURE 16. Haudenosaunee and Aboriginal passports coming together in Canada, 2014. Image courtesy of Callum Clayton-Dixon.

Onondagas, Cayugas, Senecas, and Tuscaroras), among the original inhabitants of what is now known as North America. The Haudenosaunee government began issuing passports in 1923—just before the recognition of citizenship for indigenous peoples in the United States—so that one of its statesmen, Deskaheh (also known as Levi General), could travel to Geneva and advocate for the acknowledgment of indigenous sovereignty at the League of Nations headquarters. In 2014, Clayton-Dixon and a delegation from the APG traveled to Canada on their Aboriginal Nations passports to meet with representatives of the Iroquois Confederacy—and to have their travel documents stamped by the chiefs of the indigenous alliance. The Aboriginal delegation was briefly detained by immigration officials as they entered Canada and then again when they returned to Australia, until their Australian citizenship was independently verified and they were allowed to proceed. Although the members of the APG reject their Australian citizenship and refused to present other forms of identification, the Australian government created a loophole to allow them to use their Aboriginal passports to reenter the country. Nonetheless, the delegation was "very proud" to have their Aboriginal Nations passports recognized by the Iroquois Confederacy.

Meanwhile, as we have noted, the Haudenosaunee passport has been dismissed as a "fantasy passport" by the European Union, as well as by the settler states that have appropriated much of the territory the Six Nations tribes once inhabited. Tribal leaders, including Tadodaho Sid Hill, chief of the Onondaga Nation, have insisted that their passport holders should enjoy "the full rights extended by the rules of international law and diplomacy" to the citizens of "a sovereign nation recognized by the United States under the 1794 Treaty of Canandaigua signed by George Washington" himself. Citizens of the Six Nations do not view the acceptance of American or Canadian passports as an option, since their people belonged to their tribal nation for millennia before the arrival of European settlers.

These conflicting views reached a crisis point in July 2010, when the Iroquois Nationals lacrosse team attempted to travel on their Haudenosaunee passports to the World Lacrosse Championships in Manchester, England. Traveling on the passports was significant not only as an assertion of national sovereignty, but also as a means to confirm the eligibility of the twenty-three team members, who would play what they consider "the Creator's game" (lacrosse originated among Native American communities as early as 1100) in the jersey of the Iroquois Nationals. With their first game of the tournament approaching, the players, coaches, and their manager, Ansley Jemison, were prevented from boarding a flight at JFK airport, precipitating a diplomatic standoff. With the team stranded at a nearby Hilton hotel, tribal leaders urgently tried to reach an agreement with the US State Department and to secure entry visas from the United Kingdom. As the standoff continued, the team was forced to forfeit its first game, though Secretary of State Hillary Clinton eventually granted a one-time waiver authorizing their departure and guaranteeing their ability to reenter the United States. Regrettably, UK authorities continued to withhold the requisite visas until it was too late for the team to participate in the tournament at all. As Hill later said, "we were barred from the championship of a game we invented and which is central to our culture." He also pointed out the absurdity of the official actions in both the United States and the United Kingdom, "since this issue began when Europeans arrived five centuries ago and seized our lands in the first place."[31]

To emphasize the sovereign status of indigenous nations, when the World Indoor Lacrosse Championships were held on the lands of the Iroquois Confederacy (the Onondaga Reservation near Syracuse, New York) in September 2015, tribal representatives stamped the passports of players and coaches from visiting nations—including the United States and the United Kingdom—with Haudenosaunee entry visas.

Good Passports Bad Passports

Let's get to know each other	*Lernen wir uns kennen.*
"Yes" is on the left-hand side,	*"Ja" ist auf der linken Seite, "Nein"*
"No" is on the right-hand side	*ist auf der rechten Seite.*
I speak German	*Ich spreche Deutsch.*
I am a resident of this country	*Ich bin Inländer.*
I have a credit card	*Ich habe eine Kreditkarte.*
I love my home country	*Ich liebe miene Heimat.*

AND SO ON. Thus intones a disembodied male voice at the beginning of Helena Waldmann's 2017 dance production *Good Passports Bad Passports: A Borderline Experience* (*Gute Pässe Schlechte Pässe*). As the statements continue, a group of about thirty black-clad figures, male and female, assembles on the dimly lit stage and then begins to separate into opposing camps according to that decisive command—"'Yes' is on the left-hand side, 'No' is on the right-hand side."[1] Occasionally, one of the figures seems to change her mind and scurries across the stage, as if she is confused by the statements or worried she might be caught in a lie. This sorting process is interrupted only when a male figure emerges from each group and steps forward—one downstage left, the other downstage right—to perform a series of movements, which they announce one by one in their native tongues. The figure on the left speaks in German and performs impressive acrobatics in the manner of *nouveau cirque*; the figure on the right speaks in English and performs graceful movements in the style of contemporary dance, which seem choreographed to derisively mimic his counterpart. Soon each figure is joined by other performers from his side of the stage to form two rival groups: three acrobats and four dancers. As the performance continues, the movements of the groups suggest encounters between different, often antagonistic, national cultures, including a sequence in which the dancers aggressively defend a line taped down the center of the stage from any trespass by the acrobats—even as the acrobats welcome the dancers to their side of the boundary. The small groups continually disperse and reform across the stage in a series of dramatic scenes, repeatedly evoking frontier crossings, border patrols, passport checks, and other aspects of the global migrant crisis. Eventually, after a particularly fraught encounter between a dancer and an acrobat, the rest of the cast (local volunteers from a variety of ethnic communities) reemerge from the wings and interlink arms to form a wall of bodies dividing the adversarial groups from one another. But when both groups start to push on the human barrier, it begins to rotate slowly around the center of the stage, gradually accelerating, as the performers lift their voices in a dissonant cry, until the centrifugal force disperses them across the entire performance space and they all fall silent.

Waldmann describes her inspiration for the piece as the simple recognition that "good" passports provide their holders a freedom of movement that is denied to those who possess "bad" passports. Traveling with dancers and show crews from various parts of the world, she has frequently witnessed those with "bad" passports being delayed and subjected to intense questioning, while Waldmann, with her "good" German passport, was able to navigate the customs and immigration process with ease and expediency. Of course, she is not alone in such observations. In *Step across This Line,* for instance, Salman Rushdie describes a day spent at the immigration area of Heathrow airport, watching how passengers were treated by passport control officers: the one factor that seemed to make all the difference was the possession of a US passport, which enabled travelers to move quickly on their way, regardless of their ethnic features or presumed associations. He concludes that for "those to whom the world is closed, such openness is greatly to be desired. Those who assume that openness to be theirs by right perhaps value it less." *Good Passports Bad Passports* provides a highly charged recognition of this basic duality.

FIGURE 17 The wall of bodies in *Good Passports Bad Passports* (*Gute Pässe Schlechte Pässe,* 2017) stands behind dancer Lysandre Coutu-Sauvé, holding a passport. Photo by Wonge Bergmann. Image courtesy of Helena Waldmann.

In doing so, the dance production evokes the mounting importance of passport indexes, such as the one compiled by Henley & Partners (the self-described "Firm of Global Citizens"), which ranks travel documents "according to the number of destinations their holders can access without a prior visa."[2] In 2017, the Henley Passport Index ranked Germany at the top of its list (followed closely by Sweden, Denmark, Finland, Italy, Spain, and the United States), with the capability to travel to 176 nations visa-free, while Afghanistan could be found at the bottom (just behind Somalia, Syria, Pakistan, and Iraq), with just twenty-four nations opening their borders to its passport holders without a visa. An Afghan or Somali passport may assert both the personal and national identities of its holder, but it collapses them in a way that essentially imprisons the individual within her nation of origin. In effect, the list codifies the very sentiments that Rushdie expresses at the beginning of his book: that while his British passport has "done its stuff efficiently and unobtrusively," the Indian passport he held as a boy in the 1950s was "a paltry thing." "Instead of offering the bearer a general open-sesame to anywhere in the world, it stated in grouchy bureaucratic language that it was only valid for travel to a specified—and distressingly short—list of countries."[3] The "bad" passport decrees that its holder will be waylaid, interrogated, possibly detained or turned back at airport checkpoints and border controls around the globe. If a "good" passport, under the current regime, is the key to unlocking the doors of international travel, providing freedom of movement and unfettered opportunity, then a "bad" passport locks away its holder, as the inmate of an "undesirable" national community, unwelcome in most of the wider world.

Good Passports Bad Passports ends by offering the image of a future beyond its titular dichotomy. When the statements of the spectral voice resume at the conclusion of the production, a new option is posed: "I believe that one day national borders won't exist / *Ich glaube, dass es irgendwann keine Landesgrenzen mehr geben wird.*" With this prompt, the entire cast steps to the front of the stage and, for the first time, performs a gesture of unanimity as they interlock arms and gaze out into the audience. It is an arresting tableau. At the same time, however, the production has provided a visceral reminder to its spectators in Stuttgart, Bolzano, Beirut, Tel Aviv, and elsewhere that, for now, "good" passports provide bodies with security, mobility, opportunity, which is denied to the bodies of persons just as deserving as those with superior travel documents. It serves notice of the differential value of passports, often ignored by those who enjoy documents with significant economic and political value, even as it is sensed acutely by those who face overwhelming obstacles to travel and migration based on nothing more than their citizenship or country of origin. Even so, as the line of multi-ethnic, multigenerational bodies forms at the front of the stage, coming together in the semblance of a single global community, we also glimpse the possibility of a borderless world, where our current international system of separation, obstruction, and detention no longer holds. We see a sign, if only momentarily, of what Rushdie calls the "post-frontier," which might just help us to imagine a new age of unrestricted movement.

Yet the vision of a world without borders may be far too utopian to expect in our geopolitical reality anytime soon. For the time being, the passport remains (and becomes continuously more) an object with immense political, personal, and financial significance, one that has created a global hierarchy of haves and have-nots, all subject to the little book that is presented at border crossings and airport checkpoints. More than ever, the rights we enjoy depend not just on the fact of our citizenship or our possession of a passport, but on the color of the passport, the seal on the cover, and the status of the issuing country in the international community. Our passport defines who we are in the geopolitical order, where we can travel, reside, work, and on and on. At present, there is little international effort dedicated to increasing hospitality across the sovereign nation-state system or seeking practical means to collapse the inequities in the international passport regime. The United Nations might proclaim that "everyone has the right to leave any country, including one's own, and to return to one's country," but the fact of the matter is that not all passports are created equal or treated with equal respect.[4]

It should not come as a surprise that, in such circumstances, a market for second passports has emerged and grown almost exponentially in the twenty-first century, as passport holders seek to enhance their status in the international system. Henley & Partners, along with other firms such as Sovereign Man and Nomad Capitalist, have emerged to advise their clients, usually high-net-worth businesspeople and investors looking for new prospects and tax breaks, on the various means to attain a new citizenship and a second passport. These methods include, of course, citizenship by ancestry and by naturalization, but also by investment, sometimes without ever having to step foot in the issuing country. For the price of a property purchase (starting at about $250,000) and/or a government fee (starting at about $25,000), depending on just how "good" the document is, individuals can acquire passports from small nations such St. Kitts and Nevis, Dominica, Cyprus, Vanuatu, and Comoros. There are significant financial barriers, then, to the attainment of "global citizenship," just as there is obvious clout associated with the phrase "I possess two different passports / *Ich besitze zwei verschiedene Pässe.*" The precious books promise investors more political stability, or perhaps enhanced opportunity, though, as might be expected, these programs have often met with charges of corruption.

．　．　．

At border crossings and airport checkpoints, as we have observed, even a "good" passport is often dependent on its relation to a body and a name, which are subject to the same kinds of judgment and categorization that are directed at the document. Sarah Ahmed, whose scholarship is positioned at the intersection of feminist, queer, and race studies, has written incisively about what she calls the "politics of mobility"—that is, the "politics" of who has the ability to move without difficulty across frontiers, of "who gets to be at home and who gets to extend their bodies into inhabitable spaces."[5] She starts with the observation that some bodies are "stopped" more than others, subjected more often to interrogation by agents of the state, including policemen, border guards, customs officials: "Who are you? Why are you here? What are you doing?"[6] These questions, the familiar mode of interrogation associated with conditional hospitality and state sovereignty, are directed most insistently at bodies determined to be "suspicious" or "out of place" by virtue of skin color or surname, suggesting a "wrong" (or "bad") ethnic lineage, a "wrong" (or "bad") national affiliation. These interrogations, that is, are directed at bodies that cannot be interpolated within the ideological coordinates of the nation-state as belonging to citizens who recognize and enjoy that status. Instead, they subject bodies to stasis: these interrogations deny them freedom of movement and simultaneously indicate that they do not belong within the space of the nation-state. Moreover, the questions leave their mark on these bodies, transforming them into sites of intense social stress and official scrutiny in the process of being "stopped."

Ahmed exemplifies this phenomenon with a story from her own experience at a US Customs and Immigration checkpoint not long after the September 11 terror attack:

I arrive in New York, clutching my British passport. I hand it over. The airport official looks at me, and then looks at my passport. I know what questions will follow. "Where are you from?" My passport indicates my place of birth. "Britain," I say. I feel like adding, "Can't you read. I was born in Salford," but I stop myself. He looks down at my passport, not at me. "Where is your father from?" It was the same last time I arrived in New York. It is the question I get asked now, which seems to locate what is suspect not in my body but as that which has been passed down the family line, almost like a bad inheritance. "Pakistan," I say, slowly. He asks, "Do you have a Pakistani passport?" "No," I say. Eventually, he lets me through. The name "Ahmed," a Muslim name, slows me down. It blocks my passage, even if only temporarily. I get stuck, and then move on.[7]

This is not, as Ahmed emphasizes, an isolated incident in her experience. Her name and her skin, these twin legacies from her father, repeatedly elicit this kind of interrogation (even though she has a "good" passport) precisely because they connect Ahmed with her Pakistani heritage (and its association with a "bad" passport). These personal birthrights have become, in a word, politicized. When she flies out of New York a week later, she learns that her name has been added to the "no fly" list and she must again stop until the situation can be rectified by a Transportation Security Administration (TSA) supervisor: "to inherit a Muslim name in the West," she writes, "is to inherit the impossibility of a body that can 'trail behind,' or even to inherit the impossibility of extending the body's reach." To be recognized as Muslim, or even potentially Muslim, by virtue of her name and her body is to be subjected to a certain discomfort in these spaces, where she must be constantly on guard against new infringements on her "rights of passage."

Like Waldmann, Ahmed recognizes a simple reality: that passports allow "some bodies" to flow easily across borders, but that they do not work this way for everyone. For Ahmed, however, this is not just a matter of "good" passports and "bad" passports: "having the 'right' passport makes no difference if you have the wrong body or name: and, indeed, the stranger with the 'right' passport might cause particular trouble as the one who risks passing through, or passing by." To be sure, contrary to what Rushdie observes, Ahmed suggests that a perceived schism between a "good" passport and a "suspicious" body can produce new forms of strain and stress: "If the nationality of the passport does not seem to follow the line of the name, and such judgments exercise histories of normative thinking, then the body is suspect." Suspicious bodies generate questions: "Where are you from? Where are your parents from?"[8] And on and on. Her experience of being "stopped" in this manner, then, is not only a question of being waylaid or inconvenienced. Instead, being stopped reorients the attention of the passport holder back to herself, as her body does not just "come along" with her, but rather draws the wrong kind of attention from the officials of the state. "Some bodies" are recognized as belonging to strangers, aliens, while "some bodies" are recognized as being "at home," so that their passports enhance or extend their mobility—and simultaneously enhance their social mobility, their access to opportunity, to safe haven.

Nation-states show no sign of letting go of the passport as a means of identification and movement control to support their claims to sovereignty. Instead, with the implementation of new technologies and design features, the passport has only become more prominent in its role of defining what bodies are "at home" and what bodies are "out of place" in the age of Brexit, Trumpism, and other populisms. When a new British passport design was presented at London's Globe Theatre in 2015, it contained images of cultural icons such as William Shakespeare, John Constable, and Ada Lovelace; of technical advancements such as the London Underground and the Penny Black stamp; and of cultural landmarks including the Houses of Parliament, the London Eye, and Edinburgh Castle. Perhaps incongruously, in an apparent concession to the idea of a multicultural Britain, the document also displayed images of several major works by the renowned Bombay-born British sculptor Anish Kapoor (but we might note that while the face of Shakespeare can be found throughout the passport, it is only the abstract sculptures of Kapoor, and not his bodily presence, that are seen in its pages). This new passport, designed to celebrate the "Creative United Kingdom" of Great

Britain and Northern Ireland over the past five centuries, also boasted the latest technologies for preventing forgery, making it one of the most secure documents in the world, according to UK minister for immigration James Brokenshire.

It was not long until the design of the British passport became a talking point in the political hurly-burly around the Brexit referendum: in August 2016, soon-to-be Brexit Party leader Nigel Farage took to social media to demand, "We want our passports back."[9] For Farage, this meant removing the words *European Union* from the cover of the British travel document as a symbol of "taking back" his country, his nationality, and his vision of Britain, while closing the door to what he deemed to be undesirable immigration from other parts of the EU. Here, then, was a crucial emblem of national sovereignty for the Brexit backer and his followers. In August 2019, Farage used social media again to post a picture of himself smiling smugly and holding his new "EU-free" passport, which reads simply, "United Kingdom of Great Britain and Northern Ireland" on the cover. He captioned the photo, "We got our passports back!"[10] In March 2020, continuing to shed all signs of the EU from its passport, the United Kingdom began phasing out the burgundy covers that had been used for the European version since 1988 and phasing in navy blue covers in a return to the "original" color for the British passport, first used in 1921 (though, rather ironically, the new passports are manufactured by the Dutch company Gemalto at their printing plant in Tczew, Poland). As if to double down on the symbolic import of the document, the new British passport will carry national emblems not just on its front cover, but also on the back, which has been embossed with the national flowers (and, well, one shamrock) of England, Scotland, Wales, and Northern Ireland. At the same time, the new design has dropped the images of Kapoor's art from its stamping pages.

These design changes may have pleased those, like Farage, who shout, "Make Britain great again!" and "We want our country back!," though the blue EU-free passport holders would likely be chagrined to learn that their travel documents are no longer as "good" as those of many of their EU neighbors. The 2020 Global Passport Power Ranking, based on the "total mobility score" of visa-free and visa-on-arrival destinations, places passports from Germany, Sweden, Finland, Luxembourg, Spain, Denmark, Portugal, Austria, Italy, Norway, Switzerland, and—perhaps most painfully for the British—Ireland, with their "European Union"–embossed covers, all ahead of that from the United Kingdom.[11] This situation is not likely to improve as more and more countries require UK passport holders to obtain visas to travel across their borders and as opportunities for the British to study, work, and retire in the Schengen Area continue to diminish. This is not to say that, given the relative economic might of the United Kingdom, its passports will suddenly become "bad." Rather, it is a reminder that the hubris of nationalism is often in the service of a deeper insecurity and that sometimes it acts as a direct threat to the mobility and security of its citizens in the global system. It is also a reminder that the history of the passport is still unfolding, though not necessarily in a linear or teleological way that would result in a definitive list of winners and losers.

This is perhaps nowhere more evident than in the story of the Muslim Travel Ban and the US passport. In January 2017, as we noted in the previous chapter, President Trump signed Executive Order 13769, titled "Protecting the Nation from Foreign Terrorist Entry into the United States." In doing so, he asserted that citizens from six predominantly Muslim nations—Libya, Syria, Iran, Somalia, Yemen, and Sudan—who did not have a "bona fide" connection or "close familial relationship" to individuals in the United States would not be allowed to cross into the national territory. Here was a naked assertion of sovereign power, as the president claimed the authority to determine how and to whom the law applies: with a flourish of his Sharpie he summarily rendered certain passports "bad." Just how arbitrary this assertion of sovereign power was can be gleaned from the fact that no one from any of the countries named in the executive order had been linked to a terrorist act in the United States since 2001. Meanwhile, countries that had been the source of terrorists were not listed in the order. Capricious enforcement of the ban led to the separation of families, the abandonment of longtime US residents in foreign countries, and the stranding of travelers in airport terminals around the world. Suddenly, the national seal on their passports could leave them cast out, removed, stopped; abruptly, the rights of these citizens from elsewhere were suspended as if their lives were devoid of legal, political, or even human value.

Those who devise such bans would do well to remember that the narrative is always subject to change—that in the history of our geopolitical arrangements what goes around is always bound to come around. On the last day of January 2020, the United States declared a state of public emergency in response to the spread of the Covid-19 virus and simultaneously banned foreign nationals, other than immediate family of US citizens, from entering the country within fourteen days of being in China. Although most studies agreed that travel restrictions might slow, but could do little to contain, the spread of the virus, additional travel bans were soon implemented: On March 2, the government extended the ban to those who had been in Iran, and then, on March 13, to those who had been in any country within the Schengen Area in the previous fourteen days. The clumsy rollout of the European ban, which did not clarify the exemption of US citizens or those traveling from the UK and Ireland, resulted in chaotic scenes with thousands of travelers crammed together in airport terminals across the United States and Europe. Soon, however, the ineffective response of the Trump administration to the spread of the virus led the European Union to drop the United States from its list of countries whose tourists were welcome. In July 2020, the Henley Passport Index captured this dramatic loss of prestige in an updated ranking, which indicated that US passport holders now had access to just 158 countries, down twenty-seven from January; in fact, the US passport had fallen to a rank of twenty-fifth in the index, a precipitous drop from 2012, when the document topped the list.

Media outlets across the globe were quick to report that the US passport was now virtually, if only temporarily, equivalent to the Mexican passport in terms of the freedom of movement afforded its holders: "We see an emergence of a new global hierarchy in terms of mobility,"

Christian Kaelin, chairman of Henley & Partners, said, "with countries that have effectively managed the pandemic taking the lead, and countries that have handled it poorly falling behind."[12] The pandemic vividly demonstrated to US passport holders and their government, perhaps far too late, that the right to leave one's country, to travel freely, and to return unobstructed does not accrue to us as human beings, but rather as citizens of particular nation-states—and those rights may be revoked at a moment's notice.

. . .

Responding to both the discriminatory practices of border crossing and the human consequences of being "stopped," the Maltese poet Antoine Cassar has created a combined protest poem, art book, and performance project called *Passaport* (2009). Printed in a small format and bound in a red cardboard cover that mimics the Maltese passport, the book was originally published in Maltese; subsequently, it has been reprinted in a series of multilingual editions (English, Spanish, Slovenian, Croatian— twelve languages in all), each bound in one of three colors ("ocean blue, dried blood red, and coal black" like passports from around the world) and embossed with the image of a migratory swan circling the globe. Rather than enclosing a photograph, personal data, and the legalese of the nation-state, *Passaport* contains approximately 250 lines of verse that proclaim dissent from the wounding force of the international passport system and its often-brutal forms of exclusion and expulsion. Addressed directly to the holder of the little book, the poem begins by acknowledging the physical presence of both the passport and the passport holder:

> Yours, old or new friend, of the heart and of the skin,
> who grasped me with both hands, strong and caressing, and welcomed
> me with a warm and open face, . . .[13]

This is a document that promises the possibility of mobility for all bodies, regardless of national origin or skin color, in a kind of utopian reverie, imagining a world without the stress of border crossing or the fear of being "stopped." Instead of prompting interrogations, that is, *Passaport* offers reassurances:

> you can enter and leave without fear, there is no one to stop you,
> no one to jump in the queue, or send you to the back, there's no need
>   to wait,
> no one to say *Ihre Papiere bitte!*, quickening your heartbeat with the
>   pallour of his finger,
> no one to squint or glare at you according to the gross domestic product
>   per capita of the nation you've left behind,
> no one to brand you stranger, alien, criminal, illegal immigrant, or *extra-
>   communautaire,* nobody is extra...[14]

Here is a document that cannot be denied, cannot be turned against its holder, cannot be used to label her "suspicious" or "out of place":

> yours
> this passport
> for all peoples, and for all landscapes,
> take it where you will, there is no need for a stamp or visa,
> you can leave or stay as you please, it does not expire,
> you can renounce it, it is not the property of the government, duke or
>   queen, you may even have several...[15]

Passaport, then, is more properly understood as a kind of "anti-passport," a document that imagines a world where passports will no longer be labeled "good" or "bad," ushering some bodies along while waylaying others. It is a radically utopian object that, in the guise of a travel document, dispatches all the assumptions—about nations, about borders, about aliens, immigrants, and others—that have been attached to our passports. It is a document that, as Cassar puts it, imagines "a world without customs and checkpoints, without border police out to snatch away the dawn, without the need for forms, documents, or biometric data ... A world without the need to cross the desert barefoot, nor to float off on a raft, on an itinerary of hope all too quickly struck out by

FIGURE 18. Antoine Cassar reading *Passaport* in Singapore, 2016. Photo by John Gresham. Image courtesy of Antoine Cassar.

the realities of blackmail and exploitation."[16] It is, in other words, a precious object that helps us to envision the "post-frontier."

The poet, who grew up between England, Malta, and Spain and subsequently studied and worked in several other countries across Europe, has traveled the world performing the poem to spread his vision. At festivals and conferences on four continents, he has invited his audience to bring their "real" passports to his performances and then to symbolically "renounce" their national identities during the reading. Cassar has also committed to donating the proceeds from sales of the little book to grassroots organizations that support universal freedom of movement and assist refugees in fourteen different countries.

What does *Passaport* suggest about the possible futures of the passport? How can such a utopian document help us to reconceive the functions of our actual documents? What does the limitless hospitality postulated by Cassar suggest about the interests and potentials of a geopolitics-to-come? As we have seen, passports, in one form or another, have been with us for more than three millennia, although in their most recent manifestation—the one that has served to reinforce borders, bans, and the sovereignty of the nation-state—they are an eminently modern phenomenon. The passport, then, for all its promise of mobility, escape, and freedom has served as a reminder that human beings, in all our vulnerability, are subject to the current status of our paperwork far more than to the basic fact of our humanity.

Recent developments betray no signs that this historical trend will soon abate. In addition to its blue cover and national emblems, the new British passport has introduced a series of technical advancements to ensure the security of the document, most notably a laser-engraved polycarbonate biodata page with an embedded radio-frequency identification chip, which duplicates the biodata to prevent forgery. The passport thus becomes an ever more invasive, definitive, all-but-indestructible document of our identities. Meanwhile, the passport inspection ritual has been "enhanced" with the use of fingerprint, iris, and even facial scanning. Nation-states from Canada to Japan, the Netherlands to Australia, have begun to collect more data from not just their own citizens but also international travelers passing through their airports. Of course, the reasons for the nation-state to use identification documents for security are numerous, but these enhanced procedures also raise myriad concerns about how much data we are comfortable with our governments collecting and how much we want to open ourselves to surveillance. Amid the Covid-19 pandemic, the discussion of health passports with proof of vaccination or negative test results has only exacerbated these concerns. Collectively, these new developments ensure that now, more than ever, we *are* our documents: they tell the world who we are, where we come from, and where we can go—although it is our bodies that must match the document, not the other way around, in order to vouch for our identity and ensure our mobility and protection. It is all rather dystopian.

Looking ahead, some commentators have perceived the recent digital transformations of our travel credentials as a sign that the end of the passport-as-we-know-it is near. They foresee the day when the smart phone will replace the passport book, just as it has progressively replaced other forms of print media, from the boarding passes that allow us through the passenger gate to the books and magazines that we read in flight to the cash we once used to purchase drinks and duty-free items. Those who promote these advancements promise that digitization will improve the security and reliability of identification documents, increase the efficiency of the border control process, and thus upgrade the "passenger experience" at airports and other checkpoints. But most versions of this brave new world also require increased storage and sharing of "passenger-related information." For instance, passengers departing Dubai International Airport can use an app called "Smart UAE Wallet" on their mobile phones (and a scan of their fingerprints) to pass through "smart gates": in the initial phase, the wallet contained their passenger ID, passport details, and smart gate card data, with further plans to link to "all the data of Emiratis and residents."[17] Similar programs have emerged in recent years through both single-state and international initiatives around the world.

Meanwhile, the World Economic Forum (their motto: "Committed to Improving the State of the World") and Accenture PLC (theirs: "To Deliver on the Promise of Technology and Human Ingenuity") have recently collaborated to "enhance security in world travel," with the use of biometric authentication, blockchain technology, and identification databases. The ambitious initiative, called "Known Traveller Digital Identity" (KTDI), promotes itself as "the first end-to-end intervention to streamline the entire travel experience by enhancing the ability of authorities to get the information they need when they need it, so that they can move people swiftly across borders."[18] In an attempt to allay worries about mass data storage or centralized data registers, the KTDI program has emphasized its use of a blockchain-based data-sharing system that would dispense with the need for such archives. One possible model for this system would operate on the so-called "self-sovereign identity concept," allowing travelers to store their personal data on their mobile phones, while the system would hold only the certificates and proof of validity for this data. There is perhaps some solace in this, though the KTDI program, for all its innovation, still retains the basic model of the passport as a document that limits freedom of movement by authenticating personal identity and national affiliation.

Let us be clear: an improved "passenger experience" is not the same thing as unlimited hospitality. *Passport,* as an anti-passport, calls on us to have the courage to question the articles of faith on which the modern passport is founded, including the holy trinity of nation, state, and territory. The anti-passport provokes us to be always alert for ways to be more open and accommodating to the other: it envisions what Derrida calls "pure hospitality," which "consists in welcoming the new arrival before imposing conditions on them, before knowing and asking for anything at all, be it a name or an identity 'paper.'"[19] Such hospitality demands doing everything possible to address the other, to grant them a proper name, while eschewing the conditions of official interrogation, information registration, and direct border control. But the philosopher acknowledges that, if pure hospitality is to be more than a utopian ideal, our desire for it must always exist in relation to the laws of hospitality (the rights and protections of sovereignty that are necessarily conditioned and conditional). The passport-as-we-know-it functions only insofar as the nation-state betrays the principle of pure hospitality in order to protect the homeland against the unrestricted access of the other, but also to protect its guests from the dangers that pursue them to the border. There is no easy way to resolve the tension between these modes of hospitality. In this sense, the passport, whether in paper or digital form, will remain a crucial nexus for our geopolitics, where we negotiate (and perhaps reimagine) the balance between conditional and unconditional hospitality, the rights of the citizen and the rights of man, the continued strength or final decline of state sovereignty—and our own places within these relations.

NOTES

NOTES TO THE INTRODUCTION

1. Salman Rushdie, *Step across This Line* (New York: Modern Library, 2003), 381.

2. Rushdie, *Step across This Line*, 368.

3. Salman Rushdie, *Joseph Anton: A Memoir* (New York: Random House, 2012), 484.

4. Paul Fussell, *Abroad: British Literary Traveling between the Wars* (New York: Oxford University Press, 1980), 24.

5. Fussell, *Abroad*, 30.

6. Fussell, *Abroad*, 30.

7. Ernest Hemingway, *A Farewell to Arms* (London: Penguin, 1929), 210.

8. Hemingway, *Farewell to Arms*, 217.

9. Hemingway, *Farewell to Arms*, 243–44.

10. Graham Greene, *The Confidential Agent* (London: Heinemann, 1939), 13.

11. Greene, *Confidential Agent*, 14.

12. Leo Mellor, "Early Graham Greene," in *The Oxford Handbooks Online* (Oxford: Oxford University Press, 2018), n.p.

13. Rushdie, *Joseph Anton*, 122.

14. *The Terminal*, dir. Steven Spielberg (Amblin Entertainment, 2004).

15. Giorgio Agamben, "No to Biopolitical Tattooing," *Communication and Critical/Cultural Studies* 5, no. 2 (June 2008): 201.

16. *The Terminal*.

17. Salman Rushdie, *The Satanic Verses* (New York: Viking, 1989), 4.

1. "La momie de Ramsès II ne sera pas exposée à Paris," *Le Monde,* May 10, 1976, www.lemonde.fr/archives/article/1976/05/10/la-momie-de-ramses-ii-ne-sera-pas-exposee-a-paris_2942690_1819218.html; translation by author.

2. Boyce Rensberger, "Ramses' Illness Was Fabricated, Scientists Allege," *New York Times,* November 8, 1976, 7, www.nytimes.com/1976/11/08/archives /ramses-illness-was-fabricated-scientists-allege.html.

3. Yvonne Rebeyrol, "La cure de 'rajeunissement' de Ramsès II pour une nouvelle éternité," *Le Monde,* November 22, 1976, www.lemonde.fr/archives /article/1976/11/22/la-cure-de-rajeunissement-de-ramses-ii-pour-une-nouvelle-eternite_3121881_1819218.html; translation by author.

4. "Ramesses II: The First (and Probably the Last) Mummy to Receive a Passport!" *Random Times,* February 5, 2020, https://random-times .com/2020/02/05/ramesses-ii-the-first-and-probably-the-last-mummy-to-receive-a-passport.

5. A. Leo Oppenheim, *Letters from Mesopotamia* (Chicago: University of Chicago Press, 1967), 134.

6. Quoted in Mario Liverani, *International Relations in the Ancient Near East* (London: Palgrave, 2001), 73.

7. See, for instance, Judith Butler, "Performativity's Social Magic," in *Bourdieu: A Critical Reader,* ed. Richard Shusterman (Oxford: Blackwell, 1999), 113–28.

8. Raymond Westbrook, "International Law in the Amarna Age," in *Amarna Diplomacy: The Beginning of International Relations,* ed. Raymond Cohen and Raymond Westbrook (Baltimore: John Hopkins University Press, 2000), 30–31.

9. Pierre Briant, *From Cyrus to Alexander: A History of the Persian Empire,* trans. Peter T. Daniels (Winona Lake, IN: Eisenbrauns, 2002), 1197.

10. Quoted in Briant, *From Cyrus to Alexander,* 364–65.

11. "Read the Sermon Donald Trump Heard before Becoming President," *Time,* January 7, 2017, https://time.com/4641208/donald-trump-robert-jeffress-st-john-episcopal-inauguration/.

12. John H. Kroll and Fordyce W. Mitchel, "Clay Tokens Stamped with the Names of Athenian Military Commanders," *Hesperia: The Journal of the American School of Classical Studies at Athens* 49, no. 1 (1980): 86–96.

13. Roy Harris, "Speech and Writing," in *The Cambridge Handbook of Literacy,* ed. David R. Olson and Nancy Torrance (Cambridge: Cambridge University Press, 2009), 50.

14. T. Corey Brennan and Hsing I-tien, "The Eternal City and the City of Eternal Peace," in *China's Early Empires: A Re-appraisal,* ed. Michael Nylan and Michael Loewe (Cambridge: Cambridge University Press, 2010), 202.

15. John Torpey, *The Invention of the Passport* (Cambridge: Cambridge University Press, 2018), 21.

NOTES TO CHAPTER 2

1. Marco Polo, *The Travels of Marco Polo,* trans. Ronald Latham (New York: Penguin, 1974), 35.

2. Polo, *Travels of Marco Polo,* 44.

3. Polo, *Travels of Marco Polo,* 44–45.

4. Quoted in Hans Ulrich Vogel, *Marco Polo Was in China: New Evidence from Currencies, Salts, and Revenues* (Leiden: Brill, 2013), 85.

5. Mark B. Salter, *Rights of Passage: The Passport in International Relations* (Boulder, CO: Lynne Rienner, 2003), 11.

6. "Conduct," *OED Online,* www.oed.com/viewdictionaryentry /Entry/38617.

7. Thomas Edlyne Tomlins and John Raithby, *The Safe Conducts Acts* 1414: *The Statutes at Large, of England and of Great Britain—From Magna Carta to the Union of the Kingdoms of Great Britain and Ireland* (London: George Eyre and Andrew Strahan, 1811), 2:320–26.

8. "Passport," *OED Online,* www.oed.com/viewdictionaryentry /Entry/138557.

9. See Ernst Hartwig Kantorowicz's landmark study *The King's Two Bodies: A Study in Mediaeval Political Theology* (Princeton: Princeton University Press, 1957), 7–23.

10. John Buxton and Bent Juel-Jensen, "Sir Philip Sidney's First Passport Rediscovered," *The Library,* 5th ser., 25, no. 1 (March 1970): 42.

11. Quoted in Buxton and Juel-Jensen, "Sidney's First Passport," 44.

12. John Buxton, *Sir Philip Sidney and the English Renaissance* (New York: Palgrave, 1988), 73.

13. "Passport," *OED Online.*

14. Laurence Sterne, *A Sentimental Journey* (New York: Penguin, 2002), 67.

15. Jesper Gulddal, "Porous Borders: The Passport as an Access Metaphor in Laurence Sterne's *A Sentimental Journey," Symplokê* 25, nos. 1–2 (2017): 47.

16. Sterne, *Sentimental Journey,* 82.

17. Sterne, *Sentimental Journey,* 85.

18. Quoted in Craig Robertson, *The Passport in America* (Oxford: Oxford University Press, 2012), 27.

19. Quoted in John Torpey, *The Invention of the Passport: Surveillance, Citizenship, and the State,* 2nd ed. (Cambridge: Cambridge University Press, 2018), 36.

20. Giorgio Agamben, "We Refugees," *Symposium: A Quarterly Journal of Modern Literature* 49, no. 2 (1995): 117.

21. Torpey, *Invention of the Passport,* 68.

NOTES TO CHAPTER 3

1. George Gordon Byron, *The Letters of Lord Byron,* ed. Mathilde Blind (London: W. Scott, 1887), 104.

2. George Gordon Byron, *Don Juan,* in *The Works of Lord Byron: Complete in One Volume* (London: J. Murray, 1837), 715 and 730.

3. Jesper Gulddal, "Paper Trails: The Austrian Passport System in Stendhal's *La Chartreuse de Parme,*" *Arcadia* 49, no. 1 (2019): 58–73.

4. Stendhal, *The Charterhouse of Parma,* trans. C. K. Scott Moncrieff (New York: Boni, 1925), 260.

5. Byron, *Letters,* 157.

6. Stendhal, *Charterhouse,* 231.

7. Stendhal, *Charterhouse,* 247.

8. Stendhal, *Charterhouse,* 233.

9. Stendhal, *Charterhouse,* 235.

10. Stendhal, *Charterhouse,* 247.

11. Quoted in Betty T. Bennett, *Mary Diana Dods: A Gentleman and a Scholar* (New York: Morrow, 1991), 80.

12. Bennett, *Mary Diana Dods,* 81.

13. Bennett, *Mary Diana Dods,* 229.

14. Geraldine Friedman, "Pseudonymity, Passing, and Queer Biography: The Case of Mary Diana Dods," *Romanticism on the Net* 23 (August 2001): 5.

15. Bennett, *Mary Diana Dods,* 226.

16. Gulddal, "Paper Trails," 68.

17. Bennett, *Mary Diana Dods,* 273.

18. See Steven Olsen-Smith and Hershel Parker, "Three New Melville Letters: Procrastination and Passports," *Melville Society Extracts* 102 (September 1995): 8–12.

19. Frederick Douglass, "My Escape from Slavery," *Century Illustrated Magazine* 23, no. 1 (1881): 126.

20. Douglass, "My Escape from Slavery," 126–27.

21. David W. Blight, "Frederick Douglass, Refugee," *Atlantic,* February 7, 2017, www.theatlantic.com/politics/archive/2017/02/frederick-douglass-refugee/515853.

22. Quoted in David W. Blight, *Frederick Douglass: Prophet of Freedom* (New York: Simon & Schuster, 2020), 318.

23. Frederick Douglass, *Life and Times of Frederick Douglass* (Boston: De Wolfe, 1892), 393–94.

24. Yael A. Sternhell, "Papers, Please!," *New York Times,* August 8, 2014, https://opinionator.blogs.nytimes.com/2014/08/08/papers-please.

25. Sternhell, "Papers, Please!"

26. Mark Twain, *Innocents Abroad, or The New Pilgrims' Progress* (Hartford, CN: American Publishing Co., 1869), 382–83.

27. Douglass, *Life and Times,* 713.

28. Douglass, *Life and Times,* 712.

29. Douglass, *Life and Times,* 713.

NOTES TO CHAPTER 4

1. Tom Stoppard, *Travesties* (New York: Grove, 1994), 45.

2. US Congress, *Statutes at Large of the United States of America from April 1917 to March 1919,* vol. 40, pt. 1 (Washington, DC: Government Printing Office, 1919), 559.

3. Mark Ellis, *Race, War, and Surveillance: African Americans and the United States Government during World War I* (Bloomington: Indiana University Press, 2001), 186.

4. Ellis, *Race, War, and Surveillance,* 188.

5. Rainer Maria Rilke and André Gide, *Correspondence,* 1909–1926, ed. Renée Lang (Ann Arbor: University of Michigan Press, 1952), 224.

6. Ezra Pound, *The Selected Letters of Ezra Pound to John Quinn,* 1915–1924, ed. Timothy Materer (Durham, NC: Duke University Press, 1999), 180–81.

7. Bridgette Chalk, *Modernism and Mobility: The Passport and Cosmopolitan Experience* (New York: Palgrave, 2014), 19.

8. Stefan Zweig, *The World Yesterday* (London: Cassell, 1953), 410.

9. Friedrich A. Kittler, *Literature, Media, Information Systems,* ed. John Johnston (New York: Routledge, 2012), 42.

10. Gertrude Stein, *The Autobiography of Alice B. Toklas* (New York: Harcourt, 1933), 145.

11. Stein, *The Autobiography*, 222.

12. Stein, *The Autobiography*, 206.

13. Stein, *The Autobiography*, 3.

14. Jace Gatzemeyer tells this story in detail in "How Hemingway's Joint Passport Ruined His Marriage," *The Writing Cooperative,* March 6, 2020, https://writingcooperative.com/how-hemingways-joint-passport-ruined-his-marriage-7fd023e44d6e.

15. Daniel Robinson, "My True Occupation Is That of a Writer," *Hemingway Review* 24, no. 2 (Spring 2005): 87–93; Hemingway's emphasis.

16. F. Scott Fitzgerald and Zelda Fitzgerald, *Dear Scott, Dearest Zelda,* ed. Jackson R. Bryer and Cathy W. Barks (New York: Scribner, 2019), 88.

NOTES TO CHAPTER 5

1. Marc Chagall, *My Life,* trans. Elisabeth Abbott (New York: Orion, 1960), 83.

2. Giorgio Agamben, "We Refugees," *Symposium: A Quarterly Journal of Modern Literature* 49, no. 2 (1995): 114.

3. Hannah Arendt, *The Origins of Totalitarianism* (New York: Meridian, 1958), 291–92.

4. Quoted in Richard Taruskin, *Stravinsky and the Russian Traditions,* vol. 1 (Berkeley: University of California Press, 1996), 3.

5. Vladimir Nabokov, *Speak, Memory: An Autobiography Revisited* (New York: Knopf, 1999), 215.

6. Nabokov, *Speak, Memory,* 216.

7. Andrew Field, *VN: The Life and Art of Vladimir Nabokov* (New York: Crown, 1986), 196.

8. Quoted in Field, *VN,* 197.

9. Stefan Zweig, *The World of Yesterday* (London: Cassell, 1953), 4.

10. Zweig, *World of Yesterday,* 366.

11. Zweig, *World of Yesterday,* 315.

12. Zweig, *World of Yesterday,* 408.

13. Zweig, *World of Yesterday,* 409.

14. Zweig, *World of Yesterday,* 411.

15. *The Grand Budapest Hotel,* dir. Wes Anderson (Fox Searchlight Pictures, 2014).

16. Richard Ellmann, *James Joyce* (Oxford: Oxford University Press, 1982), 738.

17. Quoted in Benjamin Harshav, *Marc Chagall and His Times: A Documentary Narrative* (Palo Alto, CA: Stanford University Press, 2004), 467.

18. Hannah Arendt, "We Refugees," in *The Jewish Writings,* ed. Jerome Kohn and Ron H. Feldman (New York: Schocken, 2007), 265.

19. Quoted in Andy Marino, *A Quiet American: The Secret War of Varian Fry* (New York: St. Martin's, 1999), 143.

20. Arendt, *Origins of Totalitarianism,* 287.

21. Arendt, *Origins of Totalitarianism,* 298.

NOTES TO CHAPTER 6

1. *Human Flow,* dir. Ai Weiwei (Participant Media, 2017).

2. Weiwei, *Human Flow.*

3. Quoted in Tom Phillips, "Ai Weiwei Free to Travel Overseas Again after China Returns His Passport," *Guardian,* July 12, 2015, www.theguardian.com /artanddesign/2015/jul/22/ai-weiwei-free-to-travel-overseas-again-after-china-returns-his-passport.

4. Quoted in Farah Nayeri, "A Departure for Ai Weiwei at the Royal Academy in London," *New York Times,* September 14, 2015, www.nytimes .com/2015/09/15/arts/international/a-departure-for-ai-weiwei-at-the-royal-academy-in-london.html.

5. *Ai Weiwei Drifting: Art, Awareness, and the Refugee Crisis,* dir. Eva Mehl and Bettina Kolb (DW Documentary, 2017), available at https://youtu .be/9MkcTIoo_uw.

6. Quoted in Marie Seton, *Paul Robeson* (New York: Dobson, 1958), 95.

7. Quoted in Martin Duberman, *Paul Robeson: A Biography* (New York: Ballantine, 1990), 389.

8. Quoted in Adam Feinstein, *Pablo Neruda: A Passion for Life* (London: Bloomsbury, 2004), 239.

9. Quoted in Gerald Horne, *Robeson: The Artist as Revolutionary* (London: Pluto, 2016), 146.

10. Paul Robeson, *Paul Robeson Speaks,* ed. Philip Foner (New York: Citadel, 1978), 415.

11. Quoted in Paul Robeson, *Here I Stand* (London: Dennis Dobson, 1958), 77.

12. Robeson, *Here I Stand,* 74.

13. "The NSK State," https://passport.nsk.si/en/about_us.

14. Slavoj Žižek, "Es gibt keinen Staat in Europa," in *Irwin: Retroprincep, 1983–2003,* ed. Inke Arns (Frankfurt: Revolver, 2003), 51.

15. Inke Arns, "The Nigerian Connection: On NSK Passports as Escape and Entry Vehicles," in *State in Time,* ed. IRWIN (London: Minor Compositions, 2014), 94.

16. Quoted in Arns, "Nigerian Connection," 91.

17. Benjamin Ramm, "A Passport from a Country That Doesn't Exist," *BBC,* May 16, 2017, www.bbc.com/culture/article/20170515-a-passport-from-a-country-that-doesnt-exist.

18. Quoted in Slavoj Žižek, *Like a Thief in Broad Daylight* (New York: Seven Stories, 2018), n.p.

19. Žižek, *Like a Thief.*

NOTES TO CHAPTER 7

1. *The Man Who Fell to Earth,* dir. Nicolas Roeg (British Lion Films, 1976).

2. "Alien," *OED Online,* www.oed.com/viewdictionaryentry/Entry/4988.

3. "Alien," *OED Online.*

4. Quoted in John Szwed, *Space Is the Place: The Lives and Times of Sun Ra* (New York: Pantheon, 1997), 29.

5. Szwed, *Space Is the Place,* 278.

6. *Space Is the Place,* dir. John Coney (North American Star System, 1974).

7. *The Simpsons,* season 26, episode 12, "The Musk Who Fell to Earth," dir. Matthew Nastuk, written by Neil Campbell, aired January 25, 2015 (Fox, 2015).

8. Quoted in Catherine Clifford, "Multi-Billionaire Elon Musk: 'I Arrived in North America at 17 with $2,000,'" *CNBC,* June 12, 2018, www.cnbc.com/2018/06/12/telsas-elon-musk-tweets-he-arrived-in-north-america-at-17-with-2000.html.

9. Quoted in Catherine Clifford, "Why a Science Fiction Writer Is Elon Musk's 'Favorite Philosopher,'" *CNBC,* July 23, 2019, www.cnbc.com/2019/07/23/why-hitchhikers-guide-author-is-elon-musks-favorite-philosopher.html.

10. Elon Musk, June 22, 2020, https://twitter.com/elonmusk/status/1275264504725528576.

11. Quoted in Dan Evon, "Was Elon Musk an Undocumented Immigrant?" *Snopes,* February 11, 2016, www.snopes.com/fact-check/elon-musk-illegal-immigrant.

12. Elon Musk, January 28, 2017, https://twitter.com/elonmusk/status/825502618680045568.

13. Quoted in PowlowNiber, "From Brooklyn to Bo-Kaap," *Rolling Stone,* December 6, 2018, www.rollingstone.co.za/musicrev/item/3171-from-brooklyn-to-bo-kaap.

14. Quoted in Siobhán O'Grady, "Mos Def Was Arrested in South Africa for Using a 'World Passport.' Yes, That's a Real Thing," *Foreign Policy,* January 15, 2016, https://foreignpolicy.com/2016/01/15/mos-def-was-arrested-in-south-africa-for-using-a-world-passport-yes-thats-a-real-thing.

15. Quoted in Garry Davis, *My Country Is the World* (New York: Juniper Ledge, 1984), 54–55.

16. Quoted in "Yasiin Bey's (Mos Def) Official Representative Maintains South African Arrest Allegations Are False," *Okay Africa,* January 15, 2016, www.okayafrica.com/yasiin-bey-mos-def-representative-maintains-south-african-arrest-allegations-false.

17. *The World Is My Country,* dir. Arthur Kanegis (Future Wave, 2014).

18. Garry Davis, "World Passport Issued to Snowden," World Service Authority, July 7, 2013, https://worldservice.org/roundup.html?s=4#11.

19. Edward Snowden, "Statement from Edward Snowden in Moscow," *Wikileaks,* July 1, 2013, https://wikileaks.org/Statement-from-Edward-Snowden-in.html.

20. "World Service Authority," https://worldcitnews.org/articles/wsaofs.html.

21. US Department of State, *Foreign Affairs Manual,* 9 FAM 403.9-3[A][1], https://fam.state/gov/fam/09FAM/09FAM040309.html.

22. *Information Concerning the Non-Exhaustive List of Known Fantasy and Camouflage Passports, as Stipulated by Article 6 Of Decision No 1105/2011/EU,* https://ec.europa.eu/home-affairs/system/files/2021-21/list_of_known_fantasy_and_camouflage_passports_en.pdf.

23. "Apply for an Aboriginal Passport," Aboriginal Provisional Government, July 13, 2017, http://apg.org.au/passports.php.

24. Jennifer Scherer, "Julian Assange Has Been Given an Aboriginal Passport," *Special Broadcasting Service,* June 13, 2019, www.sbs.com.au/nitv/article/2019/06/13/julian-assange-has-been-given-aboriginal-passport.

25. Sara Dehm, "Passport," in *International Law's Objects,* ed. Jessie Hohmann and Daniel Joyce (Oxford: Oxford University Press, 2018), 354.

26. Joshua Robertson, "Tolerance of Travellers with Aboriginal Passports Amounts to Recognition, Says Activist," *Guardian,* April 20, 2015. www.theguardian.com/australia-news/2015/apr/20/tolerance-of-travellers-with-aboriginal-passports-amounts-to-recognition-says-activist.

27. "Apply for an Aboriginal Passport."

28. *United Nations Declaration on the Rights of Indigenous Peoples* (A/RES/61/295) (United Nations, 2008), 3.

29. Mark Rifkin, "Indigenizing Agamben: Rethinking Sovereignty in Light of the 'Peculiar' State of Native Peoples," *Cultural Critique* 73 (Fall 2009): 89.

30. Leti Volpp, "The Indigenous as Alien," *UC Irvine Law Review* 289 (2015): abstract.

31. Sid Hill, "My Six Nation Haudenosaunee Passport Is Not a 'Fantasy Document,'" *Guardian,* October 30, 2015, https://www.theguardian.com /commentisfree/2015/oct/30/my-six-nation-haudenosaunee-passport-not-fantasy-document-indigenous-nations.

NOTES TO THE EPILOGUE

1. Helena Waldmann, "*Good Passports Bad Passports*—Official full-length video," March 2, 2022, https://www.helenawaldmann.com/works /goodpassports-badpassports/.

2. "The Henley Passport Index," Henley & Partners, www.henleyglobal .com/passport-index.

3. Salman Rushdie, *Step across This Line* (New York: Modern Library, 2003), 367.

4. United Nations, *The Universal Declaration of Human Rights,* 1948–1998 (New York: UNDPI, 1998), article 13(2); available at www.un.org/en/about-us /universal-declaration-of-human-rights.

5. Sara Ahmed, *Queer Phenomenology: Orientations, Objects, Others* (Durham, NC: Duke University Press, 2006), 142.

6. Ahmed, *Queer Phenomenology,* 139.

7. Ahmed, *Queer Phenomenology,* 140.

8. Ahmed, *Queer Phenomenology,* 142.

9. Nigel Farage, September 13, 2016, https://twitter.com/nigel_farage /status/775735864743829505.

10. Nigel Farage, August 19, 2019, https://twitter.com/nigel_farage /status/1163423674780856320.

11. "Passport Index by Rank," Passport Index, www.passportindex.org /byRank.php.

12. Quoted in Ollie Williams, "US Passports Are Now on Par with Mexico as Freedoms Are Cut," *Forbes,* July 7, 2020, www.forbes.com/sites

/oliverwilliams1/2020/07/07/us-passports-are-now-on-par-with-mexico-as-freedoms-are-cut.

13. Antoine Cassar, *Passport,* trans. Albert Gatt and Antoine Cassar (n.p.: Passport Project, 2010), 5.

14. Cassar, *Passport,* 8.

15. Cassar, *Passport,* 16.

16. Antoine Cassar, "Passaport (2009)," https://antoinecassar.net /passport-2009.

17. Quoted in Ali Al Shouk, "Now, Smartphone Is Your Passport in Dubai" *Gulf News,* June 7, 2017, https://gulfnews.com/uae/now-smartphone-is-your-passport-in-dubai-1.2040149.

18. "Accenture World Economic Forum Known Traveller," YouTube, August 9, 2018, www.youtube.com/watch?v=tThqjC2KWnM&t.

19. Jacques Derrida, *The Paper Machine,* trans. Rachel Bowlby (Palo Alto, CA: Stanford University Press, 2005), 67.

INDEX

Ernst, Max, 103–104, 136–138
European Union, 188, 203–204
exile, 34, 41–42, 55, 91, 95–97, 142–143, 151, 154–155

Farage, Nigel, 203
Field, Andrew, 130
Fittko, Lisa, 143
Fitzgerald, F. Scott, 110–111; *The Beautiful and the Damned,* 110; *Tender is the Night,* 111; *This Side of Paradise,* 110
Fitzgerald, Zelda, 110–111
Foucault, Michel, 66–67
France, 23–24, 52–54, 59–63, 72–73, 82, 85, 109–111, 130, 135–145; Calais, 169; French Revolution, 62–63; Marseille, 137–141, 143, 145; Paris, 23–26, 57–61, 91, 103–110, 115, 123–124, 130–131, 135–136, 141–142, 160–161, 184; Vichy, 130, 139–142
Franklin, Benjamin, 61
Freud, Sigmund: *Moses and Monotheism,* 33
Fry, Varian, 137–142
Fussell, Paul, 8, 10–11, 16, 101

Gaddafi, Muammar, 189
Germany, 97, 127–131, 140–142, 163; Berlin, 98, 115, 127–129, 137, 149–150, 153
Gide, André, 100, 101, 185
Gogol, Nikolai: *Dead Souls,* 121–123
Grand Tour, 57–59, 76–77, 85, 116
Greece, 37–42, 148–150; Athens, 37–39
Greene, Graham: *The Confidential Agent,* 12–13
Guggenheim, Peggy, 138
Gulddal, Jesper, 60, 67, 74

Hanks, Tom, 15, 18
Harris, Roy, 39

Hemingway, Ernest, 108–110; *A Farewell to Arms,* 11–12, 109; *The Sun Also Rises,* 109
Hemingway, Hadley, 108–109
Henry IV, King of England, 51
Henry V, King of England, 51–54
Hill, Tadodaho Sid, 193–194
Hitler, Adolf, 128, 131
Holinshed's Chronicles of England, Scotland, and Ireland, 52–53
Hoover, J. Edgar, 158, 162
Horkheimer, Max, 142–143
hospitality, 12, 15–18, 131–132, 136, 199; conditional, 6, 128, 200; unconditional (pure), 149, 208, 211
Hsing I-tien, 42–44
Hughes, Langston, 113–117; *The Big Sea,* 116; "I, Too," 116–117; "The Negro Speaks of Rivers," 113
human rights, 144, 169, 185–187

immigration, 75, 132, 180–182, 203; illegal, 5, 82, 175, 187
Iran, 3, 14–15, 205. *See also* Persia
Ireland, 95–96, 205; Dublin, 91, 94
Italy, 10–11, 45, 68; Genoa, 57, 116; Padua, 57–58; Parma, 67–68, 70; Trieste, 91, 93; Venice, 45, 47–49, 57, 64, 66, 116, 167–168

Jeffress, Robert, 36
Jemison, Ansley, 193
Joyce, Giorgio, 93, 135
Joyce, James, 91–96, 102–104, 116, 134–136; *Finnegans Wake,* 134; *Ulysses,* 91, 95, 103, 135
Joyce, Lucia, 93, 135
Joyce, Nora, 93–94, 135
Juel-Jensen, Ben, 55–56

Kaelin, Christian, 206
Kahlo, Frida, 156
Kaikhatu, 48

Turkey, 14, 109, 155
Tushratta, King of Mitanni, 29, 32
Twain, Mark: *Innocents Abroad,* 84–85
Tzara, Tristan, 95, 104

United Arab Emirates, 210
United Kingdom, 82, 98, 193–194,
  203–204. *See also* England
United Nations, 5, 184–185, 190; Universal Declaration of Human Rights,
  185–186, 199
United States of America, 75, 78, 113,
  157–161, 171, 175, 180–183, 193–194;
  Department of State, 137, 158–163,
  187–188, 193; law enforcement, 16,
  158; New York, 16–17, 78, 81, 112, 131,
  137–138, 176, 201; Supreme Court,
  82, 163; visa system, 17, 137, 143, 181,
  204; Wartime Measures Act, 99
utopia, 165–166, 170, 206–208

Videla, Gabriel González, 160

Waldmann, Helena: *Good Passports Bad
  Passports: A Borderline Experience,*
  195–198

wars: Anglo-Irish, 95; Cold, 157–158;
  February Revolution, 96; First
  World, 11, 91–93, 99, 123; Greco-
  Turkish, 109; Korean, 158; Russian
  Civil, 124; Second World, 12, 130,
  134–135, 145–146, 150, 157, 184;
  Seven Years, 60; Spanish Civil,
  157; Ten-Day, 164; US Civil,
  83–84
Westbrook, Raymond, 32
Wilde, Oscar: *The Importance of Being
  Ernest,* 96
Williamson, John, 162
Wilson, Woodrow, 100
World Service Authority, 184–185,
  188

Yugoslavia, 164–165

Žižek, Slavoj, 165, 168–170; *Like a
  Thief in Broad Daylight,* 169;
  Refugees, Terror, and the Trouble
  with Neighbors,* 169
Zweig, Stefan, 95, 101–103, 129, 131–132,
  134; *Jeremiah,* 95; *The World of
  Yesterday,* 101–102

Founded in 1893,
UNIVERSITY OF CALIFORNIA PRESS
publishes bold, progressive books and journals
on topics in the arts, humanities, social sciences,
and natural sciences—with a focus on social
justice issues—that inspire thought and action
among readers worldwide.

The UC PRESS FOUNDATION
raises funds to uphold the press's vital role
as an independent, nonprofit publisher, and
receives philanthropic support from a wide
range of individuals and institutions—and from
committed readers like you. To learn more, visit
ucpress.edu/supportus.